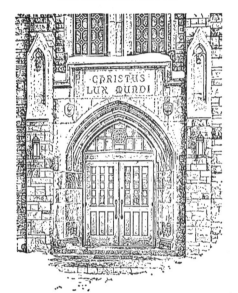

Charlemagne

Charlemagne, by Dürer
(*Radio Times Hulton Picture Library*)

Charlemagne
a study

E. M. Almedingen

Martha Edith

THE BODLEY HEAD
LONDON SYDNEY
TORONTO

© E. M. Almedingen 1968
SBN 370 00402 7
Printed and bound in Great Britain for
The Bodley Head Ltd
9 Bow Street, London, WC2
by C. Tinling & Co Ltd
Liverpool, London and Prescot
Set in Monotype Baskerville
First published 1968

MEMORIAE
OLGA ANTONII FILIAE DOBIACHE
QUAE
APVD VNIVERSITATEM OLIM
PETROPOLITANAM
HISTORIAM PROFESSA
IN STVDIOSIS ERVDIENDIS
ARTEM PRAESTABAT ABSOLVTAM
AMICITIAM INDECLINATAM
HVNC LIBRVM DEDICAT
DISCIPVLA

CONTENTS

ACKNOWLEDGMENTS

The theme of this book has been in my mind for a long time. It is with deep gratitude that I acknowledge my debt to the late Dr F. J. S. Raby of Jesus College, Cambridge, for his invaluable suggestions concerning in particular Alcuin and the Palace School of Aachen; to Miss F. M. Pilkington for drawing the map, turning my own most untidy notes into a faultless genealogical tree, for typing the entire MS, and for making the index; to Mr J. S. G. Simmons of All Souls College, Oxford, for his help with the Dedication, and to Miss Anne Pickles of the Somerset County Library, for her great help in providing the not easily obtainable books I had to use for my study.

E.M.A.

ILLUSTRATIONS

GENEALOGICAL TREE

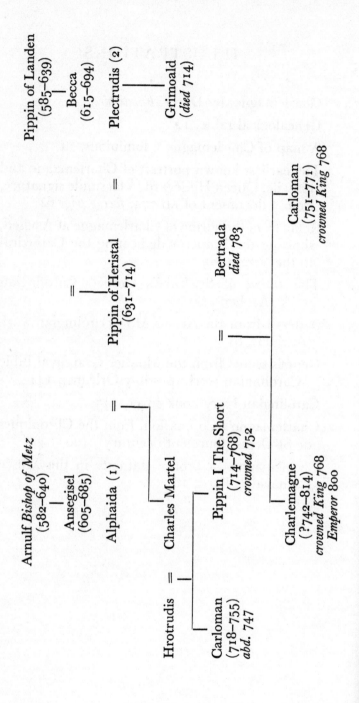

Pippin of Landen
(585–639)

Becca
(615–694)

Plectrudis (2)

Grimoald
(*died* 714)

Arnulf *Bishop of Metz*
(582–640)

Ansegisel
(605–685)

Alphaida (1)

=

Pippin of Heristal
(631–714)

=

Bertrada
died 783

Charles Martel

Pippin I The Short
(714–768)
crowned 752

=

Hrotrudis

=

Carloman
(718–755)
abd. 747

Charlemagne
(?742–814)
crowned King 768
Emperor 800

Carloman
(751–771)
crowned King 768

AUTHOR'S NOTE

In normal terms, a biography should cover the distance from the cradle to the coffin. But such an orthodox treatment would hardly answer in Charlemagne's case. In the first place, practically nothing is known of his childhood and boyhood. Next, he owed an incalculable debt to the Frankish past, to which the first part of the book is devoted; the second describes his country as he found it on coming to manhood. Another reason for the departure from the commonly established pattern and, as it seems to me, the most weighty one, is that all the public activities of Charlemagne stemmed from one common root: his faith in God and his allegiance to Christ's Church. Charlemagne fought his wars, carried out his reforms and rekindled the love of learning with no other aim but that of rendering glory to his Maker.

Separate considerations of these three aspects of Charlemagne's life therefore precede the section dealing with his personal life, his habits, foibles, virtues and vices, which throws a sharp light on the curious and admittedly unpleasant halvedness of Charlemagne's moral make-up.

The two remaining parts, concerning his coronation as Emperor and his last year, follow the chronological canon. His legend is dealt with briefly since it has no connection with the central theme.

There follows a short bibliography which by no means mentions all the books consulted. The sources were the first to be studied.

A few words should be added about the dedication. I was fortunate in being trained by a scholar of international repute, the late Olga Dobiach, Professor of History at the Petrograd University. The training was severe: none of her pupils were allowed to use anything except sources in their research. I well remember Dr Dobiach's scathing rebuke when, in an essay on the travelling routes of the Northmen between the eighth and the tenth centuries, I allowed myself to use rather copious quotations from a French authority on the subject, a book published about a hundred years ago.

At the beginning of my very first term at the University, Dr Dobiach gave us a course of lectures on the life in France during the twelfth century. She prefaced the first lecture by telling us that we had come to college not to be crammed with theories, dates and facts but to learn to use our minds. In my own immeasurably smaller way, I have tried to follow my teacher's words.

E. M. ALMEDINGEN
January 1968.

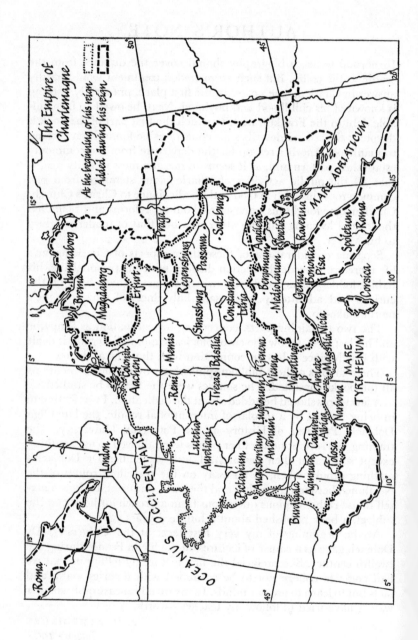

The Empire of Charlemagne

At the beginning of his reign
Added during his reign

I

THE COUNTRY
BEFORE HIS COMING

The matter of Gaul was woven into Charlemagne's inheritance, the same Gaul of which her first chroniclers would sadly say that she was '*vexata et afflicta*,' and they certainly had good reason for their lament.

She was conquered, fortified and partially colonized by the Roman legions, but the conquerors thought little of the inhabitants. Caesar's opinion is well enough known[1], Livy's judgment was even more scathing, and other writers insisted that the Gauls were boastful in their speech and known for their inconstancy.[2]

Centuries passed. The power of Rome grew weaker and weaker until it could be compared with a splintered reed. The last legions left Britain and Gaul. Yet the leaven of the Roman civilization had left its imprint – particularly in Southern Gaul.

Now sporadic encroachments of the barbarian became an avalanche. New blood, new ideas, new customs poured into Europe. Great waves of Germanic infiltration broke westwards from the Danube and southwards across the Alps. The Huns were routed, but the Germanic expansion continued growing. They swarmed, but they did not always ravage. Theirs was a peculiar hunger for land, for spaces where they could settle down, wrest a livelihood from the soil, and be able to draw a breath after their long wanderings. All unaware of it, they had a contribution to make to the lands they engulfed with their women and children, their horses and cattle, and their primitive household gear. It was a healthy and inevitable movement.

Those tribes were many. Among them, the Visigoths pressed
further and further west and, finally, swept into Spain. The
Ostrogoths turned southwards, crossed the Alps and conquered
Italy. Burgundians, Allemannians, Riparian and Salian Franks
reached the European plain and went no further. By the end of
the sixth century the Salian Franks were established in North
East Gaul. The much more war-like Riparian Franks settled
along the banks of the Rhine and the Moselle. They were
a savage people, far less developed than other Barbarians
from the East, but there was an indefinable quality about
them.

The wanderings were over. The scattered tribes became
kingdoms in little, their focal points at Cologne, Tournai,
Arras, Cambrai, and other places. According to Duchesne[3], it
was the Franks who *'eurent raison des autres barbares, s'imposèrent
à toute ancienne Gaule, lui rendirent unité politique en y créant un
puissant état.'*

Yet little of that brilliant future could be discerned at the
time.

Rome, pillaged, sacked, and robbed of the imperial dignity,
might have suggested a ship about to founder. She did not
founder. The Pope had not gone to the Bosphorus. The city
remained far more than a dusty symbol: she was at once a
challenge and a necessity.

The first Frankish chief known to History was a Salian Frank,
one Merovech, destined to christen a dynasty. The servility and
awe of contemporaries and the imagination of those who came
after endowed him with a divine descent. Merovech's son,
Childeric, made Tournai his capital, and war on all his
neighbours was the only matter to engage his attention. The
victories won by him pleased his people exceedingly. They
showed their pleasure after his death in 481, by which time the
whole country between the Somme and the Rhine was theirs
by savage conquest. Childeric had been their chief. Now they
felt they deserved a king. In 481, at Tournai, they raised
Childeric's son, Clovis, on a shield and clanged their swords
against shields to announce his kingship. A faint pattern of
unity began to emerge.

Childeric had lived and died a pagan. His people too clung

to the old faith, but Christianity had spread throughout Gaul
long before the day of Merovech[4], though the Franks were the
last but one among barbarian peoples to enter the comity of
Christendom.

Clovis inherited fully his father's passion for war. He
considered his dominions and thought them too small. Between
the Loire and the Somme lay Armorica ruled by Sygarius. To
the south was Aquitania all but under the heel of the Visigoth.
To the east were the turbulent Allemannians, and in the north
petty Frankish chiefs spent their time in troubling Clovis's
boundaries.

His wife, Clothilde, a Burgundian princess, was a Catholic.
Not her prayers but his good fortune in war decided Clovis to
become a Christian. After his great victory at Soissons in 485,
he marched from success to success. In the end, his conquests
made him master of the whole country from Amiens and Rheims
to Nantes and Orléans. He defeated the Allemannians and gave
little breathing space to the Visigoths in Aquitania. In the
north he crushed the Frankish princelings, and he made Paris
his capital. The Merovingian Frankland comprised the entire
modern France with the exception of a narrow strip to the
south, the Low Countries, Switzerland and Germany except
for Hanover and Westphalia held by the savage Saxons. All
unaware of it, the crowned savage who had learned the
rudiments of statesmanship on battlefields became the
architect of the greatest power in Western Christendom. Yet
it is open to doubt whether Clovis would ever have become a
Christian had the fortunate sequence of his victories been
broken by a reverse. As it was, it took him fully eleven years to
adopt his wife's religion. On Christmas Day 496 Clovis was
baptized into the Catholic Church and compelled his people
to follow him.

It was a gesture of consummate statesmanship.

The Franks became Christian in the orthodox fashion unlike
so many of their neighbours who professed the Arian heresy
condemned at Nicea in AD 325. 'If the Father begat the
Son, – ' argued Arius, 'He that was begotten had a beginning
of existence; hence it is clear that there was a time when the
Son was not. It follows then of necessity that (the Son) had

His existence from the non-existent.'[5] Nicea's answer was both negative and positive, the former by pronouncing a solemn anathema on the heretic, the latter in formulating the great Nicene Creed. But the condemnation of the Council did not kill the heresy. Nation after nation fell under the seductiveness of Arianism. Arian emperors sat in Byzantium and corresponded with Arian rulers and bishops in Visigothic Spain. Both Burgundians and Ostrogoths professed the heresy.

By his refusal of Arianism Clovis won the support of all the Catholics in Gaul in his further struggles against Burgundy and Spain. That baptism would determine the courses of Frankland down many generations to come. It turned Clovis into the most powerful representative of orthodoxy in the West, and he took shrewd and ample advantage of that attitude. Theocratic breaths soon enough became evident in his dealings with the Church as, centuries later, they would govern Charlemagne's policies. The Gallo-Roman hierarchy having supported Clovis in many struggles, he repaid them in rather surprising coin by passing a law whereby no man might be admitted to the priesthood without the sanction of the king or his representative, the only exceptions being made for sons or direct descendants of clergy.

The Franks were Christian by compulsion, having first been deeply imbued by a far older religion, and the conquest of Clovis had done nothing to uproot it. The ancient faith of Gaul easily engulfed what other worldly elements there were in the ethos of the race. The tenets of the old Gallican faith had been handed down by word of mouth, no other record being permitted, from one generation to another. It was animism at its crudest. Mountains, rivers, fields and woods were supposed to be inhabited by deities, one Vosegus being worshipped in the mountains later known by his name, and one Arduinna elsewhere. Winter solstice and Midsummer Day were kept with rites, their origins going back to unrecorded seasons. Some classic authors, Suetonius in particular, mention the unspeakable cruelty of human sacrifices offered in propitiation. There was a goddess of fertility, whose image would be carried about at sowing time. An abundant harvest ended in orgiastic thanksgiving. A disastrous spell of drought was interpreted as the goddess's anger, and children would be sacrificed to appease her.

The efforts of the first Christian missionaries had little effect. In the fourth century, St Martin of Tours waged a life-long battle against pagan practices, but he was seldom successful. In one instance, the people permitted him to pull down a shrine, but he was prevented from felling an old tree standing close by. Later, we do hear of venerated oaks, elms and thorns being cut down at bishops' orders, but lay Christians would not make the least use of the timber for fear of the gods' vengeance. In the days of Caesarius of Arles (c. 470–542), appointed bishop by Clovis, the January Calends were kept in his diocese. Men, wearing skins and horns of stags, performed a ritual to the singing of prayers for abundance to fall upon their fields in the year to come. The Church turned Midsummer Day into the Feast of St John, but synodical decrees meant little to the people who preferred to cling to the ancient observance. So fires would be lit in the places hallowed by immemorial custom, and men and women, revolted at the idea that high honours should be paid to the Forerunner, spent the night in dancing, singing, drinking and plain debauchery. – '*Cantica diabolica, amatoria, et turpia*,' as Gregory of Tours described it.

There were also milder, less unpleasing diversions. To prevent ravages by mice, rats and moths, a special day was set aside to propitiate them by offerings of bread, cloth and linen left in a particular manner in appointed places. '*Sortes Sanctorum*' continued for centuries in the teeth of all synodical fulminations, and ancient deities were often invoked together with Christian saints. Important decisions, such as the choice of bride or bridegroom, would be made on the strength of omens read in a ripple of water, the fall of a twig, or the number of acorns found at the foot of an oak. During eclipses, Christian Franks would secretly gather together in places purposely away from any church or hermitage, beat drums, and wail in their efforts to recall the sun from its place of exile where, as they firmly believed, a malignant deity had sent it. Stolen goods could be recovered once the thief's name was revealed by a kindly god who did not deny his service so long as the applicant refrained from making a single sign of the Cross.

Credulity knew no limits. Dr Joan Evans mentions beads of paste and glass 'being in common use in ancient Gaul under the name of serpents' eggs; they were thought to be generated from the breath of many serpents congregated together, who shot them into the air from their hissing jaws.'[6]

Synod after synod went on forbidding this traffic with heathenry, but in far too many cases admonitions and curses fell on stony ground. The Frankish mind was too firmly rooted in ancient uses, and the Frankish imagination saw no harm in offering hospitality to pagan gods, the Trinity and Christian saints together. One bishop complained that the evil was all the more difficult to extirpate because the very names of week-days derived from ancient gods and served as constant re-minders of an unhallowed past.

Most of those darkly coloured practices, certainly with the exception of human sacrifices, would still be there in the Carolingian days.

* * *

In the second book of his 'Historia Francorum'[7], Gregory of Tours is almost at a loss to find adequate words to praise Clovis! 'Daily would God lay his enemies under his hand, and He increased his kingdom because [Clovis] walked before Him, his heart upright, and he accomplished what was pleasing in God's sight.'

Now, the architect of the Regnum Francorum was a cruel, treacherous and vicious savage, who became Christian solely because his 'conversion' answered his political purposes. Yet the first historian of France should not be accused of nauseating hypocrisy. All his misdeeds notwithstanding, the first King of the Franks had a vision and a purpose which included more than a narrowly personal ambition. He was jealous for the honour of a tribe become a nation.

His subjects were Franks who lived in Gaul, its boundaries lying from the Pyrenees to beyond the Rhine. The country included the whole of present day Belgium and parts of Holland as well as large pockets of modern Germany. Clovis was sovereign of the ancient Provincia where the Roman culture had sunk deepest, of the central Gaul where that tradition had been assimilated but patchily, and over the North which, though conquered by Rome, had never attracted settlers from the south. In northern Gaul, the widely spaced towns were so many garrison posts. By the time the Franks came, many Roman forts were in ruins. Clovis's military triumphs swept over Bavaria, Allemannia and Thuringia, crippled the Burgundian power, chased Arianism out of Aquitania, and vanquished the Visigoths at Poitiers. The Saxons escaped his grasp, and he never ventured beyond the Alps. All these vast possessions came under the ancient Frankish custom of inheritance and would, in consequence, be most disastrously divided among the king's four sons after his death in 511.

But never again would it be a tribe, its courses swayed this way and that at the whim of an unruly assembly. A pattern had been evolved in Clovis's life-time. It was a *Regnum Francorum*, governed by a king, not led by a chieftain. The kingdom was a property to be defended against all aggression, to be increased as chance offered, to be enjoyed as taste and mood dictated. The old tribal laws were put together, amended, amplified, and became a code in 500 – known as *Lex Salica*.

None the less, the country was governed in a peculiar fashion.

Clovis's power was absolute, and he would bequeath it to his successors. They had counsellors but not ministers, and they had the so called '*Missi dominici*', officers of the Crown, whose duties were those of supervisors. The royal '*palatium*' was the household kept continually on the move: Clovis's own capital was Paris, but he seldom stayed there. His constant wars required his presence along the frontiers of the kingdom. His innate restlessness made him prefer unending perambulations to a settled domestic pattern.

The kingdom was divided into '*pagi*', each under the authority of a count ('*comes*'), a name given to the holder of office and not a hereditary dignity. They were appointed by the king, their term of office dependent on his pleasure. The count's court, '*placita*', was held three times a year. To administer the law was no easy matter since the Salic Code had not eliminated various ancient laws and customs followed in different parts of the kingdom. Thus a Burgundian had the right to be tried by Burgundian law even when living away from his native land.

The king's exchequer travelled about with his '*palatium*'.
The counts were responsible for local tax collections and other
fiscal matters. Much of the tax revenue was in kind. In broad
terms the king and his household lived off the land.

Such, then, was the skeleton of the Merovingian administration, some of it borrowed from Rome and the rest improvised
by Clovis, and its substance would be in force under the
Carolingians. The administrative structure certainly had its
defects, but it might have answered if the right of primogeniture
had been recognised by the Franks.

As it was, they stood committed to the ancient customs, and
on the death of Clovis the kingdom was parcelled out among
his four sons, each of whom was entitled to the style of '*Rex
Francorum*'. All the four were married and had sons of their own.
Within less than a century, the dynastical matter of Frankland
might have resembled a patchwork quilt were it not for the
fact that no Merovingian had any care for the well-being of his
kin. They poisoned, hanged, burned, drowned and beheaded
one another with such a zest that King Lothair I, who died in
611, could logically style himself '*Rex Francorum*', there being
no kinsman living to challenge his right to the dignity. Yet,
unlike most of his predecessors, Lothair I had a father's heart.
He never murdered any of his four sons. But he should have
introduced the law of primogeniture.

After his death the unfortunate country was again plunged
into the bloody turmoils of internecine war. Gregory of Tours
admitted himself 'bored' when he came to that point in his
'History'.[8] In his opinion, the unspeakable excesses committed
by Clovis were praiseworthy since they stemmed from the
king's zeal for the Faith. His successors, however, had no such
purpose to redeem their misdeeds.

After eighteen years, however, peace came to Frankland;
power was once again in one man's hands, and it is pleasant to
reflect that at least one Merovingian should have walked both
into legend and into song as '*le bon Roi Dagobert*' (629–639).
Arts, letters and a gentler way of living prospered under him,
and he enjoyed his sovereignty without having recourse to
gibbet, stake, or poison. During his all too brief reign, the land
breathed more happily and the epitaph, calling him '*dulce caput*

populi Dagoberte,' speaks of a people's devotion rather than a scribe's sycophancy.

The year of Dagobert's death rang the virtual knell to the Merovingian fortunes. The dynasty was to endure for more than a hundred years more, spinning out its existence in a twilight shot blood-red with violence. Economically and politically, Clovis's kingdom entered a stage of decay.

* * *

The Emperor Justinian died in 565. Three years later, the Lombards, led by Alboin, swept into Italy, and Byzantium was no longer able to render help. She had a Persian war on her hands, and had to deal as best she could with the Bulgarian inroads. She had neither men, nor ships, nor yet money to spare for her Italian possessions. The Lombards came and they stayed. In the end, Byzantium retained some few parts of the peninsula, including the Exarchate of Ravenna, but her supremacy was shaken to the roots. Italy, parcelled out between Byzantium, the Lombards and the Papal See, was a house divided against itself.

But for Frankland there were perils nearer home. To the east of her borders the savage Avars were spread over the Danubian plain. The Saxons, entrenched between the lower Rhine and the Elbe, were continually troubling the Frankish boundaries. Within a mere ten years (622–632), Mahomet's followers swept like a flame over parched stubble. Long before the end of the century, Syria, Persia, and Egypt were in their hands. It was obvious that the Middle East could not contain them. Islam had its eyes on Europe. The seventh century teemed with new problems and brought a challenge to the European door, but Frankland, once the mightiest upholder of orthodoxy in the west, could not meet it.

According to a theory offered by the late Henri Pirenne[9], the decay in Frankland was due to Islam. His arguments are most persuasive. Yet, in reality, how far was Islam responsible for the dead hand laid over Frankish economy?

It is true that the gradual disappearance of papyrus was due to the capture of Egypt by the Moslems, and a number of other shortages may be attributed to the Islam mastery of the

Mediterranean. It is also true that travel overland was fraught
with ever growing risks and, in certain cases, proved more
expensive than sea voyages. Still, routes over the Alps, however
infested by robbers, had been used by the Franks who traded
with Lombardy, Ravenna and Byzantium. Such routes were in
no peril from the Moslems, and yet fewer and fewer Frankish
merchants came to use them during the second half of the
Seventh Century. It is true that by 675, the whole of Tunisia
fallen to Islam, Moslem pirates were able to launch their
attacks in force upon the shipping in the Mediterranean until
Genoa and Pisa were virtually cut off from all sea-trade with
the East, and the great Provençal ports came to resemble so
many dead cities.

Those are proven facts. None the less, the impact of Islam,
however sharp its ramifications, cannot wholly explain the
Frankish economic decay. In the first place, far too much
emphasis has been laid on the effects of Moslem piracy. They
were by no means first comers in those waters. The freedom of
the Mediterranean had rarely been unchallenged in the past.
Vandals, for example, were champion pirates, and their fleets
would control the Corsican and Sardinian waters long before the
Islam conquests, but Vandal depredations, their volume and
savagery notwithstanding, did not succeed in killing all
activity in Provençal harbours.

Again, though exports of papyrus ceased to go to Frankland,
Egypt did not discontinue exporting it altogether since papyrus
was being used in Italy well into the Tenth Century. Finally,
if Islam had really blocked the Mediterranean against European
trade, economic decay would not have spared either Italy or
Byzantium. But we have no traces of such a parallel. Italy
certainly was a sufferer, with Genoa and Pisa denied their
accustomed outlets, not so Venice and Byzantium, who if
anything grew wealthier.

The decay in Frankland had set in long before; its causes
were many, but their common root lay in the lack of a sane
and constructive policy during the reigns of Clovis's successors.
For one thing conquest as such seemed to sum up their
purposes. The vanquished *Provincia* added an immense strip
of sea-shore to their dominions, but not one of the Merovingian

kings ever thought of building a navy. Such Frankish ships as sailed from Frankish Ports were all privately owned and used for passenger traffic and freight.

Their conception of what a kingdom should be could not but play its part in the economic impasse. Clovis and his successors were '*Reges Francorum*', not '*Reges Franciae*'. They were kings of a people. The country was their property to handle as they pleased. They lived off it. Any property considered in terms of income must be managed as an investment. Such a conception would have been utterly alien to the Merovingians. They took all they could and they put nothing back. There is ample proof in the pages of Gregory of Tours that, even had there been no Moslem conquest, the Frankish economic doom would have fallen upon the country because of an administration impotent to shape the mere rudiments of a sound fiscal policy.

The financial mismanagement suggests a trend of thought verging on lunacy. The country was flooded by bad money. The king had a royal mint attached to his '*palatium*', but privately struck coins passed for legal tender throughout Frankland. It was a privilege granted by the king, though there may well have been cases when coins would be struck without any such sanction. The privilege granted frequently and sometimes indiscriminately ended by introducing chaos in fiscal matters until the Merovingian specie, debased to the utmost, had no value outside the country. Foreign merchants began to insist that all imports to Frankland should be settled in gold bezants, the ubiquitously honoured specie of the period. Such gold had to be borrowed, and Byzantium, for all her wealth, had little gold to spare for a borrower of proved bad credit.

And what had Frankland to export? Little enough! Timber, skins of wild animals, and slaves – mainly prisoners of war such as Belgics, Saxons and Slavs.[10] The timber trade was certainly important, but its volume could not offset Frankish imports reaching the country for the use of the king, his household and a small moneyed minority. Olive oil from North Africa, silks and other textiles from Egypt, Byzantium and Persia, spices from Asia Minor, gold and silver plate, precious and semi-precious stones, – all those came in great bulk, and such cargoes suggests a healthy mercantile climate in Frankland. But the ever widening gulf between imports and exports, to say nothing of large indebtedness, led to a great many shortages.

In some measure, the dwindling imports checked the decay. For one thing, they led to a quickened tempo of activity among the Franks. Olive oil had to be replaced by wax and fats. Landowners, both ecclesiastical and secular, realized the importance of extensive bee-keeping and better organized cattle-breeding. Attention was drawn to the usefulness of vegetable fats. Imports of wine from Italy and Asia Minor dwindled so sharply that such monastic houses as could afford the expense began planting vineyards on the banks of the Rhine and the Moselle. Luxuries such as carved ivories, beads of jade and amethyst, furniture supports of malachite and porphyry and, above all, delicately tinted silks vanished altogether. Fredegarius commends the industry of the Frisians who wove a coarse serviceable cloth. By the middle of the Seventh Century 'frieze' was no longer used solely for the smock of a serf.

Spices ceased to come in, and the privileged minority had to eat their meat unseasoned. Finally, there were no more imports of papyrus. It was replaced by parchment so much more expensive that fewer and fewer manuscripts came to be copied in monastic *scriptoria*. That particular shortage led to the abandonment of the generously flowing uncials which were replaced by the crabbed minuscule script. In the royal chancery alone was papyrus still used for charters.

The market pulse beat more and more faintly, and what trade remained was mostly in alien hands. Syrians, Greeks and Jews sold the little there was to sell, though it should be remembered that foreign merchants and pedlars were by no means newcomers in Frankland. Gregory of Tours mentions a well established Jewish merchant colony at Clermont Ferrand, and there was one at Orléans. Possibly, there were others.

Far fewer barges plied up and down the rivers. Most roads having fallen into a state beyond repair, travelling was whittled down to a minimum. There were instances of pilgrims trudging along for hours without meeting a single man or woman.

Something of an anti-urban breath swept over the country. Landowners lived on their estates, and the common folk looked to them for subsistence as well as for protection. In the heart of the country about the only economic relationship in existence lay between a landowner and his tenant based on services rendered and paid for in kind.

The basis of manorial life was a vigorously maintained self-sufficiency. The lord and his men wore boots of leather tanned on the estate. The women spun and wove cloth and linen for shifts, tunics, and cloaks. Horses were shod at the manor smithy. Shields, spears and axes were made for the battlefield, cauldrons and cups for the hall. Potters fired platters and pots for common use. Some among the workmen were free men, others slaves. The former received their wage in kind – not greatly differing from the slaves clothed and fed according to the steward's discretion.

The manor was a peculiar social unit. With very few exceptions it had no financial commitments either within or without its walls. Even the alms given to a neighbouring monastery might take the form of a silver cup or a jewelled buckle, so many loads of timber, so many baskets of fish. It was a narrowly banded horizon, and there always remained the risk of climatic vagaries working havoc upon the harvest, of cattle epidemics and similar misfortunes.

Certainly, life was hard for many. But mediaeval chroniclers had a habit of plunging into the waters of deep despondency. Expressions such as '*heu mihi*' and '*proh dolor*' were worked to death. Yet what tangible evidences we have of the Merovingian era are proof enough that, in spite of their twilit skies, men had taste for beauty and leisure to give it expression.

*   *   *

The Merovingian story was told by Gregory of Tours and, after his death, continued by a far less capable chronicler, Fredegarius.[11] It makes horrible but oddly compelling reading, and it suggests a gigantic diptych: revolting cruelty, frustration, inertia and misgovernment on the one side, and on the other – a kindlier, warmer landscape of lives spent in work, thought, wonder and prayer. The tribe could not become a nation without the cost of birth-pangs, and savagery remained part of its inheritance. But, having once settled down and taken some measure of the surroundings, the people learned – however slowly – that they were living among the evidences of a civilization already old at the time when their own forebears hunted wolf, bear and other wild beasts in forests far away to the east from the Rhine and the Danube. They did not accept that civilization except patchily: tribal memories lived long, and a certain streak of dichotomy ran through their lives. Yet, such as they were, they had entered the European comity, and one of the greatest Popes, Gregory I, showed insight in welcoming their arrival.

Charlemagne's own day cannot be understood apart from the Merovingian era because he was a Frank of the Franks.

It is pleasant to turn to the brighter side of the diptych. Economic decay and administrative chaos did not lead to the twilight of the mind. As will be shown below, books were written and were copied in Frankland all through that thorny era. People danced and sang, listened to pilgrims' stories, enlarged their knowledge of the outside world, wrote poetry, worked in silver and gold, marble and precious stones. Kings and queens were not wholly occupied with daggers and poisoned wine. They had ample means and they found leisure to build churches and monasteries. Letters were written to Pavia, Rome, Ravenna and Byzantium, to Ireland, Northumbria and Spain. Scribes, drafting royal charters, took care to observe what formalities were handed down from the days of old imperial edicts, The Merovingian Latin was barbarous and the scribes' spelling puzzling in the extreme, but the beginning and the ending of every charter were copied out with an enviable exactitude.

Pilgrimages were made in the teeth of all perils on the road. There were feasts which demanded a heightening of ordinary observance, and the Church never wearied of trying to instil an orthodox consciousness into the Frankish mind. She was not wholly successful: for centuries to come, a certain nostalgia for the pagan past and a stubborn clinging to many unhallowed observances would stay with the people, some pagan ideas closely interwoven with the strands of the new dispensation.

Clovis's successors lacked his iron will. His dealings with the Frankish hierarchy were not exactly those of a pious Catholic. But under his successors, the balance of power shifted from the secular to the ecclesiastical. The Church became the main heartbeat of the country. She grew wealthy, and made the Crown acknowledge that her vast properties were inalienable at law because all she owned was in reality her Master's. She went much further to safeguard her independence from all lay encroachment. In the words of M. Latouche:[12] *'L'Eglise est devenue une personne morale dotée de capacité juridique.'*

And, in a certain sense, it was right.

A Merovingian bishop had his 'seat' in a town formally committed to the authority of a count appointed by the king and responsible to him alone. Under the Merovingian administration, many among those counts, together with their clerks and particularly tax collectors, considered their appointments as an easy channel to self-enrichment. The king's conception of the kingdom in terms of property was here repeated in little. It was left to the bishop to stand as an intermediary between his flock and bureaucratic rapacity.

It is true that all episcopal appointments were in the king's hands, and that certainly explains much of the later decadence of the Frankish Church but, once given his see, a bishop usually stayed there till his death, unlike the king's counts who were often moved from place to place at their master's pleasure or displeasure. A city, therefore, belonged to the bishop in a permanent and much more intimate manner. Its interests and privileges and also its hazards were shared by him. Being a man of substance, he often spent money on urban development and embellishment, and Gregory of Tours mentions bishops keeping roads in fair condition and organizing famine relief in kind. Perpetuus, Bishop of Tours in the later fifth century, referred to the poor of the city as his 'beloved friends in the Lord',[13] and his will included a generous provision for them. By virtue of their office, bishops could mediate between their flocks and the king's representative, and their relations were not always strained. The same Perpetuus bequeathed a mule and a horse to the count, speaking of him as 'my most beloved son.'[14]

None the less, the Merovingian climate of violence, teachery and venality ended by affecting the Frankish Church, and Columbanus's fulminations against it were grounded on facts. Little by little, chiefly owing to the difficulties of communication, the link with Rome weakened. Again, episcopal appointments were in the hands of the king, and few of them, Dagobert I excepted, were fit to make proper nominations. Young men and even boys, laymen of no moral stature, indifferently bred sycophants, who haunted the king's '*palatium*' for no other purpose than that of worming their way to a preferment, many such sat on episcopal thrones during the worst Merovingian period. The comparatively few, who were honourably fitted for their high office, often paid with their lives for a gesture of courage and candour.

There was yet another factor playing a sad enough part in the moral decay of the Frankish hierarch: the national law of inheritance. As a body, they professed their allegiance to '*Rex Francorum*', but all too often the crown would be disputed by three or even four men. Such a parcelling-up of sovereignty inevitably led to dissensions among the episcopate. Their synods, however infrequently held, became occasions for brawling and open violence. The more temperate men wished they might appeal to Rome, but Duchesne[15] can cite only one such case, and few, if any, Frankish bishops are known to have crossed the Alps during the whole of the seventh century. Moreover, so parochial did they become that they lost all interest in the affairs of other churches. The only far-flung outlets of Frankish spiritual activity were confined to pilgrims, but the majority of bishops had grown too indolent to undertake pilgrimages. To add to other evils, simony crept to the foreground: men, their hands deeply stained by bloodshed, learned that croziers and mitres could be had at a price.

Against such a background, however, quite a number of names shine as brightly as the stars on a winter's night, and Gregory of Tours[16] must have been happy when writing of them. There were prelates like the gentle Nicetus of Lyons, whose goodness and generosity could not be described; Remigius of Rheims, who dedicated himself wholly to the poor and unblessed folk, Caesarius of Arles, whose moral standards 'reached up to the mountains', Agericus of Verdun, 'never bitter in word or deed'; Avitus of Vienne, of whom another than Gregory said 'by him all the common people, all travellers and pilgrims were comforted . . . [*aluntur*];[17] and, finally, Praetextatus of Rouen, who had 'bitter words' with Queen Fredegund when she threatened him with exile because of his fearless sermon against the iniquities of the court. 'In exile and out of exile I was and am and shall be bishop, but you have not always been queen,' he told Fredegund, and went on to accuse her of her crimes, and warned her that she would not escape the judgment of God. Shortly afterwards, in the morning of Easter Day, Fredegund had the bishop murdered in the sanctuary of his own cathedral. Gregory of Tours adds that other prelates witnessed the horror but 'they did not come to the rescue of Praetextatus'.[18]

* * *

For all its chaos, horrors and darkness, to say nothing of the frustration gyving the land, the sixth century did not crush to dust the liberties of the mind. It produced a man like Gregory of Tours, the first historian of France. A Gallo-Roman of noble descent, he was born in 530, and could claim as kinsmen thirteen out of eighteen predecessors on the episcopal throne of Tours. As a chronicler, he was honest and painstaking. However barbaric his Latin, he yet possessed the gift of a telling phrase. A good man, he once said that he had 'a multitude of friends', and Venantius Fortunatus was among them.

Born at Treviso in 536, brought up and educated at Ravenna, Fortunatus found himself 'compelled' towards Frankland after a severe eye-complaint of his had been cured by a relic of St Martin of Tours kept at San Vitale in Ravenna. Fortunatus' learning sat lightly on him, but he was poet rather than scholar. He crossed the Alps, a clerk of no renown, little substance in his scrip but many songs on his lips. He could not then have foreseen that the see of Poitiers was to be his ultimate harbour.

He reached Paris. It did not please him, and he wandered westwards. In the end it was Gregory of Tours and Queen Radegund, then Abbess of St Cross at Poitiers, who accorded him both sanctuary and friendship, and assured him a livelihood.

'*Singulière destinée que celle de cette grande dame transplantée de la plus lointaine Germanie* [Radegund came from Thuringia] *pour y protéger en la personne d'un clerc italien les dernières aspirations de la muse latine*,' says Duchesne[19] for here, indeed, many casual and varied circumstances were welded together into a most rewarding and happy alliance. Fortunatus' resolve to tramp to Frankland ended in the introduction of most harmonious notes in the strident cacophony of the Frankish orchestra. The candles of learning were burning low: there were still a few men writing and copying ponderous theological commentaries, but nobody thought of poetry, and the very fluency of speech had vanished. Articulacy became an abrupt and clumsy matter. Dialects jostled one another at markets and other meeting-places, dialects still remote from the birth pangs of a national tongue. Latin had fallen low, its majesty as a great *lingua franca* in shameful tatters. Avitus of Vienne is said to be the last Merovingian ecclesiastic to have had a good style. Gregory of Tours, for all his knowledge of Virgil and Seneca, wrote a barbaric Latin. Still, grammar and style apart, he could at least tell a story in a living manner. Fredegarius[20] could only limp from one woodenly worded sentence to another.

Fortunatus brought a new breath into that climate. To him, every thread of life came as a line of a poem. Nothing he saw, felt, or heard but translated itself into an image of delicate beauty. Except for one occasion, he was a poet of little things. His verse-letters touched on orchards, sunsets, books, winter clothes, fruit, flowers and weather. Many among them are gracefully turned acknowledgements of the Queen-Abbess's gifts of violets, apples, vegetables, medicines and books and of skin coverlets to keep him warm through the winter months. Once, in a few lines of chiselled beauty, Fortunatus thanked the Queen for the gift of a garden. To read his poems is something of a reconciliation with the iron reality of his day. His work – from the great Passion hymns to the delicate little pieces about a spring morning or the apple-trees in Poitiers garden – is a reminder that circumstance, whatever its horror, should not blur the vision or deaden the imagination. '*Gallia vexata et afflicta saepius fuit*', remarks his biographer, marvelling at a gift so disciplined as not to be silenced by the turmoil all about the man.

A happy chance led a queen and a scholarly bishop to recognise the genius of an obscure Italian traveller. It was improvisation at its boldest and most rewarding. All unknown to the contemporaries, it created a precedent for Charlemagne who, in his turn, would choose the men best fitted to answer his own hunger for beauty and mental enlightenment.

*   *   *

By this time, the *Regnum Francorum* created by Clovis's ferocious energy was no longer an undivided entity. Well to the east, between the Rhine and the Moselle, lay Austrasia, wholly Germanic in its ethos, the people virtually untouched by Roman culture. To the West, between the Channel and the Loire was Neustria, its population still largely Gallo-Roman, preserving something of the language and customs from the past. Burgundy stretched all along the south-eastern border of Neustria. Aquitania, with Visigothic Spain for a turbulent neighbour, was rather loosely attached to Neustria. All those frontiers, however, were fluid, constantly subjected to territorial changes born of the box-and-cox sequence of victory and defeat. Communal life was like a tangled quickset hedge. In particular, testamentary dispositions were difficult to honour, and lawyers reaped good harvest from cases where defendant and plaintiff did not recognise the validity of one and the same law, each enjoying the right to be tried according to the law of his country of origin. In 614, a synod of bishops won their case at the court of Clotar II whom they petitioned to give a general assent to all bequests made to the Church in any part of the kingdom. Earlier, many such legacies had been contested by the testator's kin and declared void in provincial courts under the plea that, say, a Burgundian testament could not be enforced by the Salic Law.

It was in the reign of Clotar II (d.629) that a certain office, attached to the king's '*palatium*', began gaining more and more prominence. At the beginning a Mayor of the Palace used to be the chief officer of the household. His duties were many and some of them arduous – particularly during spells of famine when he must exert all his ingenuity to secure the victualling of the '*palatium*'. But, little by little, the simple domestic pattern of the office was enlarged both in scope and in importance. Some of the kings could not govern and the country would have been in a perpetual state of anarchy. The office became the major administrative post in Frankland. Mayors of the palace still professed allegiance to the king, decrees were still issued in his name, and counts in the provinces were still nominally responsible to him alone. In reality, by mid-seventh century, the three Mayors of the Palace in Austrasia, Neustria and Burgundy were virtual rulers of the country.

*   *   *

With the death of King Dagobert I in 639, the Merovingian day began drawing to its sunset. It is true that the dynasty survived well into the next century, but from now on a sovereign's person and sovereign power had little if anything to do with each other. '*Les rois fainéants*' were just a chaplet of names on little regarded charters. Many of them died young, exhausted by debauchery and drunkenness. Pale, thin shadows of men, they spent their entire lives scarcely aware of the confusion on their right hand and on their left. Some measure of contentment was theirs so long as they could live on what estates the Mayors of the Palace apportioned to them, enjoy their mistresses, their meat and wine. Fredegarius's abrupt entries are telling enough. 'AD 640. In those days Clotar the King, smitten by severe fever, died whilst still young, having reigned four years', and a little further on we are told about an unfortunate child being elected as 'King of the Franks'. 'They elected little Clodoveus to be King. After a few years the said King Clodoveus died of insanity',[21] and Fredegarius's anonymous 'continuator' echoed the judgment passed by Caesar and Livy upon the Gauls when he turns from the dryly factual record to acid comment. The Franks, according to him, were seldom certain of themselves, and 'great were the tumults among them'.[22]

Charlemagne's biographer in chief Einhard,[23] says of those days . . . 'the authority and strength of the realm were held by the prefects, who were called *majordomos* and [they] exercised full authority'. The king was content with its shadow. He wore his hair long according to the immemorial custom. He was poor since the Mayors of the Palace gave him but a meagre allowance (*precarium vitae stipendium*). If health allowed him to travel, he went to the *palatium* to receive ambassadors and sat there in a majesty shorn of all but a few trappings. He also attended the yearly assemblies of his people, and there spoke to them, repeating the words his mentors had taught him. Thousands and thousands among his subjects would not even know his baptismal name. Apart from the few great occasions, he appeared in the plain national dress and, when health did not permit him to ride, he would be driven in a cart drawn by a pair of oxen, a cowherd holding the reins. But be it said here that such a humble mode of travelling did not start with '*les rois fainéants*'. Dagobert I and his predecessors had not scorned to appear in a cart drawn by two oxen.

Those '*fainéants*' were indeed puppets. They were also a symbol and they were a necessity. However empty their title, it justified itself in that it reminded the people that – even though nominally – they were still ruled in the name of a man who alone among them could claim divine descent. Two centuries of Christian allegiance had not destroyed the legend of Merovech's miraculous origin.

Sovereignty was in the hands of three Mayors of the Palace in Austrasia, Neustria and Burgundy. Power was their daily bread, and they meant to rule, not to misgovern but, unfortunately, all three had a dream and a vision, its heart the matter of a united Frankland. The three men realized that the unification could not be accomplished except at the cost of a total defeat of the two among the three. So they sharpened their swords and axes for a long drawn out struggle. Each of the three was assured of support from the hierarchy and the landowners in their part of the kingdom. As to the unprivileged folk, their counsel was not asked for and their reaction regarded as much as a spent breath.

The landowners' loyalty and active help would prove a decisive element in the struggle. For some time past, a new leaven had been threading its way through the social structure of Frankland. A new aristocracy, still not hereditary, their wealth determined by the acreage they held, was coming forward. They owed nominal allegiance to 'the King of the Franks', but they were sworn vassals and servants of the Mayor of the Palace. They appeared at the *palatium* and the annual assemblies, but they were not hampered by the restrictions and obligations of any administrative status. Living on their vast estates, they were no more and no less than uncrowned kings in little. At a time when brigandage, rapine and murder were commonplace daily details, it was but natural that unendowed folk should commend their safety to the nearest powerful neighbour. Such protection would be accorded but, once given, it demanded an exchange of service. The landowners' armour would stand between a tenant and what jeopardy might fall across his path. But in return the manor fields, woods and mills must be worked by the tenant. In broad terms, vassalage suggests one circle enclosing another since the landlord himself owed fealty and service to the sovereign.

In what concerned land ownership, the interests of this lay aristrocracy were here and there interwoven with those of the Church. The great monasteries held large domains of their own, mostly bequeathed by the faithful. In principle, all Church property was inalienable. In practice, and that in spite of the law, some testamentary dispositions would be contested by the testator's kin usually with the result of the plaintiff losing the case. The Frankish Church being at the time cancered with venality, it often happened that 'justice' being meted to a lay defendant was in direct proportion to the palm oil at his disposal, and it also depended on his standing with a neighbouring religious house. Frankish laity were illiterate, but many monks were versed in law as well as in patristics. Old documents were consulted in search of new material for more lay demands on the Crown. The monasteries knew that all such services would be amply rewarded on the landowner's death.

The necessity of having lay landlords' support in the coming struggle made the Mayors of the Palace consent to have many of such demands embodied in the law. The ancient customs defining the right of pannage and suchlike were gradually raised to the level of binding edicts. There were laws about the snaring of game birds, rabbits and hares, about fishing and mill dues. Anything grown on the land was subjected to legislation, and a peasant's daughter, filling her basket with wild berries in a wood, was, if caught, proved to be a transgressor.

But lay lords and secular prelates were by no means the greatest landowners in Frankland. Monks' domains stood well to the forefront.

Monasticism was introduced into Gaul by St Martin of Tours and Ligugé in Poitou is supposed to have been the first monastic foundation. St Martin died in 397. With Honoratus on the Île de Lérins, Cassian at Marseilles in the fifth century and Caesarius at Arles in the sixth, monastic life spread into all the corners of Gaul, the native effort being gradually helped by missionaries from Ireland and Northumbria. The influence of a house like Marmoutiers extended all over Aquitania and beyond.

It was a grimly exacting life of prayer and manual work, but it answered a particular need of the day and it certainly lightened the darkness of the Merovingian sky. The monks gave up the world's delights but not the world's burdens. In an age of tattered moral values, they stood for integrity and, for the violence raging outside their gates, they offered peace. Finally they were the champions of mental enlightenment. Plough and harrow, hatchet and fishing-rod, a monk's hand was well trained to use all those. Equally, it knew how to use a pen. There would have been little, if any, literacy in those years if it had not been for the monks who taught the illiterate and copied manuscripts in their *scriptoria* – often enough in conditions to tax the endurance to the utmost. Winters could be cruel in Frankland. Only one room in any house had a fireplace in it, and that room was the infirmary, not the *scriptorium*.

By the sixth century, all alienation of Church land was forbidden by law, and M. Latouche remarks[24] that the monastic movement had '*la chance inésperée de naître et de se multiplier à une époque où les rois barbares . . . héritiers des immenses latifundiae légués par les empereurs romains disposaient de richesses foncières presque inépuisables . . .*'

From the Pyrenees to the Loire and from the Rhône to the Vosges men were settling down to a life known as '*via Dei*', i.e, God's road. At the very start, foundations were usually in wild, inaccessible places where the ground must be conquered inch by laborious inch. The monks tamed the wilderness. They cleared vast forests, reclaimed great stretches of marsh and bog, cultivated enormous reaches of apparently barren land. Some among them, permitted to go on pilgrimages to Rome and the East, brought back seeds of valuable nutritive plants unknown in Frankland.

The royal house, for all their preoccupation with war, rapine and murder, early enough recognized the importance of the movement. There were numerous royal foundations, the donors' generosity not always pleasing to the secular hierarchy. Even the terrible Fredegund and Brunhild, whose 'pastimes' all but turn the Borgias's trespasses into a parlour game, would endow monastic houses – in between devising fresh schemes for murdering their kin. Childebert I was the founder of St Vincent's Abbey near Paris, Clotar I created St Médards near Soissons, and Queen Radegund was the foundress of St Cross' at Poitiers. The kings were unstinted in their benefactions.[25] Some allowance should be made for the stilted language of the charters, the clerks in the royal chancery being anxious to follow old imperial usages. Still, the frequency and richness of grants of land and various other bequests make it obvious that even the most undeserving '*rois fainéants*' had a strong desire to promote monastic development and since the latter was undoubtedly for the good of the kingdom, it did not greatly matter that royal generosity had selfishness and fear for its roots. To endow a monastery was a guarantee, assuring monks' intercessory prayers before and after the donor's death. The bone of a formula '*ad laudem et stabilitatem regni nostri*' was no empty phrase.

Great lay landowners lost no time in following the royal example, since king and commoner stood on the same level in what concerned their chance of eternal salvation. To found a religious house meant a guaranteed stream of prayers which might well mitigate and shorten the afflictions of Purgatory, or even rescue a benefactor from the flames of Hell.

Little wonder that within less than two centuries after St Martin's death, monks in Frankland were the largest landowners.

*　　　*　　　*

The patristic thought had already been shaped, some great Biblical commentaries written, and the conciliar utterances brought together. Some of the classic authors found their way to the shelves of monastic libraries, but the corner-stone of mediaeval learning had been placed by St Augustine. God and the soul mattered alone. All knowledge to be acquired by man should be directed to one final aim – that of knowing God, and the means of achieving the aim lay in Holy Writ. Not a single question to engage man's curiosity but had its answer in the Scriptures. Natural facts had their value in so far as they offered confirmatory evidence of the truths in the Bible. St Ambrose, in his commentary on the Book of Genesis, held that physical phenomena knew no other law than the will of God, and in his 'Histories' Orosius spoke of God's *'ineffabilis ordinatio'* of all recorded events. The entire creation was shaped by a miracle, an expression of Eternal Will projecting into Time, and man's life was nothing if it did not answer the Maker's purpose to run the course for it appointed. Whatever unhappy deviations happened in life were due to man's weakness in succumbing to the nefarious lures of Satan.

A little later, one Salvianus, Belgic by origin, a priest at Marseilles, produced a book which was to bring great comfort to the mediaeval mind. The eight parts of his *'De Gubernatione Dei'*[26] deal exclusively with the fifth century, but much in them is applicable to any age. Salvianus looked upon the world of his day – with Rome falling into decay, barbarian hordes sweeping into Europe, and a sense of further disasters crippling the courage of many. Salvianus did not belittle either the misery or the danger, but he begged his readers to remember that happiness was to be found in the faith even when the drift of cruel circumstances seemed to deny it.

The theme was elaborated still further by a pupil of Salvianus, Salonius, Bishop of Vienne[27] and a Gallo-Roman by birth, who, in a commentary on the Book of Proverbs written in the form of a dialogue, asks why it is wrong to say that the past was better than the present. The answer is, because 'The one God is the Maker of past, present and future.'

Venantius Fortunatus died at the very threshold of the seventh century which certainly lacked the amplitude of

independent thought. But the riches of the past were not left to
gather dust on the shelves. *'Florilegiae'* came into their own,
those enchanting mediaeval anthologies, usually compiled in
monasteries, where the cream of patristic thought would be
gathered together for the benefit of such religious houses as
could not afford large libraries of their own. Negligible as was
the volume of purely creative activity, the church still offered
both material and incentive to keep the warm embers from a
grey death. A few hymns glided in among the commentaries
and works of hagiography, one being the well-known compline
poem – *'Christe, qui lux est et dies'*.[28]

In loose terms, all of it may be called a literature of acceptance and assimilation. Thought was by no means paralysed
but busied with an activity, its importance not dwarfed by the
dearth of outward expression. The polished turn of a good Latin
sentence was indeed forgotten, but men remembered the old
methods of exercising their minds. If fewer books were written,
many were copied, and they were read creatively. The patristic legacy stood in need of breathing space commensurate
with its volume. The process was slow, but the apparent lack
of original intellectual activity all through the seventh century
and through most of the eighth carried the seeds of the Carolingian age when the orchard would break into the promise of
fruit.

*   *   *

All its barbarity notwithstanding, the Merovingian age was
not barren of beauty. If creative literature was at a low ebb,
not so architecture and the little arts. Certainly, there was much
indebtedness to Italy, Byzantium and Asia Minor, but each
such borrowing passed through the crucible of the national
interpretation. There was much hunger for colour – gold,
crimson, purple, deep blue and hyacinth. Some articles of
domestic use and jewellery made at the time afford proofs of
taste and imagination. Both Sidonius Apollinarius and Gregory
of Tours describe the coloured magnificence of many churches
and abbeys in their day. Even when allowance is made for a
chronicler's unbridled enthusiasm the details given make it
obvious that his admiration was not evoked by daub and
wattle. Decorative detail, all the lovelier for being disciplined,

enhanced the beauty of stone. Paternus, Archbishop of Lyons, summoned artists from Ravenna to enrich his cathedral with mosaics, and Gregory of Tours describes how the wife of a bishop of Clermont was asked to choose themes for the mosaics at St Etienne's Church. She made her choice after studying some miniatures in a manuscript.

Contemporary wills mention crosses, reliquaries, cups and various ornaments of silver and gold. Eloi, friend and councillor of King Dagobert I, was the most famous goldsmith in his day. Much of his work was decorated with cloisonné, an art supposed to have come from Persia. Garnets, almandines and turquoises, brought from Asia Minor, were used for it. Designs for capital letters in manuscripts had Ireland for their place of origin.

Even the so called unprivileged people chaffering up and down a market place added much colour to the scene. The Franks were proud of their national dress and that included touches of scarlet and blue.

*   *   *

Such, then, was the Merovingian landscape in little, the cradle of Charlemagne's own inheritance. Much done or attempted by him would stem from the policy however crudely initiated by Clovis, and that included the administrative field. But where Clovis leant on the legend of his divine descent, Charlemagne's richly endowed personality – far more than his predecessors' laurels – would win the day. Both Clovis and he laboured at the foundations of the future greatness of Frankland. Both were equally and fatally hampered by their reverence for immemorial customs, a reverence having no other root except their conviction that no custom might be broken with impunity. Thus Clovis splintered the Merovingian fortunes by parcelling his dominions among his four sons. In their turn, Charlemagne's grandsons would precipitate the inglorious Carolingian sunset. But the imprint of a truly great reign abides whatever the chaos following it. The future reigning houses of France would stand in deep debt both to Clovis and to Charlemagne.

II

THE COUNTRY
HE CAME TO

From one point of view the beginnings of mayoral supremacy were hardly promising for the future of Frankland. The then mayors of the Palace in Austrasia, Neustria and Burgandy may well have shared a vision of a united country, but to each of them that goal appeared in terms of an inevitably bloody struggle. Very much in the manner of the Merovingian co-heirs, the three men waited for an opportunity to attack and snatch a victory, and for a time it seemed as though the national interests were all but reduced to ashes by the high burning flames of personal ambition which was inevitably encouraged to grow by the unending dynastic tangle and wrangle.

In the struggle Burgundy, with one exception, played a secondary part. The chief protagonists were Austrasia and Neustria, the former staunchly Teutonic, the latter deeply attached to the survivals of the Gallo-Roman era. In Austrasia, the Mayors' policy leant towards winning the favour of great landlords. In Neustria, for all the mayoral dictatorship, loyalty to the Crown stood to the forefront. The fact that the office was not yet hereditary, and its term sometimes determined by conspiracy ending in murder, added to the difficulties.

It was in Austrasia that Charlemagne's ancestry emerged at the beginning of the eighth century. The quarrel of the two queens, Brunhild in Austrasia and Fredegund in Neustria, helped in the founding of a new dynasty in the following century.

Once more the crown of Frankland was in dispute, Fredegund claiming the dignity for her son, Clotar, and Brunhild resolved not to surrender the rights of her infant great-grandsons. Were Brunhild to win the struggle, she and she alone would have ruled Austrasia, and such a possibility by no means pleased the people. The Mayor of the Palace in Austrasia was Arnulf, a nobleman of high repute and great possessions. Later, the Church would canonize him. Indeed, he deserved well of his God and his country, but he did not merely dislike Brunhild – he hated her, conscious as he was that her acknowledged supremacy would harm Austrasia to a bitter degree.[1]

Brunhild's downfall meant the forming of a conspiracy. Arnulf did not hurry. Gradually and surely he won the support of one Pippin of Landen, the greatest, most influential and popular landowner in Austrasia, his vast possessions stretching between the Meuse and the Moselle. The two men met several times and decided that, facing a crisis as they were, that was the moment for welding together Austrasia and Neustria 'for the future weal of Frankland'. In the end, Fredegund's son, Clotar, was invited to enter Austrasia and acclaimed as '*Rex Francorum*'. Brunhild's terrible death, however, could not but leave a stain on the escutcheon of the House of Arnulfings.

But to them nothing mattered except that the war-torn country should have peace again, and the year 613 was certainly an auspicious landmark. The young king owed his crown and sceptre to Arnulf and Pippin of Landen, and his ambitious mother had enough intelligence to see that a speedy uncrowning would have followed her son's attempt to govern independently. Some years later Arnulf, 'a man justly beloved by all the people in Frankland,'[2] retired to a hermitage having named Pippin of Landen as his successor in office. Pippin, having married his daughter, Becca, to Arnulf's son, Ansegisel, became – all unaware of it – virtual sovereign of the country, but his great qualities prevented him from blundering into clumsy and unnecessary assertions of his power.

With the accession of King Dagobert I in 629, Austrasia entered upon a golden age with a revival of arts and trade and an increased respect of her neighbours. But ten years later the country lost both Dagobert and Pippin, 'greatly regretted by all men of Austrasia, whose hearts he had won by his goodness and love of justice'[3]. Ansegisel assumed office. A shadowy figure, nothing good or bad could be said of him, but he was Arnulf's son and, in the country's eyes, that outweighed his pusillanimity and ineptitude.

The budding dynasty's fortunes were almost disastrously shaken in the middle of the seventh century when Pippin of Landen's son, Grimoald, became Mayor of Austrasia. The Arnulfings had so far ruled *de facto* but not *de jure*. To lay their hands upon the outward trappings of sovereignty had not been within their scheme. They had great ambitions but their statesmanship was firmly grounded in commonsense. They knew that the symbol of sovereignty, however shadowy its representative, was still cherished by the people. Dagobert I had been a great and merciful king. Whatever his successors' defects, there was still hope that another would arise to revive the kindly climate of a good reign.

But Grimoald thought differently. He did not covet the crown for himself but for his son. In 656, King Sigibert, a true *fainéant*, died, nobody remarking his death. But he left a legitimate heir. Grimoald's rôle in being the architect of a plan as stupendous as it was foolhardy offers ample material for a thriller. He laboured arduously and secretly. Sigibert's heir was seized, sent to Ireland, and there forced to enter a monastery. At the next annual assembly Grimoald had the temerity to proclaim his son, Childebert, '*rex Francorum*', but not a single arm moved to have the boy raised on a shield. 'The people,' according to the chronicler, 'were most indignant.'[4] Even those to whom the Merovingian matter meant nothing began asserting their loyalty to 'a house of divine descent'. Grimoald's supporters lost no time in melting away. He was seized, carried off to Paris, tried for high treason and executed 'with great torments'.

His nephew, Pippin of Heristal, son of Becca, succeeded him as Mayor, but the Austrasian mood had hardened against the Arnulfings. A spell of chaos followed, a bitter price to pay for one man's ambition, and Ebroin, then Mayor of Neustria, saw a chance to assert his supremacy in Frankland. First, in order to deny a possible ally to Austrasia, he overran Burgundy. In the long run, however, that proved a Pyrrhic victory; Pippin of Heristal was a true grandson of the Lord of Landen and of

Arnulf. Wise, just and patient, he succeeded in winning back
the people's affection, and Austrasia soon came to forget
Grimoald's mad trespass. Ebroin died in 681, his ambition to
break Austrasia unrealized.

The lord of Heristal had his own idea of a united Frankland,
and he followed it in the teeth of one obstacle after another.
The Arnulfings were most unpopular in Neustria, and it took
Pippin fully eight years to carry out his design. 'He wants the
Crown,' – alleged his enemies. 'Like uncle, like nephew', but
the calumny fell on deaf ears in Austrasia. The people knew
that Pippin did not mean to supplant the Merovingian, and
they trusted him to lead them to victory. The way was rough,
long and wearying. Not till 687, at Tétry near St Quentin, did
the Austrasian host win a decisive day. By its fruits Pippin of
Heristal became the only Mayor of the Palace in Frankland.
The Franks were united, their dominion stretching right across
the Rhine with the Bavarians and the Allemannians under
Pippin's hand. The fortunes of the Arnulfing house rose to an
unprecedented height, and Pippin was now formally styled as
'*Dux Francorum*'.

But the high honours won by him involved many responsibilities. The victory of Tétry, for all its far-reaching and
abiding results, was no magical cure for many old wounds. The
long war had all but drained the exchequer, and it asked for
courage to raise taxation which, within the social framework
of the day, hit hardest at the men of Pippin's own rank. Land
was about the only criterion of wealth and yet vast reaches of it
lay ravaged after drawn out carnage. The pulse of urban life
beat faintly, and trade was all but moribund. A crushed
Neustria did not mean that Frankland had no enemies:
Pippin had to defend its northern and eastern boundaries from
Frisians, Saxons and various savage Slav tribes. Towards the
end of his life the European skies grew dark indeed with the
Arab invasion of Spain.

Pippin did not spare himself, and he deserved well of his
people. Unfortunately the man at the helm of public affairs
and the man within the comparative privacy of his own
palace had little, if anything, in common with each other. The
one was brilliant as statesman, soldier and administrator. The

other was in the habit of listening to women's gossip and harmful advice, and capable of stumbling into one blunder after
another. With nearly fatal results for the future of Frankland,
the uxorious puppet in Pippin of Heristal gained ascendancy
over the wise 'Dux Francorum' towards the very end of his life.

Fortune smiled at the Arnulfings, but there ran a curious
streak of dichotomy in them all. It almost looks as though they
had a demon for their familiar, compelling them to risk
everything on a game of absurd and occasionally disastrous
hazard. Pippin of Landen had given his only daughter in
marriage to a shadowy fool. Grimoald had all but entombed the
Arnulfing cause by his effort to satisfy an insane ambition; with
Pippin of Heristal, a woman's intrigue very nearly wrecked the
future dynasty.

Two names only are associated with him – that of Alphaida,
who bore the architect of Frankish greatness known as Charles
Martel, and that of Plectrudis, 'a harsh and domineering
woman',[5] whose own son died leaving an illegitimate boy, one
Theudwald, in his grandmother's care. To Plectrudis, the
child became the earnest of her own ascendancy in the land.
It was Pippin's privilege to name his successor in office.
Charles was his obvious heir, and Plectrudis hated Charles.
Too astute to follow in the steps of Brunhild and Fredegund,
Plectrudis did not have her stepson murdered but she succeeded
in poisoning her husband's mind against the only possible
candidate for the high office. She kept telling Pippin that
Charles cared for nothing except war, that he nursed the
ambition to wear the crown, that he was known to mock at
church ceremonies and to have no respect for the hierarchy.
Her voice was not the only one at the Mayor's Palace: she had
a crowd of sycophants and it was easy to persuade them to
echo her strictures. Pippin was old, ailing and weary. He had
reached his deep winter and his wife's unending complaints
about Charles seemed in accord with the season. So Pippin
named Theudwald, aged eight, as his successor, and died. It
happened in 714. The Arabs had overrun the Iberian Peninsula
three years before.

Flushed with her triumph, Plectrudis promptly had Charles
imprisoned. She might have had him killed. She did not, and

her apparently incomprehensible restraint in this instance must stand to the unending credit of this otherwise detestable woman. The future of the entire Europe would have run a darkened course if Plectrudis had followed in Brunhild's steps and had Charles assassinated.

Her sun set all too rapidly. She had meant to govern but she needed wise counsellors and sycophants had not the making of statesmen in them. Neustria would have none of her and, fortified by the support of the Frisians, attacked Austrasia. So did the Saxons in the north. One defeat followed on the heels of another until in 715 Charles escaped from prison and sent a summons to his people who lost no time in rallying under his standard, and vociferously acclaimed him as the rightful '*Dux Francorum*'.

It was a moment of danger, with a deadly enemy standing well within the Frankish doorway, but to Charles Martel danger was a breath of life. He neither sought nor provoked the greatest campaign of the century. He certainly welcomed it. The battle-cry of the Franks may well have been 'death to the infidel'. To a Dagobert I, such a war would have appeared as a holy crusade. The Frankish hierarchy so regarded it, and the lack of piety in Charles Martel made them mistrust him all the more. At least, one of his stepmother's allegations bore the seeds of truth: Charles had little reverence for the Church. When the exigencies of the moment demanded it, he confiscated Church properties – in mocking defiance of the law passed in 614. He bestowed vacant prelacies and abbacies on any but deserving laymen in his retinue. He interfered between the hierarchy and their tenantry, and he regarded the Arabs as his enemies because they had dared to invade Frankland.

* * *

In 711 the Visigothic Kingdom of Spain had fallen under the Moslem onslaught. A few years later the Arabs crossed the Pyrenees, reached the heart of Burgundy, and overran Provence at a time when Charles Martel was still in prison. The Arab advance halted, and the long respite certainly played into Charles's hands.

By the spring of 732 the Arabs decided the moment had

come for the final conquest of Frankland. A great host, led by Abderrahman, routed the Duke of Aquitania near Périgord, and pressed on until Poitou lay under their heel and the fair city of Poitiers had been put to the sack. The invaders' way seemed clear to Tours and Paris.

A lesser strategist would have given battle long before. But Charles Martel preferred to wait, and his own great army trusted him to a man. He led his forces to a plain between the rivers Clain and Vienne, and there he encamped.

The Arabs, leaving the smoking roofs of Poitiers well behind them, galloped on until they came to the banks of the Clain and saw the Frankish camp, and Abderrahman was rather discomforted by its size. Himself a good general, he decided to let the Franks have the first chance, and he had no doubts about the outcome. The dice were certainly loaded in his favour: his army was invincible, and all the men were mounted, whilst the Frankish rabble were on foot.

A week passed. The Franks would not attack. At last, the Arabs moved forward – to be checked not by a single counter attack but by the immobility of the enemy. The Franks stood like a wall, 'as though they were frozen to their places by the cold breath of winter', said the chronicler. To a man, they obeyed their leader's order of the day. Nor did they shout. Standing still, many dying where they stood, they parried thrust for thrust and blow for blow, their swords and axes unerring in striking and hewing down. No sooner would a Frank fall than a comrade leapt into the gap. The battle went on through the day. The dark fell on unbroken Frankish ranks, and wave upon wave of superstitious terror swept up and down the Arab host. Was it the Christian God helping the enemy, or Satan lending them what seemed supernatural strength? The Arabs could not tell.

At dawn, the tents were there for the Franks to see. Charles Martel ordered an advance and his men reached those sumptuous tents of red and yellow silk to find nothing except immense booty awaiting their pleasure. The Arabs had fled during the night and the grim legend of the Moslem invincibility was broken for ever.

The battle of Poitiers was an immense landmark. For one

thing, it proved the Frankish unity. They had won the day, Austrasian, Neustrian, Bavarian and Burgundian standing shoulder to shoulder. Pilgrims and travellers talked of the miraculous victory. Minstrels composed lays to be sung from the Pyrenees to the Alps and even beyond. Embassies were sent to Frankland to be received not by a Merovingian king but by the *Dux Francorum*. The Church promptly forgot his impieties and ordered solemn Te Deums to be sung all over the country. Aberrahman having been killed at Poitiers, neither friend nor foe could explain the Frankish victory except as a miracle. It did not greatly matter to Charles what the bishops thought of it. He and his people had won the day. The rest was immaterial.

Charles was a king in all but the title. The Arnulfings had won their way to the throne, but he would not mount its steps. He had no need of regal trappings, nor any leisure to give to an insignificant matter. The throne of Frankland meant much less than the people of Frankland, and his particular genius knew well how to serve them. Moreover, he was very busy. There were the Frisians and Saxons to deal with in the North, the savage and cunning Avars to keep in check in the East. Nor did the battle of Poitiers put an end to the Arab arrogance. Within a few years they returned and, having crossed the Rhône, overran and devastated Provence. This time, to the Pope's sharp displeasure, Charles Martel had an ally. His brother-in-law, Luitprand, King of the Lombards, came to help him. Within a short time Provence was in Frankish hands, the Arabs retreating once again.

The Pope, Gregory III, congratulated Charles in rather lukewarm terms. His own patrimony, said the Pope, was being constantly menaced by the Lombards and, surely, it behoved 'the most pious Franks' to come to the help of the See of St Peter. The leader of the 'most pious Franks' had many faults and vices but disloyalty was not among them. Luitprand having proved himself a true ally, Charles would not interfere in the quarrel of the Papal See. Besides, the Pope's ambassadors were told, the *Dux Francorum* had his hands full fighting the savage Saxons.

He came back, a tired and sick man, and in October 741 he

D

died at Quierzy-sur-Oise. They buried their hero at St Denis, laying the stone coffin side by side with that of a crowned king.

Charles's last act was in full and unfortunate accordance with the Arnulfing genius for blundering. He had scorned the Canon Law and many ecclesiastical observances but the roots of a differently coloured loyalty lay deep in his heart. It would be too sweeping to say that Charles Martel was a Frank before he was a Christian. Still, the immemorial customs of the tribe were sacrosanct to him. A king in all but name, he directed that the whole of Frankland was to be divided among his three sons, Carloman, Pippin the Short, and Grifo, and the Franks were pleased with their leader's adherence to a custom far older than the provisions of *Lex Salica*.

It was certainly an inconsistency when we remember Charles Martel's efforts towards the unification of Frankland, but that particular streak was evident in much of his policy. His dealings with the Frankish Church were occasionally odd, to say the least. His lay abbots and prelates were by no means pillars of piety, but he sponsored the missionary cause with a zeal which justly earned him papal approbation. St Boniface was his intimate friend, and Willibrord and other Northumbrian missionaries were greatly encouraged by him in their work among the Frisians. Finally, it was during Martel's tenure of office that friendly relations were re-established with the Papal See, and Gregory II was among the first to recognise his quality.[6]

His grandson's reign would rather overshadow the accomplishments of Charles Martel but it was he who, perfecting the work of Clovis, placed Frankland on a pinnacle and left a fair heritage to his renowned grandson.

The division of the country willed by Charles Martel did not really weaken Frankland because it did not last long. Grifo, the youngest of the three brothers, wholly unversed in the ways of government, was deposed peaceably, his passing unremarked by the people. Carloman, his conscience troubled by his father's lapses from grace, decided that it was his duty to atone for them, and within a few years he retired from the world. Carloman did not seek refuge in any Frankish monastery. He crossed the Alps and made his vows at Monte Cassino.

Pippin the Short was left alone in Frankland, a king in all but name. A feeble-minded Merovingian puppet sat on the throne, easy enough to be disposed of – by poison or any other means. But Pippin was too wise to repeat Grimoald's mistake. The king must remain until the people wished him gone. At the spring assembly of 751 the question was put. The lay approval of Pippin's idea was unanimous. There remained the hierarchy, and Pippin the Short did not share his father's ideas about the Church. The whole body of Frankish landowners clamoured for him to assume kingship. He answered them by sending an embassy to Rome in the summer of 751. It was headed by Fulrad, Abbot of St Denis, who was to be the spokesman of the people of Neustria, and Burchard, Bishop of Würzburg, who represented the Austrasian interests. The ambassadors were instructed to consult Pope Zacharias 'concerning the kings of the Franks who were of royal race . . . but had no power . . . except only that grants and charters were [still] drawn up in their name.' The bishop and the abbot explained to the Pope that 'the King of the Franks did all things in accordance with the Mayor's pleasure.' According to the ancient custom, the king made a public appearance on the first day in March to receive the customary gifts of the people. On that occasion he wore the crown and the royal mantle, and sat on the throne, the army mustered behind him and the Mayor of the Palace standing near the throne. The king, thoroughly briefed for the occasion, informed the assembly that such and such new laws were to be passed, thanked them for the gifts they had brought, and prayed that God's blessing should be upon them. The ceremony marked his only appearance among his people. For the rest of the year, the king stayed on what estate had been allotted for his use, enjoyed his mistresses and his meat and wine, received no one, and interfered in no state matters.

When Pippin's emissaries had presented their case, Pope Zacharias replied that it seemed better for one who had power in the kingdom to be called king. It followed that Pippin of the House of Arnulfings should be styled King of the Franks.[7]

The bishop and the abbot, well pleased with such an answer, travelled back to Frankland. In the following November, a great assembly came together at Soissons to see Pippin, not raised on a shield and acclaimed king, but anointed and crowned by Boniface, Archbishop and missionary. The people's cheers were deafening. They wanted Pippin for king, and the Church sealed their approval with a rite never before seen in the country. It was the birthday of the Carolingian dynasty. The Merovingian era stepped into the past, its last representative, Childeric III, vanishing into the silence of the cloister.

It was a revolution in little and, as such, it had no juridical basis. Zacharias had no authority to raise Pippin to the throne, to depose Childeric III, or to absolve the Franks from their oath of allegiance to the Merovingian. But it should be remembered that the authority of the Mayor of the Palace rested solely on the conjunction of circumstances and had no legal backing. The event of November 751 was undoubtedly arranged *pro bono publico*. It is doubtful if Charles Martel would have an affirmative reply from the Pontiff, or if Zacharias would have been so ready to comply, were it not for his pressing need of Frankish help.

We can find no mention of a nine-year-old boy being present at the ceremony at Soissons, but he and his mother would certainly have been there, Bertrada, once Pippin's mistress in chief, later his wife, and now Queen of Frankland, and Charles her first born, of whose early years we know nothing except that he was supposed to be born out of wedlock. There are no pleasing stories about the budding genius in infancy, childhood, or youth. Enough of the Frankish way of life is known to build up the boy's background: he would be early skilled in horsemanship and in the use of bow and sword, brought up hardily as befitted a soldier's son, trained in good manners by his great lady of a mother, taught to despise physical indolence and not to run away from danger, acquainted with the past of his country and taught enough Latin to follow church services and to understand ambassadors' speeches. As a boy, Charlemagne may well have been fond of his food and showed an insatiable curiosity about everything happening under God's sky. His affection for his mother and for his only sister, Gisla, must have developed early enough. We cannot tell what particular incident started his mistrust and dislike of his younger brother Carloman, fully nine years his junior. For the rest, Charlemagne's later life would prove the scope and the depth of his imagination. The unprecedented splendours of that November day at Soissons must have been deeply engraved in his memory and stamped his piety in a very particular way.

His biographer in chief, Einhard, tells us[8] that he could find neither written records nor any oral traditions about his hero's early years, and there was nobody living at the time who could acquaint him with any such facts. Now Einhard came to Charlemagne's court about 791 and remained with his patron until his death in 814. It is difficult to imagine that Einhard never met anyone who had known Charlemagne in his childhood and that by 820 when the biography was being written, there was 'nobody living' able to remember the great man's youth. And yet we know enough about Einhard not to doubt his truthfulness. That fourth chapter of his book presents us with one of the most teasing historiographical puzzles. We shall never know the grounds for Einhard's decision 'to omit the unknown' ('*omissis incognitis*').

A rather wild imaginative variant has suggested that Charlemagne had an unhappy childhood – chiefly on account of his father's unkindness – and so he wished it to remain forgotten, and that Einhard, deeply in his patron's confidence, honoured the wish. But there is no historical basis for any such conjecture. Except for one ot two thickly flattering entries in the annals, we know nothing at all of Pippin's personal character. Again, Charlemagne's devotion to his mother, Queen Bertrada, is a well proved fact, and such deep affection does not quite accord with an early landscape of misery.[9]

Thus the enigma remains unsolved to this day.

*   *   *

That November day in 751 marked a particular involvement of Pippin the Short in papal affairs. Pope Zacharias had virtually bestowed the crown on him. That first coronation in Frankland screened a bargain between the Pontiff and the King, its exact terms left most adroitly undefined.

The Pope's position was no easy one at the time. He needed

allies, and where could he look for them? Neither Britain nor
Spain could afford to give him the support required by the
circumstances. In Italy, the Lombards never ceased to covet
his possessions. The Pope was the greatest landowner in the
peninsula: St Peter's patrimony included virtually the whole of
the Campagna, vast estates along the Adriatic coast, in Sicily
and in Calabria. The papal revenues were very great, but, as
Hodgkin points out[10]: '... the Pope was ... what the Emperor
had once been, the great relieving officer of Rome, not only in
the Eternal City but all over Italy . . . whenever a bishop
brought a case of distress under his notice, there was a strong
probability that he would receive a grant in aid from the papal
revenues'.

The Lombards' conquest in Italy had led to the shaping of a
most troublesome triangle of authority. Though the imperial
throne had been at Constantinople since 476, Byzantium still
retained her Italian possessions, the Venetian archipelago
among others. All those properties were administered by the
Exarch of Ravenna, an imperial nominee. The entire valley
of the Po, most of Tuscany, the Appenines and Apulia belonged
to the Lombards. Arians at the beginning, they later entered
the Catholic fold, but that did not prevent them from showing
open hostility to the Pope, whose own position was the last word
in anomaly. He was Patriarch of the West, but the dignity was
either blandly ignored or rudely challenged by Constantinople.
He was a sovereign in his own right, but that sovereignty had
no real basis to it since he was a subject of the Emperor and, as
such, answerable to the Exarch of Ravenna.

There had been much friction before Pippin's day. Earlier
in the century the rabid iconoclasm of the Emperor Leo III had
widened the gulf between East and West. Tension thickened
when Leo's Italian subjects refused to submit to his decrees and
retained sacred images in their churches. Nothing but the
patience, prudence and charity of the reigning pontiff (Gregory
II) averted a disastrous clash. Now, in mid-century, King
Aistulf of Lombard took Ravenna and ended the Exarch's rule.
However troublesome the latter, it was still preferable to the
iron heel of the Lombard. Pope Zacharias was no Gregory II.
He knew only too well that no aid could be expected from

Byzantium, gravely harassed by Bulgarian inroads and her own home dissensions. There were only the Franks. Zacharias gave the crown to Pippin, appealed for help, and died at the beginning of 752, of a broken heart, said some. There is no record of Pippin's reply to the appeal. Most likely there was none because Zacharias' successor, Stephen II, lost no time in sending a passionate letter to Frankland. Aistulf, not content with the capture of Ravenna, was now threatening the duchy of Rome, 'raging as furiously as a lion'.[11]

Charles Martel had received a similar appeal from Gregory III in 740, and had answered it by sending costly presents to Rome. Yet Pippin was no Mayor of the Palace but a dedicated king. When Stephen II followed the first letter by a private message: 'would the Most Christian King of the Franks arrange a meeting with the Pope?', Pippin's reaction was prompt. Chrodegang, Bishop of Metz, and Duke Autchar, the king's chief councillor, were at once sent to Italy to fetch the Pontiff and to bring him to Frankland.

Unfortunately, just about the time of the departure from Rome, the papal party was delayed most uncomfortably. Byzantium, having turned a deaf ear to all appeals for help against the Lombard aggression, now awoke to the fact that Ravenna had been filched from her, and emissaries of the Emperor Constantine V appeared in Rome, bringing an imperial command to Stephen II. He was to make for Pavia and argue Aistulf into restoring Ravenna and other cities to the imperial rule. It was a peremptory command of a sovereign to a subject, and nothing was said about any aid coming from Byzantium.

The Pope dared not disobey even though he knew that any such attempt would be futile. To get Ravenna restored to the Empire was no matter to be decided at a council table, and Aistulf's probable reaction to the imperial demand would mean, as the Pope had good reason to expect, a wholesale spoliation of St Peter's patrimony.

The mission failed, and Aistulf kept Stephen II at Pavia for as long as he could. It was high honour to entertain such a guest, he alleged, trying to screen his reluctance to let the Pope cross the Alps. Not until late autumn 753 could Stephen leave

Lombardy. Spent by anxiety and the hazards of travel, he reached St Maurice's Abbey at Valais in the Swiss Alps. The first to welcome the Pope was not the Abbot but a tall, fair, good-looking boy with a pleasant smile and exquisite manners. King Pippin's first honour paid to the Pope was to send his eldest son to meet him.

This is the first recorded appearance of Charlemange – *'filius regis Carolus'* came to Valais there to await the arrival of the Pope. But the teasingly brief entry carries deep significance and leaves its stamp on the years to come.

Charles was either eleven or twelve at the time.[12] By that time his parents were duly married. He had a sister, Gisla, and an infant brother, Carloman. Frankish childhood was of no long duration, and a soldier's son would have been removed from the care of nurses at the age of four or five. By the time he met the Pope, he would have travelled about with his father, learning the art of war in Aquitania and along the Saxon border. He would have met ambassadors coming to Pippin's court. The conversation and behaviour of the King's intimates would have enlarged his horizons and informed his mind, and there were quite a few men of note at Pippin's court – Chrodegang, Bishop of Metz, Abbot Fulrad of St Denis, Burchard of Würzburg, said to be an Englishman, and Autchar, soldier and statesman, to name but a few.

At the Valais meeting, however, Charlemagne was his father's representative for the first time.

The stay at the abbey had to be prolonged because of the old Pope's exhaustion. Not until the day of Epiphany 754 did he reach Pippin's court.

Stephen's sojourn in Frankland was a long one. There were many conferences. Three times did Pippin send messengers to Pavia, but Aistulf refused to listen to any persuasion. Pippin, having pledged his support to the Pope, realized that war was inevitable. But there loomed difficulties. He was no autocrat: great decisions must be made at the national assembly, the consent of those present being an imperative, and the Frankish mind regarded an Italian campaign with disfavour. Charles Martel had refrained from picking a quarrel with Lombardy, and who were they to say that Charles Martel had been wrong?

So much needed to be done at home, and they had Arabs and Saxons to fight. If Byzantium did not choose to protect her own possessions in Italy, should it be the business of the Franks to attempt a hazardous journey and shed their blood in a thankless task? It was rumoured that Queen Bertrada, for all the sincerity of her devotion to St Peter's chair, regarded such a campaign with misgiving, and the people knew that Pippin listened to his wife's advice.

But he had pledged his word, and little by little, encouraged by his best councillors, he succeeded in changing the sullen reluctance into an eager anticipation of great glory to come to the arms of Frankland. To fight the Arabs was certainly a fitting task for a champion of Christendom. To protect St Peter's patrimony became a height of honour.

And just at that time there occurred yet another twist in the curious Carolingian mentality.

King Pippin's brother, Carloman the Elder, had been a monk at Monte Cassino since 747. In the early summer of 754 he appeared in Frankland – not to support the Pope's cause but to plead with his brother not to start fighting the Lombards. For a moment, all was confusion at Pippin's court. Carloman argued that the King of the Lombards was no enemy of the Pope, that Byzantium was no friend of Italy, and, generally, that war against Lombardy would mean a dishonour for Christendom. Carloman's arguments were too fantastic to be taken seriously, but he was the King's brother and even his histrionics could not pass unnoticed. Pippin did not let him return to Monte Cassino. Carloman was taken to a monastery near the Breton border where he died soon after. His vehement championship of Aistulf remains one of the lesser enigmas of history.

Meanwhile, preparations for the Italian campaign were going ahead. Almost on its eve, in the middle of July 754, thousands of Franks crowded into the Abbey Church of St Denis. Fulrad stood in the abbatial stall, but the main protagonist was the Pope. Pippin, his two sons, and the entire household knelt in the choir. Stephen II re-anointed Pippin, bestowed on him the title of a Roman patrician, and crowned his two sons as their father's co-heirs. That done, Stephen II 'blessed Queen Bertrada' and the nobles of the Frankish nation and . . . he bound them under penalty of interdict and excommunication never to presume to elect a king who should come forth from the loins of any other than these persons whom Divine Providence had raised to the throne, and who . . . had been consecrated and confirmed by the hands of the Pope.'[13] As Freeman remarks[14] 'The house of Pippin and Arnulf . . . was [then] definitely established as the royal house of the Franks . . . The main point is that the unction of the two sons of Pippin as well as their father declared the kingliness of the whole house.'

In bald terms, the ceremony concluded a bargain. The so-called 'Donation of Pippin' is no longer extant, and it is doubtful if it ever existed in spite of the claims made by later papal apologists. Pippin was supposed to restore to the Pope much more than the Exarchate of Ravenna, and such liberties with the Italian terrain would hardly have been tolerated by Byzantium. In more sober terms, however, the bargain was a fair one. The primate of western Christendom and the first ruler of the West concluded an alliance to the benefit of both. That Ravenna should be wrested from the Lombards and joined to the papal dominions was but a secondary point, and is one of the terms proved in the sources.

Charles Martel would hardly have agreed to any terms but no Pope would ever have been Martel's guest. Pippin, 'that devout and most mild mannered king', accepted them.

In the spring of 755, the Frankish host set out for Italy. The chronicles make no mention of Charlemagne accompanying his father, but it is unlikely that the prince would have been left at home. He was almost fourteen, and Frankish boys learned the art of war at an early age. That first Italian campaign must have proved a good school. Pippin had learned strategy from Charles Martel and so deployed his troops that the Lombards were checked at every turn until Pippin encamped outside the walls of Pavia and Aistulf had to ask for a truce. Pippin's terms were in accord with his agreement with the Pope. They were harsh, but the Lombard agreed to abide by them. No sooner had the Franks recrossed the Alps than Aistulf broke his pledge, and Pippin was in conscience bound to carry on with the job. Once more his army marched into Lombardy, and from a later

incident it is obvious that Pippin's wife was against the resump-
tion of hostilities. But Pippin seldom listened to women. He
pressed on, and the Lombards were routed. In the late spring
of 756 Pippin's camp was set up in the great plain outside
Pavia.

Here, the emissaries of the Emperor found him. They had
travelled by sea to Marseilles, made overland to Paris, and
learned that Pippin had left for Italy. They hurried southwards.
Their request was surprising. His business with the Lombards
was his own affair, they said, but Ravenna and all the other
territories of the Exarchate were to be restored to Byzantium,
such was the Emperor's command. The emissaries argued the
case with all the adroitness of well-trained Greek diplomats,
and Pippin heard them out, but they did not succeed in
bending the strong will of that most Christian and benign man!
Pippin refused their request without any hesitation. And more:
he affirmed with an oath that not to win the favour of any
mortal man had he twice addressed himself to the fight but
solely for the love of St Peter and for the pardon of his sins, and,
that no amount of 'money would induce him to take away what
he had once given to St Peter'.

The Greek emissaries carried that reply back to Byzantium,
and Byzantium accepted it. Pippin's answer deepened the cleft
between East and West, and he must have been aware of it,
but he could have done no other.

The climate was radically changed in the following year.
Aistulf died and Desiderius succeeded him. In Rome, Stephen
II died of a broken heart, as some said. His successor was Paul I
(757–762), whose letters to the King of the Franks suggest a
mental see-saw. Now the King of the Lombards is 'our most
excellent son come humbly to Rome on a pilgrimage.' In the
very next epistle, Paul I is at a loss to find strong enough
epithets to describe the perfidy of Desiderius. 'He is a traitor,
determined to spoil the Lord's heritage'. Soon after, the
Lombard becomes the pattern of all Christian virtues. The most
Christian King of the Franks should help his brother. Once
again Desiderius 'has broken all the promises he made, he has
restored none of St Peter's territories, and he is threatening
Rome. Come and save the Apostles' heritage.' Paul I begged

for help most piteously, he sent jewels, relics, and books to his most beloved son Pippin, and among his presents was the rarity of a clock so cunningly contrived that it could be used at night.

Pippin acknowledged the gifts and sent his own presents to Rome, his emissaries invariably charged to assure the Pope of the King's unfailing good will towards him. Such exchange of courtesies, however, began and ended the matter: Pippin had no intention of crossing the Alps for the third time. For one thing, as will be seen, he had quite enough on his hands. For another, the Pope's epistolary effusions made it evident that the man did not know his own mind and Pippin's arrival in Lombardy might well have coincided with an outpouring of papal affection for his 'beloved and noble son, Desiderius'. The first Carolingian king could not afford to appear in a fool's motley because of the Pope's moods.

Thus the matter of Lombardy was shelved, to be finally determined one day by Pippin's son.

The first Carolingian reign was coming to its end. Pippin was spared the indignities of shattered health and old age, but all the hardihoods of a soldier's life began taking their toll soon enough. He was still in his early fifties and he was spent. His kingdom had grown. So had his cares, but Pippin could contemplate the years behind him and not feel ashamed of them. The long war with Aquitania was drawing to its close, and now the south-western boundaries of Frankland brushed against the Pyrenean foothills. Narbonne was wrested from the Arabs. Constant vigilance was still needed in the north where Frisians and Saxons were determined to safeguard their savage liberties by repeated intrusions on the Frankish soil, but those were irritants: they did not threaten the unity of the land. Byzantium's home affairs prevented her from displaying hostility towards the West. It is true that trouble had broken out in Bavaria where Pippin's nephew, Duke Tassilo, having married Luitberga, King Desiderius's daughter, openly refused allegiance to his uncle and declared his duchy to be independent. But that complication, Pippin felt, would have to be solved by his heirs.

He had lived busily, honourably and recklessly. We know

nothing of his moral habits but his death proved his other excesses. Towards the end of 767 his health began breaking up. Within a few months he died in Paris of dropsy, – 'apud Parisios morbo aquae'.[15]

If Pippin left a will, we have no trace of it. The law of primogeniture was not followed by the Franks. Having buried their king with due honour, those closest to the court called a solemn national assembly. By common assent, Frankland was divided between Pippin's two sons. The elder, called Carolus, was then 26; the younger, Carloman – barely sixteen. The division of the kingdom might well have had unfortunate repercussions if it had lasted. Charlemagne's portion was larger in area but it carried many more complicated responsibilities. It comprised Austrasia, part of Neustria and the north German lands. Carloman received Provence, Schwabia where the Allemannians lived, and the western part of Neustria.

Einhard tells us that a measure of concord[16] was maintained by the brothers, but the following three years were by no means easy for Charlemagne. The war with Aquitania not being concluded at Pippin's death, Carloman pledged himself to help his brother and broke his promise. Various administrative measures in Neustria demanded the joint consent of both Kings: Carloman either neglected to give his, or withdrew it. Married to one Gerberga, daughter of a wealthy Frankish landowner, he was said to be under her influence, and she disliked her brother-in-law. There were dark rumours of plots against Charlemagne. He ignored them all, and never permitted the strained relations to flame into an open rupture. Fortunately after less than three years, Carloman died of an unspecified disease.[17]

Some conspiracy against Charlemagne must have been maturing at the time. For no other reason would Carloman's widow, Gerberga, have fled the country together with her two infant sons and her husband's chief councillors. Her choice of sanctuary was rather singular: she placed herself under the protection of Desiderius, King of the Lombards. Charlemagne accepted her flight without protest. We have no evidence of his making a single effort to make her return to Frankland. The elder of Carloman's infant sons was naturally his heir, but

Gerberga's action made dust of the child's chances of succession. In Frankland, a national assembly was held, and the Franks unanimously assented to make Charlemagne sovereign of a united country. He was nearly thirty at the time.

*　　*　　*

At first glance, the fourth chapter of Einhard's biography suggests a thickly woven curtain never to be lifted by anyone's hand. Einhard had no use for frothy anecdotal treatment. Unlike Notker Balbulus of St Gall, he, choosing Suetonius for his pattern, did not gather his facts second or third hand. Of Einhard's matchless integrity we know enough[18] to accept the portrait he painted, yet the comparison with a thick curtain does not really answer.

Einhard's silence about Charlemagne's childhood and youth does not really prevent us from filling in the lacunae left by the biographer. We know enough of his happy relations with his mother, Queen Bertrada, and his sister, Gisla. A single entry in a chronicle tells us of his early apprenticeship in diplomacy. His long and arduous schooling in warfare under Pippin's generals, his quickness in mastering the art of strategy as practised by his father and Charles Martel, his thirst in wanting to learn more than his teachers could give him, the clear conception of the world he was born into, the matter of Byzantium, the East, the Papal See, Lombardy and, nearer home, the problems presented by Arab, Avar, Saxon and Frisian, all of it gathered down the years was now in evidence. Charlemagne's ability to tell friend from foe, and his genius for friendship, were there too. The uneasy consciousness that the brutal necessity of establishing and guarding the vast national frontiers left little money and less time for many pressing reforms at home was not born in Charlemagne on the day he became king of the whole country. He did not come to the throne unaware of many chaotic streaks in the administration, the ignorance of the laity and the backslidings of the hierarchy, and, finally, the Gordian knot of fiscal matters.

If his energies were those of a giant, his curiosity bade fair to outstrip them. Truly, it was a *res mirabilis*. The twenty books of Etymologies of Isidore of Seville must have been his companions together with Augustine's 'City of God'. Isidore's work, which Helen Waddell so happily called 'the mediaeval Encyclopaedia Britannica', covered every subject of interest to the mediaeval mind – from grammatical subtleties to food and drink – and Charlemagne's curiosity was such that every detail of life must have been compelling to him. Einhard tells us that he abhorred idleness above all else.

His physique was in full accord with his mind. Broadly built and inclined to corpulence, Charlemagne looked every inch a king. The large grey eyes could hearten and also frighten because his displeasure was as terrible as his kindliness was amazing. His subjects had early learnt him to be easy of approach, but the habitual accessibility in no way lessened his dignity. He was devoted to his mother, whose counsels he valued, and to his sister, now Abbess of Chelles, whose prayers he needed greatly. When not occupied with warfare, Charlemagne spent his leisure in hunting, swimming, listening to songs and stories, and reading. Unlike his predecessors, wine had no attraction for him, but good food in large quantities was his delight, and the frequent Church fasts tried him severely.

But all those were widely opened windows in the large house of a personality which had no equal in his day. That house had a very carefully furnished room where ambition and resolve stepped back to give place to a dream and a vision.

Charlemagne dreamt not of an ideally administered state but of a world created after the pattern of God's own city. Catholic faith in all its fullness was to be the cornerstone not of Frankland only but of the whole of Europe, and he held it to be his duty to work towards that purpose because he knew himself to be king by the grace of God rather than by the will of his people. Hence, everything dreamt about, planned and accomplished by him stemmed from the same viewpoint.

He regarded the Church as Christ's visible kingdom on earth, its pivot being the See of St Peter. With the exception of Adrian I,[19] those pontiffs were of no remarkable stature either mentally or spiritually. Popes like Leo the Great, Gregory I and Gregory II would certainly have made far more rewarding contemporaries for Charlemagne. He revered the office. He did not always trust its holders.

The rupture between East and West was still three centuries
distant, but its signs were already on the horizon in Charlemagne's day, and the iconoclastic struggle brought the
divergences into sharp light. Charlemagne's attitude towards
Byzantium was that of a prudent statesman, but the statesman
was wholly Western and the road trodden by the Greek mind
said very little to one nurtured in the tradition of Augustine,
Ambrose and Leo the Great. With all his thirst for learning,
Charlemagne mastered enough Greek to follow ambassadorial
speeches, but he never learned to speak it.

With church observances entering every detail of his daily
life, the entire weft and warp of Charlemagne's activity as king
was informed by the conviction that, since he was a Catholic,
it behoved him to steer the ship of state through the waters of
Time into the ocean of Eternity. It was, as it were, a supra-
imperial ideal, and, as such, wholly beyond the reach of one
man, whatever his genius, but with Charlemagne its accomplishment was even less accessible because of the cleavage
within him.

It is true that the mediaeval mind looked almost indulgently
upon adultery. It was no sin against the Holy Ghost; it was
regarded as a pitiful concession to man's frailty, and it could
be absolved again and again. Ample and enduring provision
would be made for the shortening of the purgatorial period.
Abbeys and priories were founded and endowed for no other
purposes. In cathedrals and parish churches chantries were
built and weekly and sometimes daily masses were said for the
remission of the sins of the flesh. Men of substance would make
suitable provision in their wills always for the same purpose.

The Franks were neither better nor worse than any of their
neighbours. The burden of the original sin lay heavy upon all;
infants were cleansed from it by the rite of baptism, but no
man, whatever his piety, could escape its persuasion through
life. The sexual urge came quite clearly from the Devil. It was
rather clumsily sanctified by the sacrament of marriage, but the
state of virginity, extolled by the early Fathers of the Church,
held its pride of place.

In brutal terms, sex was an appetite. In the case of a king,
there were certain privileges since his choice of a wife was

The earliest known portrait of Charlemagne and his wife, Queen Hildegard
Below: a facsimile signature, from a document of AD 775
(*Radio Times Hulton Picture Library*)

Relief from the shrine of Charlemagne at Aachen, showing the Emperor dedicating the Cathedral to the Virgin

inevitably restricted. The Church steered a middle course, at once withholding both condemnation and approval. She could do no other so long as anyone's sexual behaviour was expressed in normal terms. She came down heavily enough on any cases of homosexuality and sodomy.

Charlemagne was clear of those. He had mistresses without number (the chroniclers prudently restricted themselves to name five of them) and four or five wives, and he was patently devoted to at least two of these. But to sleep with a woman meant no more to him than to enjoy a good dinner. It is true that he cared for the bastards begotten so casually. He provided for them and their mothers most liberally. He never behaved shabbily to any of his many mistresses.

But the cleavage remained. Charlemagne was at home with Augustine's Confessions and the New Testament. He knew the terrible words about adultery committed in the heart. They did not just pass him by. And they were the cause of his dream about God's Kingdom on earth remaining a dream never to be fulfilled.

E

III

THEOCRACY IN ACTION

Notker Balbulus, a monk of St Gall,[1] wrote his book at the request of a descendant of Charlemagne, the Emperor Charles III. The Carolingians were most constant and generous benefactors of the abbey. In a certain sense, Notker's allusions to 'the most pious Charles' and even 'the bishop of bishops' (*'episcopus episcoporum'*)[2] might be considered as so many expressions of a sycophant's servility. Yet they were true. Charlemagne – and that on more than one occasion – was the custodian of the Frankish Church, its problems and difficulties to be referred to him rather than to the Pope. There was something of a paradox in the situation: Charlemagne deeply cherished St Peter's, venerated the Pope's high office, defended his interests against the Lombardian and Byzantine threats, and lavished many gifts on the holder of the office. Rome rather than Constantinople was the ecclesiastical centre to him. None the less he remained a theocrat, and therefore his relations with the Holy See are marked with something like vagueness. None could really tell how much was bestowed and how much witheld.

Taylor[3] rightly says that '[Charlemagne] . . . from the nature and necessities of his own transcendent power possessed in fact the ecclesiastical authority of the Roman Emperors. . . .' All the reforms and wars he undertook were unmistakably based on the theocratic principle informed by a never flagging missionary compulsion.

If we turn to Einhard, Charlemagne's most trustworthy biographer, we find that[4] '. . . on occasion [the Saxons] would be so frightened and broken that they vowed to turn away from the worship of demons and submit themselves to the Christian faith . . .' It was lamentably true, however, that all the promises made by the Saxons were little more than spent breath, though their constant faithlessness in no way interfered with the *raison d'être* of Charlemagne's campaigns.

He was steeped in St Augustine's 'City of God', and he dreamt of becoming the architect of some such centre in Europe, but he was no mystic devoted to a life-long contemplation of 'the eternal problem'. First and last, Charlemagne was practical. As theocrat, he dealt with the Lombard, entered into theological battles with the Pope and Byzantium, administered the government of the Frankish Church, presided over episcopal synods, and planned to crush Islam as well as to eradicate paganism from Western Europe.

Yes it must be admitted that his was a somewhat qualified theocracy.

As will be seen later, Charlemagne's private life ran in sharp disaccord with Christian principles, though that in no wise prevented him from penalizing bishops, priests and monks for 'looseness of living' all the more reprehensible, according to Charlemagne, because of their solemn dedication to the service of Christ. Here, the contradiction was a glaring one: the King considered himself dedicated by virtue of his anointment, and was styled '*rex et rector regni Francorum.*' [5]

But, all the contradictions notwithstanding, the pivot of his world remained Rome, ecclesiastically imperial (for all the Emperors now lived in Constantinople), its territories held by its bishops in trust for the Lord Christ, its liturgical usages and language holding pre-eminence in all church observances, its difficulties and perils the king's paramount duty to face and overcome.

The text of Pippin's Donation has not come down to us, but the Lombard campaign, so brilliantly conducted and won by Charlemagne, is proof enough that even a menace to, let alone appropriation of, papal territories was his business to avert. Charles Martel had promised much and done nothing beyond sending legates laden with the gifts the Pope might well have done without. Pippin the Short had twice marched across the Alps and achieved something, but the Lombard problem remained unsolved, a thick cloud on the papal horizon.

Charlemagne was the first to grasp the fact that to leave Lombardy as a kingdom in Northern Italy meant a continued threat to Rome and the rest of Western Christendom. But Charlemagne did not hurry to solve the problem, and he would not strike until he was reasonably sure of success.

Its ultimate measure, though, could hardly have been imagined even by him. It is highly significant that the last Pope of Charlemagne's reign (Leo III, 795–816) dated his letters and bulls not by the years of his papacy but by those of Charlemagne's reign.

The theocracy he practised was peculiar in other respects. The papal office was sacrosanct in his eyes but that did not prevent him from disagreeing with the Pope even on points of dogma. Every diocesan in Frankland was vested with juridical rights, but the court of final appeal was Charlemagne's own court. Episcopal appointments were in his hands, though in that particular he followed the Merovingian tradition. His was the deciding voice and vote at all the Church synods. His benefactions to cathedrals, churches and religious houses were frequent and lavish, but his generosity was rather surprisingly conditional: he insisted on regular and detailed accounts being rendered to his treasury ('*ad describendas res ecclesiasticas*'). Many of the capitularies carry reiterated demands for such accounts.

A letter Charlemagne wrote to King Offa of Mercia[6] makes it obvious that on occasions disputable matters were referred to him and not to the Church courts. The letter was concerned with an English priest either staying or living at Cologne. He had been accused of eating meat in Lent. Normally, such a breach of observance should have been handled by the archiepiscopal court, but it was Charlemagne who dealt with the offence. He wrote to King Offa that, not enough evidence having been found to convict the man, he, the King of the Franks, had decided to refer the case to the priest's own diocesan in England. Canonically speaking, the Archbishop of Cologne should have written to the Archbishop of Canterbury, but Charlemagne chose to interpret canonical injunctions in his own fashion, and in Frankland his authority in matters both clerical and lay stood far above the juridical powers of a Metropolitan.

On another occasion Charlemagne wrote to King Offa[7] about pilgrims from Britain who crossed Frankland on their way to Rome. Those travellers, who were genuine 'peregrini' and undertook the long journey for the love of God and the salvation of their souls, or else as a penance in expiation of a crime, could travel through his dominions 'without let or hindrance'. Anyone caught in attempting to turn his pilgrimage into a commercial enterprise for his own profit would be subject to fines, tolls and the alien tax. Of course, a penitent pilgrim would be expected to carry some letters from a cleric in England, but not those who went on private purposes of piety. It is a matter of curiosity how Charlemagne's customs and excise officers were able to distinguish between a genuine pilgrim and an impostor. Moreover, even letters of credence were not always reliable. Faked documents were known to provide a source of income for many a cleric.

About 772 Charlemagne granted immunity to the Abbey of Lorsch[8] because 'of the great virtues' shown by its Abbot, one Gudeland, 'a venerable man, who came to our palace at Heristal'. The Abbot brought a complaint about a layman 'spreading calumnies against the Abbey and claiming its lands' on the strength of some covenant made between Lorsch and the man's parents. Charlemagne summoned the defendant to Heristal, heard his evidence and that of the Abbot, and then 'together with our faithful liegemen, counts and vassals', decided the case in favour of the Abbey. The names of four counts and four vassals appear in the text, all of them laymen. No bishop, still less a cleric of smaller importance, was summoned to Heristal to adjudge the case. The decision of the King's court was immediately followed by the grant of immunity to the Abbey of Lorsch. Soon after, the privilege of free abbatial elections was bestowed by Charlemagne on the Abbey of Fulda,[9] and the same right together with exemption from the authority of the Bishop of Constance was granted to Reichenau.[10] Each such charter at once widened the gulf between the secular clergy and the regulars and made both more and more dependent on the grace and favour obtainable from the crown only. Some time between 796 and 800 the possessions of St Martin's Abbey at Tours were 'enlarged' at the request made to Charlemagne by its abbot, Alcuin, who was a layman and fully understood his patron's policy.[11]

Such examples could be multiplied indefinitely. Under the Carolingians and, more particularly during Charlemagne's reign, the Frankish Church became subject to the sovereign's power and, since he firmly believed that his authority was God-given, there was nothing illogical in his policy. It was a system where secular threads were so closely interwoven with clerical issues as to suggest an appearance of unity – inevitably so since the Canon Law of Charlemagne's day embraced practically every detail of public and private life. Marriage and divorce, wills and frequently tangled testamentary dispositions, the relations between creditor and debtor and between buyer and seller, constantly fluctuating road and bridge tolls and fair and market dues, all were subject both to the Canon Law and to the secular judicature. This latter circumstance enormously increased the existing legal complications. Incidentally, it yielded a pleasant lining to the lawyers' purses. Litigation cost dear both to the plaintiff and to the defendant.

As has already been told, episcopal appointments were in Charlemagne's hands. He would invariably inform the Pope of his decision. He did not ask for the approval of any particular choice. We do not hear of a single case where a decision of his was referred to Rome for confirmation. Many qualities were lacking in Charlemagne, but he possessed a well developed sense of logic. To be the *Rector regni Francorum* implied wielding absolute power over Church and State.

The task, however, involved titanic difficulties. Chief among them were paganism in Frankland, loose living of the clergy both secular and regular and, finally, the greatest impediment of all, ignorance.

'The eldest daughter of the Mother Church' – such was the papal name for the Frankish Church. None the less, paganism had not been uprooted in Christian Frankland. Its roots were embedded too deeply for any laws, persecutions and savage penalties to pull them out. Paganism formed an essential part of the national ethos. It was an inheritance of a past which could not be ignored except at the cost of betraying the national identity. The Church recognized it and strove to achieve a compromise by lending a Christian flavour to the more innocuous heathen practices, such as, for instance, the blessing of water and salt. Again Midsummer Day, one of the most important pagan festivals, was given a Christian clothing and became the feast of St John. But pagan practices continued to exist in the teeth of all such compromises.

In the Eleventh Book of his Etymologies,[12] Isidore of Seville wrote that trees had a life of their own. The common folk of Frankland had never heard of Isidore and his occasionally fanciful Etymologies, yet they would have not only endorsed but enlarged the meaning of his words. They were formally Christian; they received the Church's sacraments and recited what few prayers had been taught to them, but the full meaning of the Catholic creed was beyond their understanding. It was far easier to believe that a forest should be held sacred because its heart was the seat of a deity which had no place in the Christian Pantheon. The pages of Gregory of Tours carry many stories about the worship of trees and the heathen practices at harvest-time. Pirmin (died c. 755), founder and first Abbot of Reichenau, denounced most fierily all the rites which included sacrifices made to particular oaks and thorns, but his denunciations fell on barren ground. All through the eighth century and later, Charles Martel's great victory at Poitiers was ascribed to the fact that the relic of the True Cross, venerated at a neighbouring abbey, had been carried into the battle, thus deciding the day in favour of the Christians. At this point, and at many others, orthodoxy came to be welded with pure magic and a tradition much more ancient than the Nicene Creed. If the commonalty of Frankland had been acquainted with the Great Passion hymns of Venantius Fortunatus, they would certainly have interpreted their meaning in the way familiar to their heathen ancestors.

In his capitularies and various other directives sent to the bishops and counts all over the country, Charlemagne strove to suppress each expression of paganism, but none of his attempts met with success. His commands for deforestation, badly needed in some parts of Frankland, all too often came up against the wall of sullen obstinacy and sometimes of open disobedience. If some such clearance had been effected, the peasants were certain of a meagre harvest. When that happened, the resultant hardship would be regarded as a proof of anger on the part of a god dispossessed of his sanctuary. Fines and penalties imposed for disobeying royal commands and for performing heathen rites in a Christian graveyard achieved very little. The ancient dispensation, its covenant never written down and its usages transmitted by word of mouth, lived on from one generation to another.

The other great obstacle was loose living among clergy and monks. It seems rather odd that Charlemagne should have embarked on the unrewarding task of trying to clean that Augean stable,[13] in view of his own deeply stained morality, and here we come on the sharp evidences of his dichotomy. The theocratic king in his parliament or at his court and the lust-driven male in his bedroom at the palace or in his tent in war-time, seem two distinct personalities inhabiting the same body. The wonder is that they never impinged one on the other.

In March 779, at his palace of Heristal, the king presided over an important synod. All the bishops and abbots were summoned to attend it together with counts and other laymen of note. The findings of that assembly, together with many of the others, as well as Charlemagne's famous 'Admonitio Generalis' of 789, paint a sombre picture of the conditions then prevalent in the Frankish Church. Among other measures decreed by the King, clergy were forbidden to carry arms and merchandise was not to be brought into churches. All business and idle talk were to be prohibited in any sacred building and in churchyards. Lack of stability was yet another wound on the Church's body. It was commanded in the King's name that priests were not to wander from one parish to another, monks not to leave their abbeys for 'harmful' vagabondage all over the country, and bishops were ordered to occupy themselves with their own diocesan matters only and to live in their dioceses. 'No abbess was to leave her monastery without our permission, or allow her subjects to do so'. That prohibition was particularly important because nuns caused great scandal by attending weddings and christenings among their secular kin. They would return to their houses, their minds full of worldly gossip, which, freely shared with the other sisters, greatly harmed the spiritual climate of the community. Mediaeval weddings could not be said to yield edifying themes for discussion in the cloister.

Priests and monks were strictly forbidden to gamble, enter taverns, sing and dance. Clerics 'on the run' were not to be received by anyone ('*a nullo recipiantur*'). They were to be taken in custody and sent back to their diocesans and abbots.[14]

The most illuminating source for the worldliness of the Frankish Church comes from the records of the Synod held at Frankfurt in the spring of 794. Among other things, it dwarfed a diocesan's juridical scope. The law, as Charlemagne believed, did not exist solely for punishment: reconciliation was one of its important functions, to be exercised most particularly in testamentary cases. If any bishop found himself unable to reconcile plaintiff and defendant, it was not for him to solve the case even if the available evidence made such solution possible. Bishops were commanded to send carefully detailed reports to the King, whose adjudication alone was held to be final.

All the earlier exactments and bans seem to have fallen on stony ground, and the conditions observed in religious houses caused the King much anxiety. Once again monks had to be reminded that it was their duty to abstain from all worldly business ('*saecularia negotia*').[15] The least deviation from St Benedict's Rule was to be eradicated from the cloistral daily life, and abbots were not to indulge in the luxury of their own cells but sleep in the common dorter and have their meals in the frater together with the other monks.

To his 'great indignation', Charlemagne had learned that certain abbots and priors, giving free rein to cupidity, would demand money from those who wished to enter the community. 'Therefore it is our pleasure and that of the Holy Synod ('*ideo placuit nobis et sancto synodo . . .*') that no money should be asked from any applicant and that novices should be admitted according to the ancient way ('*secundum regulam Sancti Benedicti*'). A real vocation to religious life was expected from young men and girls and not what gold or silver they could afford to bring with them. Grants of money and land were indeed permitted to be made by the kin, but such were never to be expected as a due, still less asked for. Religious houses had grown wealthy by virtue of free offerings and not through the rapacity of their heads.

At Frankfurt, one effort after another was made to separate the cloistral peace from the noisy contagion of the world. Once again, all clerics were strictly forbidden to enter taverns '*ad bibendum*'. Priests were allowed to do so but only in case of an illness in the house. Once the sacerdotal functions were over, a priest must leave the building, refusing all offers of refreshment, an injunction fatally easy either to forget or to disobey, though the more pious among the inn-keepers might ease their conscience by leaving a jug of wine outside the tavern door.

The thirtieth article is of particular interest in that it emphasizes the close link, not to say union, between the spiritual and the temporal matters. In case of any dispute concerning a cleric and a layman, the diocesan and the count were to sit together in a common court, and the case must be decided unanimously between them ('. . . *unanimiter inter eos . . .*').

The lay ignorance of the fundamentals of their faith greatly troubled Charlemagne. In one village, the common folk thought that their church was dedicated to a saint, of whose life nothing was known and whose name was Trinity. Elsewhere, the Trinity was believed to be Our Lord, Our Lady and the patron saint of the locality. The colour and the movement of religious processions, the exquisite pattern of ceremonies, and the painted and sculptured splendour of church interiors certainly moved the popular imagination, but the commonalty were unable to grasp the meaning of ceremonies and were all too often in the dark about the purpose of a procession.

Laity must be educated, insisted Charlemagne, and on several occasions, more particularly so at Frankfurt, he expressed his wish that the dogma of the Holy Trinity, the Lord's Prayer and the Creed should be preached about, explained in every detail, and taught to the faithful.[16] At the Frankfurt Synod the royal wish was expressed in terms of a command. Alas, as will be seen below, such an order proved all but impossible to carry out, chiefly because of clerical ignorance.

Some of the measures passed at Frankfurt were sharply unpopular with the Frankish hierarchy. Such, for instance, was the regulation about episcopal possessions. Bishops who

acquired any property – both movable and immovable – after
their consecration, found themselves debarred from disposing of
it by will: it belonged to the Church. Any other substance they
owned was heritable, but that only conditionally: the kin only
could benefit and such friends as were approved by a synod.
All bishops were urged not to forget 'the poor of Christ' in their
wills.

Charlemagne said his prayers in Latin, but he insisted that
it did not matter in what language a man addressed his Maker,
and that the common folk should be encouraged to recite the
Lord's Prayer in the vulgar tongue.

Finally, quite out of accord with the prevailing mood of the
century, the King disapproved of any additions to the Church's
calendar.[17] There was no formal canonization, as we know it
today, until the end of the tenth century when Ulrich of
Augsburg was declared saint by Pope John XV (c. 993). In
the early days of the Church, martyrdom and well-established
sanctity of life were adequate credentials. In the Merovingian
and Carolingian eras, bishops enjoyed the liberty of starting a
cult of any man or woman distinguished by virtue in his or her
neighbourhood, and the number of such local cults had risen
rather alarmingly. A hermit was entitled to sainthood on no
other ground than that of abstaining from all animal food.
Charlemagne laid down that no new saints were to be invoked,
no images to them must be erected in churches, or shrines
built along the roads.

All those statutes were, so to speak, matters of eclesiastical
domesticities, to be resolved or re-shaped by the royal will.
But, as theocrat, Charlemagne found himself facing an immeasurably greater difficulty when he stated reforming the
Frankish Church. Clerical ignorance lay at the root of all, and
the Frankfurt statute that no man was to be ordained priest
until he had reached the age of thirty was but the initial stage
of a prolonged and unrewarding struggle.

The capitularies are by no means our only source in this
instance. Chronicles are full of well-nigh incredible examples
of ignorance among the very people who were supposed to
be the teachers of the faithful. We find Charlemagne sending a
passionate reproach to Lull, Archbishop of Mainz, about the

culpable ignorance among his clergy.[18] The letter was polite and even rich in affectionate terms. Lull is by turn 'amiable, venerable, dearest father (*pater amabilis . . . venerabilis . . . carissime . . .*'). But its general terms are as scorching as a brightly burning rush-light. Charlemagne found it hard to believe that in the vast archdiocese committed to Lull's care scholars should be lacking. St Boniface's name alone should serve as a spur and an example, the same Boniface who met his maryrdom at the hands of the West Frisians, the book of the Gospels pressed against his breast.

Ignorance was not limited to cathedral chapters and parish churches. It spread its web over the cloister as well. That can be seen from Charlemagne's personal letter to Bangulf, Abbot of Fulda, where the King urged that more time should be devoted to the monks' studies. The frequently careless performance not only of the Divine Office but of the Mass was due to such a poor knowledge of Latin that cases and tenses were in a state of perpetual warfare against one another. There were priests unable to recite the Lord's Prayer from memory, and towards the very end of his reign, Charlemagne had to write to a bishop that no parish priest was to be allowed to perform baptism unless he knew the Lord's Prayer and the Creed by heart.[19]

Trained by his mother, Queen Bertrada, in the lucidities of the Catholic Faith, Charlemagne, come to manhood and the fulness of power, was bewildered by that quagmire of ignorance. To him, every article of the Creed was simplicity itself. To understand the Gospels was a task at once delightful and rewarding. To enter into the very heart of Church offices seemed as necessary to him as breathing. And here were men most solemnly dedicated to Christ's work, who thought far more of the green goose on their platters and the wine in their goblets than of Catholic dogmas. There was a canon at Rheims, famous in the neighbourhood for his knowledge of herbs, but the seven gifts of the Holy Ghost remained to him a mystery he could never penetrate. There were bishops to whom the traditionally sumptuous Christmas dinner meant far more than the Christmas Mass, and one man on the very eve of his consecration pledged the altar plate to a usurer to pay for the rubies and the sapphires in his ring. It was not peasants alone who believed in 'Sancta Trinitas' as a woman saint: a cleric thought it was the name of a girl martyred in Rome during the early Christian era.

Charlemagne, however bewildered, never lost hope. As will be seen in a later chapter, he engaged scholars of note to revise the Vulgate and the Lectionary, brought in several measures to educate the clergy in the liturgical sense, insisted on young men passing an examination in theology before their ordination, reduced the liturgical chaos in Frankland by adopting the Roman use, and, above all, he did not spare himself in his efforts to raise the standards of morality and knowledge among the clergy. His helpers were many; in spite of numberless failures now in one particular, now in another, it cannot be denied that Charlemagne's efforts did succeed in clearing at least one corner of that Augean stable.

If he had laymen taking part in clerical matters, he also summoned prelates to engage themselves in secular administration. Theodulf, Archbishop of Orléans, and a Spaniard by birth, was one of the King's 'missi' who were sent on annual expeditions to inspect the work done by the counts in various provinces. Again, Vulfar, Bishop of Rheims, a man exceptionally well versed in law, was frequently used as a 'missus' to promote the ends of true justice.[20]

The findings of Synods were embodied in capitularies.[21] These were carefully copied and sent out all over Frankland. A few of such capitularies were dictated by Charlemagne, and some few were drafted by him. None was valid unless fully approved by the King and 'the Holy Synod'.[22] Those gatherings must have been lively occasions. We know from Einhard that Charlemagne delighted in debates. In one sense, those synods were a school for him. Einhard mentions that he loved talking and could on occasions be even garrulous. As president of the Synod, he learned how to listen to most able expositions of theological problems.

*   *   *

From his father, Pippin the Short, Charlemagne had inherited an unfinished war with Aquitania, the seemingly endless struggle with the Saxons, who hardly ever ceased to ravage the northern borders of Frankland, and much disquiet, to call it by no harsher name, along the edge of the Breton March. He had not been king two years when he found himself involved in the matter of Lombardy. Its ultimate resolution would give a novel shape and purpose to his relations with the Papacy.

At that time parts of the Italian peninsula still belonged to Byzantium. *De jure*, the Bishop of Rome was the subject of the Emperor and, as such, had the right to expect help from Constantinople whenever the Lombards menaced the papal territories. But even in the days of Charles Martel the popes had ceased to hope for any help from Byzantium. The Greeks, perpetually harassed by their own home dissensions, and as continuously in trouble with the Arabs, the Bulgarians and savage nomadic tribes from the north, could spare neither men, nor money, nor yet ships to protect their own interests in Italy.

By 770, the Lombards, their temper but temporarily quelled by the trans-alpine expeditions of Pippin the Short, began troubling the Papal See again. They had done so in the days of Charles Martel who, having promised help to the Pope, had given none. The Lombards knew well that Pippin the Short's campaigns had been anything but popular in Frankland. They did not know that to Martel's grandson the matter was a 'duty under God'. A climax was reached during the reign of King Desiderius. Some of the threads gone into the making of that climax were extremely odd and confusing, and provided the only cause of discord between Charlemagne and his mother, Queen Bertrada.

The lady had by no means been satisfied with a consort's comparatively modest rôle during her husband's life. Pious, intelligent, good wife and mother, Bertrada saw the contemporary scene far more clearly than any woman of her generation. She was able to give advice and it pleased her to see that advice followed. But her intelligence did not prevent her from falling into awkward errors.

In 770 the Queen Mother went to Rome on a pilgrimage. To the surprise of everybody, she made a halt at Pavia on her journey back, was most royally entertained by Desiderius, and returned to Frankland, bringing the Lombard King's daughter with her – as a bride for Charlemagne. When the news reached Rome, Pope Stephen III lost his temper. According to him Charlemagne was already married.[23] The Pope ignored both Bertrada and Desiderius. He sent a vehement letter to Charlemagne in which he accused the Queen Mother of having formed a treacherous alliance with Lombardy for her own secret purposes.[24] 'What folly, what madness for a Frank to marry a woman of the stinking Lombard race, to enter into union with that brood of lepers!' Some of the expressions used in that missive were hardly in accord with papal dignity. The Pope saw himself gravely menaced by the Franco-Lombard axis, and he knew only too well that no help might be expected from Byzantium. Unfortunately, Charlemagne's reply,. if any was sent, has not come down to us.

Whatever Bertrada's motives may have been, she timed her manoeuvre most adroitly. Hilmentrud's is the first woman's name associated with Charlemagne, though it is most unlikely that she was his first mistress. She had borne him a cripple of a son, and by 770 Charlemagne was tired of her. He had her provided for most generously, sent her together with child away from the court, and yielded to his mother's wishes by marrying Desiderius's daughter, whose very name does not appear in the chronicles. The girl has no other identity than that of being *filia Regis Langobardorum* (daughter of the King of the Lombards.)

In less than a year the bride was sent back to Pavia – in spite of all persuasions of Queen Bertrada, whose anger against her son remains the only occasion of estrangement between Charlemagne and his mother. It did not last long, however.

Notker Balbulus explains the King's sudden repudiation of his bride by her incapacity to bear children, but Einhard[25] and others assert that Charlemagne 'divorced the lady for some unknown reason (*'incertum qua de causa'*).

Naturally, King Desiderius was incensed by such humiliation, Towards the end of 771 relations between Frankland and Lombardy worsened still further when Gerberga, Charlemagne's widowed sister-in-law, escaped to Pavia and put herself under Desiderius's protection for reasons best known to her alone since nobody in Frankland had any designs either against her or against her two infant sons. Charlemagne made no attempts to compel the lady's return.

About the same time, Tassilo, Duke of Bavaria and Charlemagne's cousin, whose own wife was a Lombard princess, added to the complications of the moment by forming an alliance with Desiderius. The Lombard-Bavarian axis was certainly unlawful because Charlemagne was Tassilo's overlord, and the confusion became something of a Gordian knot when the same Pope Stephen III, having showered opprobrium on 'the race of vipers and the brood of lepers', began currying favour with Desiderius and took to extolling the Lombard's 'piety and humility'.

Fortunately for Rome, that mediaeval prototype of the Vicar of Bray died in the early January of 772. Charlemagne knew that he could expect both commonsense and firm policy from Stephen's successor, Adrian I (772-795), a pure Roman by descent, who lost no time in refusing to have any relations with Lombardy. Desiderius, encouraged by his Bavarian ally, began by trying to win the new Pope's support, but Adrian I was no Stephen III, and all the overtures from Pavia came to a barren end. The King of the Lombards changed flattery for threats and found himself mistaken in his antagonist. Adrian I, unlike many of his predecessors, neither panicked nor wasted time on hysterical appeals to Byzantium. He needed instant help and he turned to Frankland.

It was not a very convenient moment for Charlemagne, then deeply committed in Saxony. He decided to try a diplomatic approach, and Desiderius mocked at it. During the annual spring assembly of 773, many Franks expressed their reluctance to start on a Lombard campaign. Charlemagne heard their arguments but his mind was made up: the Pope, whom he respected and trusted, had asked for help and that concluded the matter. In late summer of 773, leaving a few of his finest generals to deal with the Saxon business, Charlemagne started for Italy.

The campaign lasted ten months, and none better than Einhard summed up its meaning for Europe:[26] 'The results of this war were as follows: the conquest of Italy, the dethronement of Desiderius, his being sent to exile together with his son,

The *Incipit* of St Luke's Gospel – Carolingian work (Aachen)
(*British Museum*)

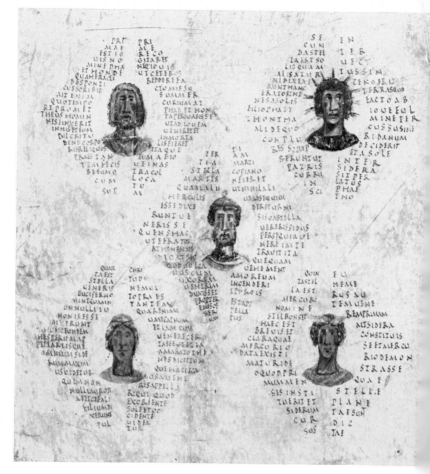

A detail from the Aratus MS. – Carolingian work (Aachen)
(*British Museum*)

Adalgis, and the restoring of St Peter's patrimony to the Pope.'

'The conquest of Italy' was to prove a heavy responsibility rather than an asset but the psychological advantages could hardly be overrated. Those among the Frankish host who had been more than lukewarm in their acceptance of the King's decision now realized that they were in the service of a sovereign who, in authority, let alone achievement, was equal to the Emperor in Byzantium.

Just before Easter 774, Charlemagne, leaving Pavia still beleaguered, marched south to Rome. At a spot some thirty miles away from the city, an enormous crimson and gold tent was erected, papal and Frankish banners waving from the roof. Here, with a pomp unfamiliar to the Franks, the King was met by representatives of the Roman nobility and acclaimed as 'a deliverer from the Lombard plague' even though the war was not yet ended. On reaching the walls of Rome, Charlemagne dismounted and walked to the Lateran Basilica where Adrian I, surrounded by all the splendour of the Roman Curia, was waiting for him. The two theocrats embraced and walked together into the basilica where massed choirs of many churches sang the Te Deum so beautifully that Charlemagne was moved to the point of tears.

On Easter Sunday after Mass at St Peter's, the Pope gave a great banquet followed by the exchange of rich presents between the Romans and the Franks. Later in the day the Pontiff and the King were closeted together in a long conference.

There is no doubt that Charlemagne then confirmed the promises made by his father, but it is highly improbable that the so called Donation of Constantine came to be mentioned.[27] The records of that Easter meeting are somewhat vague, if not confused, but one factor at least emerges clearly enough: the temporal power of the Pope enjoyed by Adrian I and his successors sowed the seeds of the later struggle between the tiara and the crown. In a different sense, Charlemagne and Adrian I may be considered as the first architects of the ultimate rupture between Rome and Constantinople.

In Rome, Charlemagne's statesmanship came well to the fore. He gave a solemn pledge to defend St Peter's patrimony, but the pledge was given at a price. With his theocratic practices in Frankland the Pope could not interfere. Now that the conquest of Italy was soon to be accomplished, the King of the Franks was the Pope's overlord. Even when every allowance is made for Charlemagne's chivalry and his deep sense of dedication, it cannot truly be claimed that the Italian campaign had sprung from a very pure motive. Italy had already entered into Charlemagne's plans of an *imperium Dei*. So Italy must be conquered, and his younger son would be crowned and anointed King of Italy, a somewhat fantastic title when we remember that Byzantium still held some parts of the peninsula.

However harassed by the Saracens, Persians, Bulgarians and others, and continually at the mercy of the mood of the army, Byzantium, though neglecting to protect her Italian possessions, had no intention of relinquishing them. The enlargement of St Peter's patrimony and even more so the Frankish successes were not welcomed in Constantinople. There followed threats of reprisals and some attempts were made to salvage a few Lombardian fragments out of the wreck. It was chiefly owing to Charlemagne's prudence and patience that none of it ended in an irrevocable rupture.

In June 774 Pavia fell to the Franks. Desiderius, the last King of the Lombards, found himself an uncrowned exile, and Charlemagne could claim the title '*Rex Francorum et Langobardorum*'. But the end of fighting by no means led to the dawn of peace. The King's victories were not accepted by the vanquished. Between 775 and 776, Hrodgaud, Duke of Friuli and a Lombard by birth, tried to regain his people's independence, and proclaimed Adalgis, Desiderius's son, King of Lombardy. But Adalgis was unpopular; Hrodgaud, failing to find many adherents to the cause, decided to claim the Lombard crown for himself. For a time the tide ran in his favour, and he succeeded in winning the allegiance of some few cities in Northern Italy. But Charlemagne was well prepared for emergencies: a Frankish army was sent across the Alps to crush the rebellion. Hrodgaud fell in battle, and all his ambitions perished with him.

Some eight years later Charlemagne appeared again in Rome, bringing his two little sons, Pippin, aged four, and

Louis, aged three. The purpose of that visit was to have the children anointed by the Pope as kings of Italy and Aquitania respectively. Pippin was left in Italy in the care of carefully chosen guardians. Louis returned with his father to Frankland from there to ride across the Aquitanian border, his clothes and armour faithfully following the Aquitanian fashion. Both children at once started learning not only the alphabet but the rudiments of kingship.

The end of the Friuli rebellion by no means resolved all the Italian complications. The Duchies of Spoleto and Beneventum tried to engage Byzantine support, and there were many sporadic revolts which made considerable demands on Charlemagne's military potential.

The real importance of the Italian campaign lay in the shaping of the closest possible intimacy between the first ruler in Europe and the Pope. Happily, Adrian's papacy lasted for twenty years. He recognized and respected the theocratic streak in Charlemagne and fully shared the other's vision of the city of God upon earth. Their friendship grew and deepened, the genius of one man in full accord with that of the other. Adrian could well understand why the King chose to direct all his activities – from the Saxon wars to the repair of old Roman roads in Frankland – to the greater glory of God. Charlemagne's theocratic gestures never troubled Adrian. In March 787 it was none other than the King who granted immunity and the right of free abbatial elections to the Abbey of Monte Cassino.

The friendship between the two men produced a peculiar climate in Europe. Pippin the Short's armies had crossed the Alps to fight battles and to win victories. But Charlemagne's excursions into the very heart of the peninsula were not confined to battlefields. Italy was the first to be drawn into the comity of nations under the banner of Christ, and it was to be a pre-eminently Western comity. However utopian the Carolingian idea may appear, it looked healthy enough at the time. The breaths of such a new climate could not but deepen the alienation of Europe from Byzantium. The Greeks of Charlemagne's generation were not very popular, and travellers to Constantinople returned with many unpleasant stories in their baggage – examples of the Greek cruelty, treachery and suchlike. In Europe they heard details of splendour – both secular and ecclesiastical – which hinted at an Asiatic provenance. Charlemagne was 'every inch a king', his dignity had not a single flaw in it, and etiquette was certainly observed at his court, but the King's dignity marched side by side with a matchless simplicity. Deep obeisances and prostrations at the foot of the Emperor's throne both bewildered and disgusted Charlemagne's ambassadors. The Frankish mind had ample room for reverence but servility was beyond its comprehension.

*   *   *

Of all the synods summoned by Charlemagne the most remarkable was the one held at Frankfurt in 794. Italian, Spanish, Irish, English and Greek prelates attended it. During the prolonged and occasionally stormy sessions a Spanish heresy was formally condemned – to the wrath of all the Spanish bishops present – and the findings of the Second Nicaean Council (held in 787, the Seventh General Council) were repudiated by a vast majority, the repudiation ending in an uproar among the Greek bishops. That Frankfurt Synod, with Charlemagne in the chair, had a definite oecumenical flavour in it, and the theocrat in the King was very much present during many debates on dogma.

The Spanish heresy was Adoptianism. That dogmatic fantasy was started by Elipandus, Archbishop of Toledo, whose fiery temper and mordant tongue far exceeded his erudition. Elipandus had begun and could not continue. The real architect of the heresy was one Felix, Bishop of Urgel. A theologian of no small stature, he astonished the Catholic world by coming to the conclusion that Christ was God's Son only by adoption. The heresy had already been condemned at Regensburg in 792 when Felix had recanted. Elipandus, however, would not change his opinion, and the majority of the Spanish hierarchy supported him.

Felix's recantation was short-lived. Once again he declared himself to be on the side of Elipandus, and Spanish bishops, encouraged by his example, sent long and eloquent letters to the Pope and to Charlemagne where they defended their position by numerous references to the Scriptures and the early

Fathers. Charlemagne's reply was a sharp rebuke. 'It is better to be a disciple of truth than a teacher of falsehood.'[28]

The Spanish bishops summoned to Frankfurt attended in full strength and argued the case as ably as they could. But the vote went against them and the heresy was formally condemned. Yet it had already spread in Spain and elsewhere. A condemnation, however solemn, was not enough. It is significant that not a prelate but a layman was charged by Charlemagne to refute the heretical idea in writing. Alcuin's famous seven books *'Contra Felicem'* succeeded in ringing the knell of the Spanish heresy, and an anathema pronounced by the Frankish Church confirmed the decision of the Frankfurt Synod. Four years later, the anathema pronounced by Adrian's successor, Pope Leo III, was somewhat in the nature of an anti-climax.

The second important matter dealt with at Frankfurt was one which by its very nature should not have concerned Frankland at all. It was the iconoclastic controversy,[29] and the fact that a synod presided over by Charlemagne should have dealt with such a problem offers a proof that the Frankish voice had become the voice of Europe even though iconoclasm, as such, made no great impact on the Western mind.

Early in the eighth century, during the reign of Leo III, the Isaurian, (717–740) the idea had gained ground that all veneration of sacred images was to be canonically prohibited. The Emperor giving it his approval, an edict was published in 726 which authorized the destruction of icons. According to the Emperor, all veneration paid to them constituted the chief obstacle in the missionary field and ground to dust all efforts made to convert Jews and Mahomedans to Christianity.

The publication of the edict together with the immediate destruction of some greatly cherished icons turned the whole of Byzantium into two camps. Germanus, patriarch of Constantinople, defied the Emperor, appealed to Rome, and was deposed. That marked the beginning of a merciless persecution of iconodules. Pope Gregory III condemned the edict. The Emperor and his sycophants mocked at the condemnation. Leo III's son and successor, the Emperor Constantine V, summoned a synod at Hieria in 753. Invitations were sent to Rome, Antioch, Jerusalem and Alexandria. Neither the Pope nor the three patriarchs attended. The assembly, brought together at the imperial command, thought it but prudent to obey the imperial directives. The synod declared that any pictorial presentation of Christ served to divide His divinity from His humanity, declared all icons to be idols, and ordered their immediate destruction. Persecutions raged all over Byzantium, and great numbers of iconodules suffered martyrdom.

The findings of the Hieria assembly produced little impression in the West. Neither the popes nor any Western Metropolitans accepted the idea that an image of the Virgin was an emblem of idolatry. But it was well understood that the Byzantine storm carried political implications. Iconoclasts gained a certain number of adherents particularly in the Duchies of Spoleto and Beneventum with the result that rebellions broke out against the Pope and the King of the Franks. 'The hateful, unmentionable Greeks', as Adrian I called them, began disturbing the balance of power on the peninsula. But Charlemagne's policy moved along conciliatory lines in spite of Byzantine attempts to resurrect the Kingdom of Lombardy.

The controversy changed its colour in 780 when the nine-year-old Constantine VI succeeded to the throne under the regency of his mother, the Empress Irene, who, herself an ardent iconodule, at once annulled the decisions reached at Hieria and the edict of 726. Her policy – at least at the beginning – was most amicable towards the Pope and Charlemagne, whose eldest daughter, Rothrud, became betrothed to the boy-Emperor.

The iconoclastic war reached a definite truce in the autumn of 787 when the Seventh General Council (held at Nicea) re-established the cult of images. Adrian I was represented at the Council but, to judge by the proceedings at Frankfurt, the Pope's legates did not understand the Greek mind and had but a scant knowledge of the Greek language. The acts of the Council were brought to Rome, there translated into Latin and sent to Charlemagne. The translation having been faulty, a great many passages lost their original meaning, and Frankish theologians took it that the Council had placed the veneration of images on an equality with the worship of the Trinity. This, to the Franks, was idolatry at its worst, and they rejected it – to the indignation of the Greeks.

It so happened that – for a wholly different reason – Rothrud's betrothal to Constantine VI was broken off. In 788 the Greeks invaded South Italy – but by then the Duchies of Spoleto and Beneventum were Charlemagne's allies, and the Greeks were routed.

Estrangement, having given place to short-lived hostility, broke into angry flame when the Frankfurt Synod repudiated the Nicean Council of 787, and Charlemagne vigorously condemned both the adoration of and the contempt for icons.

Three years later travellers' stories about the cruelty of the Greeks paled into insignificance when the West learned that, afraid of her son's popularity, the Empress had had him blinded in the very same room of the palace where Constantine VI had been born.

*   *   *

In 795 Pope Adrian I died, and Charlemagne mourned for him deeply and sincerely. Theirs had been a friendship rare to find in any age, no dusty, hidden corners in that relationship.

A few years later the King joined issue with Adrian's successor, Leo III, on a point of pure dogma – i.e. the procession of the Holy Ghost.[30] Here, Charlemagne had to meet with opposition from Rome and contempt from Byzantium.

Historically, the word '*Filioque*' was no innovation, and the idea of the Holy Ghost proceeding from the Father and the Son had the support of some passages in the New Testament as well as the authority of St Augustine. As early as 589 the Third Council of Toledo defended it. Charlemagne's logical mind had seized on it early enough. Already in 784 he sent a letter about the seven gifts of the Holy Spirit to Hildebald, Archbishop of Cologne, and asked him to have it copied and distributed among other prelates. 'What can you know if you cannot understand? Nobody can attain knowledge without wisdom and understanding . . .'.[31] Charlemagne, however streaky and fragmentary his knowledge of theological subtleties, knew his Augustine. He also knew and loved the Athanasian Creed. He firmly believed that Trinity lived in Unity and Unity in Trinity. 'And the Catholick Faith is this: that we worship one God in Trinity, and Trinity in Unity.'[32] Such was Charlemagne's faith, and to exclude the Second Person of the Trinity from the procession of the Holy Spirit seemed to him no more and no less than a cleavage in an indivisible Trinity. '*Filioque*' was but a word, but a word charged with a depth of meaning. 'However dangerous be the errors of words, much greater perils lurk in mistakes of the sense' the King wrote to his friend, Baugulf, Abbot of Fulda.[33]

Already in 796 Charlemagne instructed Paulinus, Patriarch of Aquileia, to defend the principle of the Double Procession at a Synod held at Friuli. Soon enough, '*Filioque*' was inserted into the Nicene Creed, and the use spread throughout the entire Frankland. But Pope Leo III, agreeing, however vaguely, with the theory, repudiated the practice, and received ardent support from the Patriarch of Constantinople. Byzantine theology did not greatly concern Charlemagne. The Pope's obdurate attitude did. So the King sent his very learned cousin, Adalard of Corbie, and Jesse, Bishop of Amiens, to Rome to argue it out with the Pontiff. The Frankish prelates discussed it all ably, eloquently and courteously. The Pope's manner was equally polite, but his stubbornness remained. In reply to the Frankish persuasion, he had the original form of the Nicene Creed engraved on two silver tablets which – with great and splendid ceremony – were placed within St Peter's Basilica, and not for another two centuries would '*Filioque*' be formally accepted by Rome.

Charlemagne's obduracy well matched that of the Pope. The King had won the '*Filioque*' battle at least in his own domain, and that satisfied him.

IV

FIRE AND SWORD

All free-born Frankish boys, as soon as their infancy was over, were trained in the art of warfare. They also followed their elders on hunting expeditions, these being a grim necessity rather than a pastime since wolf, wild boar, bear, bison and auroch roamed in great numbers all over the countryside and, no town being then walled, the urban population could not consider themselves safe from their ravages, particularly in wintertime. In large terms, life was a battlefield even in peace-time, and the Franks took it for granted that any boy must be made aware of it as soon as he left the care of the women in the household. A child, born of noble parents, had a small sword, axe, shield and hauberk for his toys, and he learned their use in his father's courtyard, under the guidance of men to whom the art of warfare was as familiar as the palms of their hands. It was, however, not enough to learn the use of weapons. The boy would be taught the value (or otherwise) of every move-ment made by his foot and his hand, and his eye would be trained to detect danger. Men who had fought in real wars developed the sense of direction in the boy, showing him why even a single step to the right when it should have been made to the left might easily turn into a threshold leading to an ultimate defeat.

Little by little, the courtyard exercises would shift their ground and be carried out on a difficult terrain. Hard riding, wearying marches, rough food, and all the other hardihoods of a warrior's life ended in forming a pattern where the least admission of physical fatigue spelt shame and the faintest stir of fear was disastrous.

It is true that we have no details of Charlemagne's childhood, but there is no reason to suppose that it ran a different course.

His reign lasted for forty-three years, and very few of them were years of peace. Here again he followed the tradition of his forebears, but with Charlemagne the art of war differed from the practice of Charles Martel and Pippin the Short. Those two had fought to defend the frontiers of Frankland, to extend their possessions, to acquire the booty badly needed by their frequently impoverished treasury. Such purposes were also Charlemagne's, but there was something else as well. The imperial idea of a united Europe stemmed from dedication rather than ambition. We find something of a key to all his wars in a letter, its date uncertain,[1] of Pope Adrian I to the King. 'You have made a vow to conquer the barbaric nations.'

In spite of that Christian dedication, it by no means followed that 'the barbaric nations' were vanquished in a Christian manner. The savagery of war expressed itself in a way independent of any creed. But, rightly or wrongly, Charlemagne had early succeeded in persuading himself that the savagery was little more than an accidental and that his dedication to a vaster purpose than could be achieved on a battlefield was in no way affected by it. Adrian I shared that attitude, and he rejoiced over the Frankish successes, and prayed for Charlemagne's domain to be more and more enlarged. The Pope and the King were at one. 'Your triumph is our joy,' wrote Adrian. (*Vestra exaltatio, nostra est laetitia*').

In one sense, Charlemagne planned his campaigns as though they were so many crusades. But, in spite of occasional blunders, he was much more of a strategist than any leader of crusades after his time. Einhard sums it up brilliantly.[2] The King sometimes had to face more than one enemy, but his genius for synchronization led him to make the most of his military potential. '. . . [we] may wonder which is more to be admired: [the King's] physical endurance or his good fortune. . . . [He] never refused any undertaking because of the difficulties and toil involved, nor would he ever withdraw for fear of its perils. . . . [He] was never broken by adversity nor uplifted by triumph.'

Prudence and foresight Charlemagne had in abundance, but

there were other qualities in him rare to find in that day. To him, an enemy once defeated ceased to be a foe. His magnanimity was such that the one recorded lapse from it shook the whole of Christendom – as will be seen below. He was known to weep over the news of a kinsman or a comrade fallen in battle. He possessed a certain vanity, but successes never enlarged it. His immediate reaction to them was to fall on his knees to thank God.

The *raison d'être* of all the wars undertaken by Charlemagne was to advance the day of God's Kingdom on earth, to create a Europe so united in faith and in purpose that swords and battle-axes could be turned into ploughshares, and to have fields once given over to carnage affording their hospitality to corn and roots. It was a Utopian idea hardly shared by his contemporaries and laughed at by those who came after. The very idea that St Augustine's 'City of God' could ever be interpreted in temporal terms seemed devoid of all sense. Certainly the eighth century did not suggest a background in accord with such a vision, nor did the King's private life run a course in agreement with such ideals. None the less, the vision proved a good companion to the King and the ideals, however inaccessible, played their part in redeeming many dark and sordid moments not only in his life but in that of his people.

A strategist of high calibre, Charlemagne was no soldier in the real sense of the word. He never appeared without his sword but he was seldom seen unsheathing it. During all the three decades of the Saxon campaign, the King, according to Einhard[3] met the Saxons on two occasions only, 'the first time near the Osning Mountains in the region of Detmold, and then on the banks of the river Hasa', but the plan of every manoeuvre was made by him.

Charlemagne was neither a Xerxes, nor a Hannibal. Still less did he resemble Alexander the Great, and he would hardly have shed tears on being told there were 'no more worlds for him to conquer'. To Caesar, the aggrandisement of Rome stood in the forefront of everything. Charlemagne's affection for and pride in Frankland were indeed twin jewels in the crown he wore, but the glory of God shone with an incomparably greater brilliance. That was, however, an intangible matter, and successes on that field could not be measured by any yardstick known to man.

A Teuton to the marrow of his bones, Charlemagne was a Roman in his insistence on discipline – particularly in the army. His popularity, however, never came to be dwarfed, and that in spite of the fact that his campaigns cost the country dear. Indeed, military service was the heaviest burden laid upon the Franks. To begin with, every count was commanded to set aside one half of all the fodder available in his country for the use of the army. Again, the counts were to see to the maintenance of bridges, to meet the costs of repair out of their own purse, and even to provide boats and barges for the transport of men, horses and war material. Charlemagne's counts were not necessarily big landowners; a '*comes*' did not denote a nobility rank but merely an office held at the pleasure of the Crown. To discharge those heavy obligations, a count was sometimes forced to apply to usurers, or else to borrow from the great landowners on whom the burdens of any war fell no less heavily.

Serfs only were exempt from military service, and the exemption was chiefly due to the necessity of having adequate manual labour to cope with the harvest. Every free-born Frank, no matter how thin his substance and low his social standing, had to serve and bear the costs of the service. Many capitularies of Charlemagne reiterate that it was unlawful for any man to muster an armed following for his private purposes. A war was a matter for the crown and the state to deal with.

Any free-born man, possessing twelve *mansi*, was to join the army with full armour, three horses, and a good supply of weapons, victuals and fodder. The law laid down that anyone, possessing armour and weapons and reaching the camp empty-handed, was to lose his land and all his gear, the armour included. Desertion from the ranks, the so-called '*Herisliz*', was counted as the worst trespass of all and was punishable by death, the deserter's entire property going to the King's treasury.

Charlemagne's campaigns were usually planned in late

winter or early spring. The actual fighting went on through the summer, a truce falling at the coming of winter. As soon as the plans were ready, messengers would be sent to all the counts to declare the date and place of the muster. 'Any free-born man, owning four *mansi*, is hereby commanded to provide his own equipment and to join the King's host. Whoever possesses three *mansi* only must join forces with anyone possessing one *mansus* and also help him with his equipment.'[4]

In Carolingian days 'the equipment' included more than clothing and weapons. According to the Frankish custom, anyone joining the muster had to bring enough clothing to last six months and victuals for three. The more important among the landowners were also ordered 'to provide carts and horses, flour and wine, salted pork and other meat in abundance, adzes, axes, augers and slings, and men who knew how to use them,' according to the Aachen Capitulary of 801. Armour, consisting of hauberk, shield and greaves, was expensive in Frankland and even more so abroad, and Charlemagne strictly forbade its export.

Neither Einhard nor the chroniclers make any mention of camp followers. With Einhard, the omission may well be in accord with his reticence about Charlemagne's moral laxity. The others may have thought the matter not worth their mention. We hear of no penalties for rape in enemy countries. But Charlemagne's own camp was always in the rear; his queen and whatever mistresses he had at the moment certainly followed him in his Saxon campaigns, and it is difficult to believe that his enormous household would have left their wives and mistresses behind at Aachen, Heristal or Ingelheim.

The army discipline was hard but certainly milder than the Roman. If anyone 'of whichever degree' failed to appear at the muster at the appointed time, 'he was to abstain from meat and wine for as many days as he shall have been proved to be late in coming to the muster'. No treating was permitted in camp, and water was the penalty for drunkenness, the punishment to last at the commander's discretion.

Charlemagne's campaigns, particularly those against the Saxons, brought his men into difficult country; impenetrable forests where the hazards of an enemy ambush were increased a hundredfold by the possibility of attacks from wild beasts, bare rocks which afforded no apparent foothold, rivers where the search for a ford halted the advance, and vast plains which offered no cover either from the enemy arrow or from the sun. The King insisted that no superfluities, let alone luxuries, were added to the baggage. The men in the ranks wore clothing made of light wool and of linen. Notker Balbulus[5] tells the story of a great landowner who came to the muster, his cloak, smock, belt, arms and hair glittering with jewellery. His companions laughed, but Charlemagne's wrath broke out like a pillar of flame. 'Wretch that you are! Is it not enough for you to die on battlefield without giving your soul's ransom to the enemy?' Masses to redeem and to shorten a soul's stay in purgatory were often paid for in kind – either land, or cattle, or jewellery.

All the evidences proved the campaigns to be so many crusades. The great host would be accompanied by a number of bishops, priests and monks. The latter marched with crosses held high in their arms. Important reliquaries would be carried under sumptuous silken canopies. The clerical contingent took no part in the fighting, but they shared all the hardships of the armed laity. They generally followed the baggage train, and were ready to offer their services whenever those were asked for. The host would leave the place of muster, a solemn Mass having first been sung, to the chanting of psalms and canticles. During the march, Mass would be either said or sung on Sundays and all the appointed feasts. All feasts were observed most rigidly, the two customary daily meals, i.e. dinner and supper, gave place to a single collation, and there could hardly have been a man in the army who abhorred the privation as much as Charlemagne, whose appetite (for food, not for drink) was prodigious.

At the end of every action, the clergy chanted the Gradual Psalms for the fallen, and went to the battlefield to give the last sacrament to the wounded and the dying. A certain number of physicians followed the host, and some rough medical help was available, a great many monks being skilled in the use of herbs and the making of cordials, but the men's spiritual welfare far outstripped the concern for their physical needs. Charlemagne's own physicians had a very easy time of it. He called them impostors, refused their concoctions, and held most stubbornly that starvation was the best medicine for any ailment.

In large terms, the atmosphere of the camp must have suggested a liturgically charged battery.

As has already been said, every free-born Frank learned something of war in his boyhood, but the great majority of those who joined the annual muster were wholly untrained in the practice of war. They learnt it by experience. They fought well and fiercely. If they did not win, they died 'to the glory of God and the honour of Frankland'. Harsh experiences taught them how to use any moment and any movement to the greatest injury of the enemy and to obey commands they frequently did not understand. They learned how to stand still and firm as a rock just as their fathers had stood between Tours and Poitiers and thus won the day not only for their own country but for Europe. They learned how to endure heat and storm, to climb steep mountains, and to find their way through apparently impassable forests. They never forgot that in their rear rode a man who wore the same rough clothes, shared the same victuals, knelt in their midst for prayer, and joined with them in shouts of triumph. That man was their comrade as well as their King.

They received no wage for the valour spent and the victory gained, but the unwritten law of sharing out the booty was scrupulously observed. Moreover, the weapons and other gear of a killed enemy went to his slayer.

Charlemagne's many wars resulted in giving him Aquitania, Bavaria, the Italian peninsula, the Saxon lands, and the vast Danubian plain known as Pannonia to the Romans. They established the Frankish hold along the Pyrenean border, the Breton March and Septimania.

All those wars were flung widely apart, but in Charlemagne's mind they had a common focal point where the realm of Frankland was the realm of Europe. Yet he never imposed the Frankish social pattern on the vanquished. Variety within a unity rather than a soulless grey uniformity was his ideal.

At the end of his reign a savage enemy, whom he knew but at a distance would come perilously close to the Frankish door, though even in 814 the petition '*de furore Normannorum libera nos Domine*' ('From the fury of the Northmen, Oh Lord, deliver us') had not yet found its place in the Gallican litanies.

*   *   *

Einhard wrote[6], when referring to Charlemagne's Lombard campaign, that he could say much about the physical difficulties of the march across the Alps, a march which put the Franks' endurance to the utmost test. Posterity, said Einhard, would not need detailed descriptions of trials and difficulties. The results of any war carried their own eloquence and what should be given pride of place in military history ought to fall into the background in a book, such as Einhard's, which primarily dealt with a man's life and character. Charlemagne's biographer certainly had a case. The very names of several battlefields are apt to become so many unnecessary labels.

From the King's point of view, Bavaria was part of Germania. The Duchy had intimate links with Frankland: even in the Merovingian days Bavarian princesses would bring good blood, genuine piety and rich dowries to Paris, Tournais, Rheims and Orléans. The Duke's people lived under the Bavarian law, spoke their own dialect, and jealously preserved their old customs, but underneath it all ran the deep stream of kinship with the Franks, and the Bavarians valued it greatly.

At Charlemagne's accession, the Duke was one Tassilo, the King's first cousin, and trouble broke out when he married Liutberga, youngest daughter of Desiderius. The King of the Lombards arranged the match with great subtlety. Tassilo, having the King of the Franks for his overlord, owed him allegiance. Desiderius hoped that the Duke's fealty would be weakened by a matrimonial alliance with Lombardy, and, well aware of his daughter's intelligence, Desiderius instructed her in the policy she was to follow at her husband's court. But the Lombard did not know the Bavarians, and was mistaken in his idea that a close alliance with their Duchess's country would please them. Charlemagne knew it well, and he also knew that Tassilo's Utopian vision of an independent sovereignty repelled his people. All they wanted was security, and they were well aware that the protection of the Franks could give it to them. But Tassilo, prompted by his Duchess, took to boasting openly that he would much rather be an ally of his father-in-law than a vassal of Charlemagne's.

In spite of Liutberga's unending persuasions, Tassilo was compelled to keep neutrality during the Lombard campaign. He was uncomfortably certain that the Bavarians would never have unsheathed their swords against the Franks. Desiderius was angry and Liutberga now implored, now abused him for cowardice, but Tassilo would not call his men to a muster.

When Pavia fell to the Franks, the Duke thought no more of his Lombard alliance than of a fly on the wall. He began shaping a different plan and succeeded in making Liutberga consent to it. First, he began a mild flirtation with the pagan Avars in the Danubian plain. Next, at dinner in his hall, he argued that Bavaria was far too important to remain a mere duchy. What about a king's crown for him? His wife and his counsellors echoed the ambition, but the Bavarians were not at all sure they wanted Tassilo as their king, and his flattering approaches to the heathen enemy of Charlemagne pleased them even less.

The King of the Franks knew of it all. The Lombard war ended triumphantly. Charlemagne was urged by Adrian I to try diplomatic persuasion. The Pontiff wrote that he did not give credence to gossip. Tassilo had kept his promise of neutrality and the whispers about his dalliance with the Avars may well have come from his enemies. The Pontiff reminded Charlemagne that he and Tassilo were close kinsmen and that a lasting reconciliation would be pleasing to their Maker. Charlemagne gave in, and a papal embassy went to Bavaria. In Tassilo they found an amiable and generous host, not only prepared to listen to the ambassadors but eager to agree to their proposals. He said repeatedly that he had no intention of allying himself with the heathen Avars and that his friendship with the fallen Lombard had been solely due to the kinship between them.

The Italians believed Tassilo to be sincere. According to custom, the Duchess appeared at banquets; they found her courtesy rather cloying, but she was careful not to break her silence except by echoing her husband's assurances. The Italians were not sure that they could trust Liutberga, but they kept their doubts to themselves, and their discretion was rewarded when at the end of 781, the Duke met his cousin at Worms and, in the presence of the full court, solemnly re-affirmed his oath of fealty to Charlemagne. All the Bavarian belfries pealed in thanksgiving. At St Peter's the Pope had a Te Deum sung to mark a great moral victory, but it is an open question if Charlemagne took his cousin's repentance for genuine coin. The Duchess had followed her husband to Worms. The Queen-Mother lavished presents and kindnesses on her, but Bertrada's son sensed that he could not trust a daughter of Desiderius. Her father's kingdom was shattered indeed, but the pride in Liutberga forbade her to admit that the Lombard glory was extinguished for ever. She remembered that her brother had many adherents in Italy, and took heart. She kissed Queen Bertrada's hands, was humble and prudent in her speech, but she knew that the hour of intrigues was not over.

She and her Duke went back to Bavaria, and an uneasy peace lasted till 785 when a conspiracy against Charlemagne was traced to Tassilo, Liutberga's persuasions having shaped every move and her great dowry having provided the gold. The conspirators were dealt with summarily and cruelly. Charle-magne sent a stern warning to his cousin and the Pope's faith in the Duke's integrity was all but shattered. It was gone wholly when Tassilo's flirtation with the Avars crept into the open and the friendly approaches were welded into a formal alliance. 'Tassilo is a liar,' wrote Adrian I, and threatened the Duke with excommunication. There was no further talk about the sanctity of kinship.

In the autumn of 785, Charlemagne summoned his cousin to Worms. The summons was an overlord's command, not a kinsman's invitation. Liutberga urged her husband to ignore it, and Charlemagne lost his patience. He sent no declaration of war, but the Frankish host marched into Bavaria. The un-concealed pleasure of the Bavarians frightened Tassilo into submission, and he reproached his wife bitterly. The web of intrigues she had spun would lead him to his ruin, said Tassilo, easily forgetting his own boundless ambition to gain independence.

Once again, his submission did not last. The man was like a reed swayed by the faintest breath of wind. Still young,

handsome, wealthy and gifted, Tassilo might well have taken
a place of honour at Charlemagne's council-table. Instead, he
wasted himself and all he possessed. He believed in Liutberga,
who, her intelligence notwithstanding, built plans which would
have accorded with a lunatic's aims. He also believed that
Charlemagne's popularity was grossly exaggerated by a crowd
of sycophants. Finally, he stubbornly nursed the delusion that
the Bavarians were devoted to him.

Having crushed the conspiracy and sent a grim warning to
Tassilo, Charlemagne was in no hurry to take further measures,
but the incriminating evidence of the Duke's treachery was
piling up. In the end, he was compelled to stand his trial at
Ingelheim, accused of betraying his overlord by his alliance
with the Avars and of conspiring against Charlemagne's life.
The judges allowed that Tassilo had been influenced by
Liutberga, but a crime was no less a crime when planned on a
woman's advice. Tassilo met the accusations as calmly as
though they did not concern him, and hoped that his fiery
eloquence would yet win the day for him. It did not, and when
he heard that his trespasses deserved the judgment of death,
he threw back his handsome head and replied that it would be
better for him to die than to live as a vassal on ignominious terms.
The judges condemned him to be beheaded. Liutberga and the
children were to be sent to various abbeys there to be kept for
life – not as monks and nuns but as prisoners.

The verdict had to be confirmed by Charlemagne, and he
was in no hurry to do it. According to the law, Tassilo certainly
deserved death, but Tassilo was a first cousin, and Charlemagne
was no Merovingian to whom a death sentence carried out on
their closest kin meant as much as the fall of a leaf. It was quite
a time before the King consented to the verdict and the date
of the execution was fixed.

Tassilo's head never rolled off the block. It came to Charlemagne's knowledge that his cousin had expressed a wish to be
tonsured as a monk on the very eve of the execution. 'I cannot
and I will not shed my kinsman's blood,' decided the King.
Not as a nameless prisoner but as Duke of Bavaria, Tassilo was
taken to the Abbey of Juimèges, and the cloistral rhythm
gradually quietened him. He never saw his wife again, and he

did not miss her. Once only did he leave his abbey, a humble, fully habited monk, to appear at Frankfurt in 794 there to pronounce his solemn abdication and to place the Duchy in his cousin's hands.

The Bavarian matter might well have remained a mere family quarrel were it not for Liutberga's passion for intrigues that pushed it into deeper waters, and Charlemagne owed her a debt. Tassilo's own ambitions would have begun and ended in an imaginary splendour, but an independent Bavaria, with the Avar support in the background, might well have split the continent. In spite of the later Carolingian breakdown, the surrender of the Duchy to Charlemagne laid the foundations of a united Germany.

*   *   *

The Saxon wars, begun in 772, lasted for more than 30 years though the decades were broken by many intervals of uneasy truce. Once again we must turn to Einhard[7] for a lucid and brief exposition of the scope and purpose of those campaigns.

'Never was there a war known to last so long, nor one which demanded such efforts on the part of the Franks . . . The Saxons . . . are savage by nature, hostile to our religion, and given to the worship of devils, and they think nothing of breaking the laws of God and man . . . Unfortunately, they were close neighbours of the Franks, and Frankland had suffered much at their hands in the days of the Merovingians.'

The Saxon idea of warfare was primitive and savage: it expressed itself in lightning-quick attacks on the Frankish lands. To kill, to rape, to loot, and to burn whatever they could not carry back to their thickly wooded fastnesses, such was the immemorial pattern. The ravages accomplished, they hurried back to get ready for Frankish reprisals which – in the past – did not follow as quickly as they should have done.

The immensity of the common frontier added to the difficulties. '[The Franco-Saxon] borders stretch over vast distances except where thick forests and mountains . . . make a natural rampart . . .' That borderline made attacks easier for the Saxons than for the Franks, but Einhard was too honest a historian to lay every trespass at the Saxon door. ' . . . on both sides, murder, rapine and arson kept breaking out.'

The Franks retaliated every time, but at last their patience got frayed. At the spring assembly of 772, an offensive campaign against the Saxons was suggested by Charlemagne, and his people agreed to it. Their own ultimate purpose may well have differed from his 'to the greater glory of God', but the difference in no way interfered with their readiness to follow the King.

It was to be a war *à l'outrance*. According to Einhard and other annalists, it need not have lasted for thirty odd years,[8] and Einhard gives cogent reasons for the conjecture. For one thing, however keen Charlemagne was on crushing 'the Saxon heathenry', he was not always free to give the Saxons his undivided attention, and that inevitably prolonged the war. For another, as happened so often, the King was all too ready to trust promises which should never have been trusted, and he was incapable of expecting treachery where it was most to be expected. Here we stand face to face with Charlemagne's dichotomy. That childlike trustfulness was a surprising streak in his character. It reconciled much but it never quite succeeded in redeeming his cruelty, of which the most shattering example was given to an incredulous world in his dealings with the vanquished Saxons, an example which put all his other trespasses into shade, and which, though he could not have been conscious of it, flung him back into the forest-bred darkness of his ancestors' mentality, an example which mocked at all his reforms and all but annulled his claim to the greatness that posterity would bestow on him. All cruelty, whether mental or physical, is devoid of sense. A tiger, tearing his victim limb from limb, has hunger for his excuse. Man, trampling on his fellow-man, has none.

To Frankish annalists and to Einhard the Saxons were a tiresome and savage people. But to later historians they were more than a turbulent, primitive tribe. They were Germanic and proud of their origin. They had their *'Volksthing'*, a parliament based on genuine democratic principles. They had many ancient customs and cherished them. They had a reverence for old age and womankind. They had a deep feeling for their religion, and they were passionately jealous of their independence. Each tribe chose its chieftain and obeyed him so long as their obedience did not run counter to their own wishes.

They had their settlements eastwards from the Elbe and westwards almost to the lip of the Rhine, and the name 'Saxon' denoted some few Germanic tribes united by one generic label. Having covered vast distances in their wanderings from the East, they settled down, and reconciled themselves to primitive agriculture, the land answering all their seasonal needs. But they wanted more, and the routine was enlivened by raids on their Frankish neighbours. Savage the Saxons certainly were, but savagery alone does not quite explain them. They were indifferent to trouble and suffering, and they lived too close to nature not to share in her moods.

They were fiercely jealous of their paganism and they hated Christianity no less fiercely. Any attack of theirs on Frankish lands meant burnt churches and monasteries, murdered monks and priests, and raped nuns. Such arson and slaughter, as the Saxons thought, was the most pleasing sacrifice to their gods. It was precisely their militant paganism which turned Charlemagne's war into a crusade. He was convinced that God meant him to avenge the death of St Boniface and many other missionaries. The Pope sent his blessing, a rather lukewarm one because Rome feared lest the Saxon embroglio might keep the Franks too busy for the Lombard matter. But to the King of the Franks the Saxon war appeared in a different light. The Lombards were Christian – whatever their treatment of the Pope. The Saxons, bone of the Germanic bone, were heathen, and Charlemagne was resolved to force them into the Christian household. He would pursue them over the Weser, the Ocker, the Oder, the Rhine and even beyond the Elbe. He had no doubt of the ultimate victory because he believed Christ to be on his side, though it would be futile to deny that purely territorial aggrandisement played its part in his plans.

The campaign opened in July 772, the great Frankish host accompanied by bishops, priests and monks riding and marching in the rearguard, and their presence lent its own colour to the enterprise and set the religious purpose above any other. 'I am going to convert the pagan Saxons to the Holy Faith,' the King declared to the Pope, 'and so to bring them into the fellowship of the Christian world.'

He used those words in all sincerity, but he belonged to his century, and it would have been beyond his comprehension to grasp that conversion brought about by violence was no true conversion but an unhallowed mockery of a holy thing.

The first act of violence was never to be forgotten by the Saxons. They kept to their remote fastnesses and made no move to meet the Franks in open battle. Guided by reliable scouts, Charlemagne's men reached a thick forest. In its heart they came on Irminsul, a faithful wooden replica of Yggdrasil, a dedicated column set in the middle of a sacred grove, the very heartbeat of Saxon paganism since their chief god was believed to live within the carved column. The Saxons may well have hoped that the very sight of Irminsul would not only check the Frankish advance but compel the enemy to retreat.

Instead, the huge column was cut down and burned and the temple nearby looted and destroyed, the Frankish clergy singing hymns of thanksgiving for such a signal victory over paganism. Their principal shrine ravaged, the Saxons retreated beyond the Weser. They had no heart to continue the struggle. The Franks pursued them. Many Saxons were taken as hostages, and there followed a truce.

Yet it proved nothing but a beginning. There were to be eighteen Saxon expeditions in all, stretching over more than three decades. In 774, when Charlemagne was busy in Italy, the Saxons, resolved to avenge the destruction of Irminsul, invaded Hesse. St Boniface's abbey at Fritzlar was burned down to the ground, the abbot and all the monks were put to the sword. The Saxon savagery swept over Hesse, sparing neither women nor children. When Charlemagne heard of it, his anger flamed high. He, caring for their souls, had offered them salvation and arranged an honourable truce. The Saxons broke the truce and replied to his offer by arson, murder and rapine. So the King hurried back from Italy, resolved to fight 'that perfidious nation . . . and . . . to persevere until they were either made subject to the Christian religion, or were swept off the face of the earth.'

At this point, the crusade underwent an abrupt change of purpose. Not the Lord's mercy but the King's anger became the decisive factor, and 'Be baptized or die' was the burden of

the Frankish persuasion during the campaign of 775. Untold
thousands of Saxons were found to prefer death to Christianity.
But the pagan fervour did not last. The very next year, hounded
to the banks of the Lippe, disheartened by the Frankish
successes as well as by the all too apparent indifference of their
Olympus, the Saxon chieftains got their people together, held
a hurried and harassed assembly, and sent messengers to the
Frankish camp to tell the King they were all agreed to be
received into the Christian Church. Charlemagne refused to
doubt their good faith. So many Saxons were baptized in the
waters of the Lippe that he, wholly reassured, retreated to keep
his Christmas at Heristal. At Christmas Mass he thanked God
for His help in the campaign and believed the Saxon matter
to be settled in perpetuity. Baptismal grace, so Charlemagne
assured himself, was not a gauntlet to be put on and taken off
at any man's whim.

That he believed firmly. None the less, precautions were
taken to prevent a repetition of the horrors in Hesse. Many
important Saxon hostages were retained by the Franks, well-
manned and adequately provisioned forts were built all along
the Western bank of the Lippe, and Frankish detachments were
detailed to keep a vigilant eye all along the border. The winter
passed peaceably enough. Then the spring came, and Charlemagne learned that in many cases the grace of baptism meant
less than a withered blade of grass to the heathen.

In the first place, he did not know the Saxons. Next, he had
forgotten to reckon with Widukind who, alone among the
Saxon chieftains, understood what cohesion stood for and who
knew how to win allies in the struggle against the Franks.
Widukind moved slowly. As late as in 777 Charlemagne was
able to summon the usual annual assembly at Paderborn – in
the very heart of the apparently subjugated Saxon land.
Widukind chose to be absent, but all the other Saxon
chieftains obeyed, and they declared their readiness to order
their lives in accordance with the Christian tenets. The Frankish bishops and clergy heard their assurances and prudently
made no comment, but Charlemagne was incapable of imag-
ining treachery unless its steps drowned every other sound
round about him. Widukind had vast possessions in Westphalia,

and Charlemagne believed him to be there. The King had no idea that the Saxon was much further away, arranging an alliance with Gotfried, 'the greatly dreaded King of Denmark'.

The assembly was over, but Charlemagne lingered at Paderborn, using his leisure in hunting the wild boar and the auroch. And then he heard of the Saxon-Danish alliance.

On his own, Widukind was a formidable foe. With the Danes' support behind him, he would have seemed invincible to anyone except Charlemagne. And once again, the King's immediate reaction was anger blended with bewilderment. How could Widukind enter into an offensive alliance with Denmark when the Franks and the Saxons had agreed to a truce? Widukind was still a pagan but most of the chieftains who followed him had been baptized, and Denmark was wholly heathen. How could they reconcile their baptismal vows with such an alliance? Charlemagne could not understand it. The Saxon war would certainly have been shortened by more than one decade if the King of the Franks had had a deeper knowledge of human nature.

For eight years, from 777 to 785, the Saxon matter was a duel between Charlemagne and Widukind. The Saxons' chance came in 778. Assured of a lull along the Saxon borders, Charlemagne moved his host towards the Pyrenees. Widukind did not waste a moment. He mustered his men and rushed them into the valley of the Rhine. They marched from Deutz to Coblenz, leaving pillars of smoke in their wake. Not a township or a hamlet, not an abbey or a convent but paid the price for the destruction of Irminsul. Able-bodied serfs of the Franks were driven off into Saxon slavery. Priests, monks and nuns were put to the sword.

The Frankish force left to guard the river banks checked the wild onrush at Coblenz and, fighting savagely, succeeded in throwing the Saxons back beyond Deutz, but Widukind did not lose heart. He continued to retreat, leaving the dead and the wounded behind and making the Franks believe they had utterly routed the enemy. Thus falsely assured, they halted the pursuit and relaxed their vigilance. Widukind asked for no better chance. The rout, imagined by the Franks, became a fierce assault almost overnight, and the Westphalian chieftain was triumphant.

Such, then, was then general pattern of the Saxon campaigns. Truce would be broken by either side. Mass baptism forced upon the Saxons would be followed by a mass return to paganism. Little by little the centre of the struggle shifted to the North, to Wigmodia between Bremen and Hamburg where Widukind had staunch allies – the savage Slavic tribes and the 'rex terribilis', King Gotfried of Denmark.

During those years Charlemagne committed first the major blunder of his whole reign and secondly the worst crime of the century. The blunder was made in 782 at the annual assembly held on the banks of the Lippe when the King issued the infamous Capitulary 'de partibus Saxoniae'.[9] It decreed death not only for violence and any other offences committed against the Church and the clergy but for the most trivial trespass against the Canon Law. Any Saxon man or woman would be beheaded if they had as much as a morsel of meat for their dinner in Lent. All Saxons, including serfs, were ordered to give a tenth of their substance to the Church. The poorest among them were not exempt even if the tax levied most mercilessly left them to face ruin. Over and above the tax in money or in kind, the Saxons were commanded to give a certain amount of free labour to the Church.

From beginning to end, the Capitulary was a Draconian document, the word 'mors' summing up the penalties, and it defeated its own purpose. Waves of resentment began rippling up and down the Saxon lands. The chieftains met in secret, at dead of night, in the heart of a forest, and all their people, the baptismal vows trampled down, swore to retrieve their stolen liberties. Widukind being then in Denmark, messengers were sent to him.

It is difficult, if not impossible, to understand how Charlemagne, a man of prudence and wisdom, could have stumbled on such a blunder. To have expected submission to the Capitulary suggests a total lack of understanding, and yet Charlemagne had expected it.

He was then in Bavaria, busied with the final preparations for the Avar war. Too late did he learn that Widukind, back among his people, was inspiring them all to fight for freedom. The King's cousin, Theodoric, fell in an ambush, and a little later a whole Frankish army fell under the Saxon axes at Suntal near Minden. It was no battle but a shambles, and some of the King's ablest commanders were killed.

Such, in brief, was the Saxon reply to the Capitulary.

Charlemagne's reaction was immediate, terrible, and untrue to his best self. Having made a major blunder, he followed it up by a crime, its magnitude darkening his reign.

He marched from Bavaria at the head of a bigger host than he had ever mustered. His wrath leapt even higher when he heard of Widukind's flight back to Denmark. An extraordinary assembly was held at Verden on the Aller. The assembly declared Widukind to be the instigator of the revolt, and he was condemned to death *in absentia*. The Franks had little hope of capturing him. Charlemagne, presiding at the assembly, had no use for legal subtleties at that late hour: he was no more and no less than a flame burning for vengeance. Widukind eluded him, but the Franks had over four thousand Saxon hostages, and Charlemagne ordered that they were all to be beheaded. According to some chroniclers, this was carried out in a day.

Einhard makes no mention of the Verden massacre. A jelly-minded sycophant would have piled excuse upon excuse, but Einhard was not of that company. There were no excuses. The Saxon blood split that day left an indelible stain on Charlemagne's record. That Saxon revolt had been a natural reaction to a capitulary which should never have been issued. The Verden horror was the act of a man, his whole mind conscious of nothing but the lust for vengeance.

In the end, Widukind was forced to surrender, and was baptized at Attigny in the Ardennes, Charlemagne being his sponsor, and Pope Adrian I rejoicing at the Saxon's 'true religion and perfect faith'. In Widukind's case, such an encomium rang true: he kept his vows to the end.

It is difficult to gauge how far, if at all, Charlemagne's conscience was stirred by this singular example of a genuine Saxon conversion. The facts are that, all his treacheries notwithstanding, Widukind was treated with honour, and his vast possessions in Westphalia and elsewhere were not confiscated, and he founded and endowed one of the first bishoprics in the Saxon country. It is rather tempting to conjecture that Charlemagne's incredible generosity to an enemy in chief may have been due to the reproaches of conscience for the horror of Verden.

Widukind's conversion and reconciliation with the Franks should have drawn the curtain upon the Saxon business since he alone had been the heartbeat of it, informing his turbulent and quarrelsome people with a sense of unity, a quality of far greater use to them than many thousands of axes. So it would seem. But that did not happen. Disunited, bereft of a leader, the Saxons would not surrender. Widukind's conversion made them despise him, and now they were determined to win on their own. So the troublesome war flame burnt now high, now low, sank to cinders, and flared up again.

About 792 Charlemagne was in Bavaria and an ingenious idea came to him. There, a little river, the Rezat, rises and flows northwards into the Main and, eventually, the waters reach the Rhine and the North Sea. In the near neighbourhood of the Rezat, the Altmühl flows on until it joins the Danube. Charlemagne, preoccupied with the transport problems of the Avar campaign, took to studying the terrain and decided that it might be possible to have a navigable canal dug between the Rezat and the Altmühl. He conjectured that some such canal would enable his military potential to be moved northward and thus help towards a speedier solution of the Saxon problem, and eastwards to ease his operations against the Avars.

Charlemagne had many gifted commanders in his camp but none among them could lay a claim to an extensive engineering knowledge. That did not daunt the King. A canal, as he thought, could be made by digging and by some adequate protection given to the banks. Such a job, as he visualized it, asked for brawn rather than brain, and he had a great labour force at his command. Already he imagined barge after barge, carrying men, weapons and provisions, sailing northwards, sailing eastwards, easing the perenially difficult problems of transport, and Charlemagne gave orders, calmly certain of the happy outcome.

Vast numbers of men were drafted for the digging, and they

dug zealously and willingly. But, alas, neither Charlemagne nor any among his counsellors knew much, if anything, about soil. The land between the two little rivers was marshy, and there were no experts in Charlemagne's camp to plan and to direct the necessary draining operations. A day's hard work would be undone by an hour's rain at evening. In the end, the work had to be abandoned.

By that time the King was thoroughly weary of the Saxon business. The last and faintest crusading breath had gone out of it. But, whether Christian or pagan, they were still enemies, and even the tremendous Frankish victory at Sendfeld near Paderborn did not succeed to cut the Gordian knot.

At the turn of the century Charlemagne decided to transport thousands of Saxons into Frankland, and to give their steadings to such Franks as cared to migrate. By 804, all the Saxons who lived beyond the Elbe and in Wigmodia, together with their families and what household gear they possessed, were settled in Frankland. The big landowners had their estates divided between a friendly Slavic tribe of Abodrites and such Franks as wished to settle there. Saxonia was formally divided into three bishoprics: Bremen, Münster and Paderborn. The unexpected murder of the '*rex terribilis*', Gotfried of Denmark, led to a peace being established along the northern border. The Danes had got rather bored with the Saxons. Moreover, they had their own problems to settle.

The Saxon wars, begun when Charlemagne was young and ended with old age creeping near him, brought out the best and the worst in him. The best was contained in his longing to see all the Teutonic tribes united within the Christian household, a longing which marched side by side with Charlemagne's vision of a united Europe. The idea was large and noble but it grew lamentably dwarfed because of the means he used towards its interpretation. The Draconian Capitulary with its savage penalties for trifling offences and the Verden massacre could never be wiped out. The Capitulary, acclaimed by the Pope and the Frankish hierarchy, was in a sense the forerunner of the Inquisition, and Verden a grimly atavistic gesture.

What was strange about the whole matter was that Charlemagne, himself a Teuton, remained blind to what may well have been one of the main reasons for the Saxon abhorrence of Christiantity. Treachery to an enemy was a finely developed art with them. Treachery to a friend was the worst offence imaginable. When they first heard the story of the Lord's Passion, no comprehension of the Atonement entered their minds, but to learn of Judas, of St Peter's denial, and of all the others who forsook Him and fled, was to see a landscape of such despicable perfidy that the Saxons felt it was no creed to be accepted by them. Nor did the concept of forgiveness accord with any of their ideas. All in all, it seemed a religion fit to answer the needs of fools and very young children. They never asked themselves why the Franks had come to subscribe to such principles unworthy of well-trained warriors who showed no mercy and expected none.

*   *   *

Sometime between the end of the fifth and the beginning of the sixth century, a savage nomad tribe of Mongolians, known as the Avars, ended their wanderings and settled in the Hungarian plain between the Danube and the Carpathians. They were small, dark people, who plaited their hair into pigtails, wore no beards, fed on horseflesh and mare's milk, and were horsemen of rare distinction. They bred at an alarming rate. Once settled, they developed a deep sense of cohesion. Their ruler was called *Kagan*, whose ministers were known as '*tuguni*'. According to Einhard,[10] Charlemagne's war against the Avars was, the Saxon business apart, the most important of all.

Broadly speaking, the Avars were parasites, giving nothing and taking as much as they could grasp. It was not long before they became a threat and a terror to North Italy, Frankland and Byzantium. The seventh century saw the peak of their piratical activities. They laid siege to Constantinople and, with Persia for ally, all but broke Byzantium, already weakened by ceaseless Bulgarian attacks. Twice did the Avars overrun and ravage the Duchy of Friuli. The Merovingians were routed by them in the reign of Sigebert. They rode 'faster than lightning', and their short curved swords dealt death just as swiftly. They seemed invincible, 'a race of iron and adamant', according to

Notker Balbulus, adamant being then the hardest stone known to exist.[11] An attack over, the loot packed into capacious saddle-bags, the Avars galloped back to their fastness – so constructed that none could beleaguer it.

Notker's book is of no great use to a serious historian, but here and there he can swing away from gossip and fable and give facts. In this instance[12] he says that the information about the Avar capital was given him by 'Adalbert, father of Werinbert', who must have been Abbot of St Gall since Notker speaks of his 'bereaved sons and disciples'. Adalbert, having joined Kerold's host, had taken part in the Frankish war against the Avars.

'[Their] capital,' says Notker, 'was surrounded by nine rings, or high hedges made most skilfully of thick logs, oak, ash and yew being chiefly used; each such ring was twenty feet high and twenty feet broad. The space inside was filled with stones and binding clay. The top of those rings was covered with turf. Between each of the nine ramparts, houses were built in such a way that a man's voice could reach from one ring to another. The second and the third rings were exactly like the first [in size], but with the fourth ring the circles grew smaller and smaller towards the centre where, as rumour had it, the Kagan had his palace', and there was kept the fabulous treasure, the fruits of many generations of looting.

The outer ring might indeed be reached, but the ramparts could not be pierced anywhere, and the Avars alone seemed to possess the secret of ingress and egress since no ordinary gates could be seen anywhere.

An Avar contingent attacked Bavaria in 788, and was re-pulsed. The Frankish commanders considered that the time had come for an assault upon the Ring. Charlemagne's forces were deeply committed against the Saxons at the time. However, in 789 a Frankish host made towards the Danubian plain, and came back, their objective frustrated by the absence of the enemy. The Avars avoided pitched battles and stayed behind their impenetrable fastness but, after the Franks' withdrawal, the Kagan and his councillors decided to take some precaution-ary measures. Two outposts were hastily built on the east bank of the Danube and manned by some few hundred of the Kagan's most intrepid warriors.

At the assembly held at Regensburg in the early spring of
791, it was unanimously decided to make a great effort and
put an end to the Avars' insolent pillage. 'Their place is not in
Europe', argued the King's councillors, 'they swarmed in from
Asia and they have remained Asiatic'. When the decision
became known in the country, there was a storm of applause,
and few were the able-bodied men who did not hurry to the
muster 'because of the great and intolerable malice shewn [by
the Avars] towards the Church and all Christian folk'.

Later that spring a great Frankish force started on the long
and arduous march. Presently they came within a week's
distance of the terrible Ring. The Avars were waiting, but, as
usual, they did not offer battle, trusting that their outposts
would check the enemy advance and, ultimately, trusting their
ramparts to protect them far more effectively than their gods
could do.

Just before the great host reached the Danube, Charlemagne
ordered a halt, and there they camped for three days wholly
given over to pious practices and to the construction of barges.
Masses were said each morning and Vespers chanted in the
afternoon. In between, litanies were sung and reliquaries
carried up and down along the ranks. The King decreed an
absolute fast for the first day; on the second and the third,
porridge, bread, a little bean mess and thin beer were distributed among the troops, Charlemagne sharing their fare.
Neither meat, fish nor wine were touched during the three days.

On the fourth morning, the Franks struck camp, and the
immense host was divided, one part marching along the west
bank of the Danube and the other being ferried across. Barges,
manned by Franks in their full war panoply, and carrying more
weapons and the necessary victuals, sailed up and down the
river.

The sight of such an immense force, never encountered
before, shredded the garrison's courage. Without waiting for
the Frankish assault, the Avars rushed out, flung their weapons
on the ground, and raised their arms sky-ward. But, having
expected no mercy from the Avars, the Franks gave them none,
and every man was put to the sword.

By the afternoon Charlemagne's entire host entered the

Kagan's country. They marched, meeting with no resistance, and they laid waste a great part of Pannonia. Once again they camped at no great distance from the Ring, when disturbing news from Frankland came to Charlemagne. First, the Saxons were once again in revolt, and the forces left behind were not strong enough to quell the rebellion. Next, Charlemagne's first born, Pippin the Hunchback, Hilmentrud's son, had been discovered shaping a conspiracy against his father's life. One or two attempts to storm the ramparts proving fruitless, the King decided to retreat to Bavaria.

He had failed to take the Ring but succeeded in shattering the Avar morale, and that was a victory in itself. All sense of cohesion left them. The grim sight of the ravages left in the Frankish retreat, the slaughter of the two garrisons, the acid consciousness that the Franks' next appearance would end in their ultimate ruin, all of it turned the much vaunted Avar invincibility into an idle tale. Dissensions broke out in the Kagan's palace, some among the *tuguni* clamouring for immediate surrender, others pleading that it was still possible to defend the ramparts, and some few suggesting that the great treasure should be buried deep enough out of the reach of the enemy. The Kagan listened to them all and did nothing.

Presently, the most influential among the *tuguni* escaped by stealth from the Ring and made his way to Bavaria. It was midwinter, and the King had gone to Aachen where the *tugun* and his few followers found him, and the Avar declared his willingness to be baptized and begged for permission to remain in Frankland. He was a man of great garrulity, and there were a few able interpreters at Charlemagne's court. The *tugun's* stories about the Kagan's treasure inflamed the Frankish imagination. They longed for a muster in the spring of 792, but the King knew he could not spare the men. Not until the spring of 795 did the Franks, led by Eric, Duke of Friuli, force their way into the first rampart. Yet the long interval must have restored the Avar morale: they fought ferociously, and Duke Eric was killed. Frankish reinforcements, led by a younger son of Charlemagne, lost no time in coming to the rescue, and the whole Christendom rang with the echoes of the Frankish victory. It was as complete as it was ruthless: not an

H

Avar left alive and not a single trace left of the Ring.[13]

The *tugun* at Aachen had not embroidered the canvas. Prince Charles the Younger and his intimates could hardly believe their eyes when they saw the loot gathered by the Avars during more than two centuries. Great coffers and chests were crammed with gold and silver, pearls and precious stones. Nearly twenty huge carts were needed to carry the treasure to Frankland. The King's treasury was certainly enriched, but Charlemagne refused to take a single gem until he had shared the wealth not only with the men who had fought in Pannonia but with many friends and others outside Frankland. Much of the gold once stolen from Byzantium was returned to Constantinople. Silver, gold and a profusion of precious stones went to Italy, some of the gold and gems personal gifts to the Pope, and the rest to embellish St Peter's Basilica, for which Charlemagne had a deep affection.

His purpose was triumphantly accomplished: he had cleansed Europe of 'the Asiatic poison'. But it seems strange that, the Avar stronghold levelled down to the ground, the King never thought of establishing a Frankish settlement on the land won so hardly. Pannonia, though ravaged, was rich in timber, and Frankland's wealth, however increased by the Avar booty, was not so great as to make her disregard increased exports. Yet, conquered, laid waste and wholly depopulated, the region was left alone.

Some explanation may be given by the fact that, their victory won and the booty on its way to Frankland, the Franks were in a hurry to get back, to see the last of 'the accursed country', to leave it to wild beasts and birds of prey. Fear made them hurry away. All the awesome legends, clustered round about the Avar Ring, seemed to have crowded the very air they breathed. Three centuries of Christian observance had not succeeded to stamp paganism out of the Frankish mind. They had known the meaning of the Saxon Irminsul and destroyed it, no thought of any vengeance troubling them. But the Avar Ring stemmed from an unfamiliar darkness and was all the more terrible. Charlemagne, who knew his people so well, must have understood that fear.

*   *   *

He was a strategist of no mean stature, and accustomed to plan his campaigns down to the smallest victualling detail. His ambition to release Spain from the Arab yoke was largely inherited: Charles Martel's victory had been known to him since infancy. To fight the Arabs under the banner of the Cross would be no war of conquest but a deeply hallowed enterprise. Charlemagne's crusading zeal leapt to the heights when Pope Adrian recognised it by a special blessing.

But the King's Spanish venture of 778 was a failure in military terms. It left the Iberian Peninsula under the Arab heel. Also it yielded a germ of a theme to inflame and enrich the imagination of several generations. In the end, the theme poured itself out into a mould to engay and enliven European literature for centuries to come. The rout of the Frankish rearguard in the narrow, rocky valley of Roncevalles turned a Frankish defeat into a musical phrase.

The idea of some such expedition was part of Charlemagne's inheritance. The legend of the Saracen invincibility having been shattered by his grandfather in 732, Charlemagne was, in a sense, bred in the traditional abhorrence of the Crescent. When the legates of the Abbaside Caliph came to Ingelheim to ask for help in their struggle against Abderrahman, the Caliph of Cordova, Charlemagne did not hesitate. The Arabs' visit coincided with a quietening on the Saxon front. He took it to be a summons from God, and Pope Adrian's blessing confirmed his decision.

In the spring of 788, Charlemagne crossed the Pyrenees, having first divided his army into two equal parts, each following a different route. Charlemagne led his men from St Jean de la Port over a crest in the Pyrenees towards Pampelona. 'The highest point of this road, the *summus Pyreneus* looked down on the wild and narrow defile of Roncevalles.'[14]

The siege of Pampelona, the only military action of the brief campaign, did not last very long. It fell to the Franks in the summer, and Europe expected Charlemagne to plunge deeper and deeper into the peninsula. Instead, for no reasons mentioned in the annals, he turned back, and that in spite of his alliance with Alfonso the Chaste, King of the Asturias, who would certainly have welcomed him and who sent to Charlemagne's camp at Pampelona 'a tent of great beauty', accompanied by a letter where Alfonso signed himself as 'your own man'.

The chronicles are rather irritatingly vague. Einhard says very little, his attention absorbed by the Roncevalles *débâcle*. But it seems clear that the Abbasides soon enough came to regret their decision to ask the Franks for help. They may well have thought that the troublesome Caliphate of Cordova could indeed be crushed by the Frankish heel and that then would come the turn of the Abbasides, Charlemagne making no secret of his intention to clear the whole of Spain of the Saracens.

This may well be no more than an idle conjecture but it is obvious that, except for Alfonso the Chaste, Spain did not look forward to Charlemagne's arrival. The Abbasides, having first invited him, grew more and more lukewarm. Charlemagne had no taste for unprofitable campaigns, and he turned back.

When the Frankish host had passed through the rocky defile of Roncevalles, the Basques, a savage tribe inhabiting the heights of the Pyrenees, watched them pass from their lairs. The defile was narrow, the going proved slow and hard. It was late afternoon when the last detachment of Charlemagne's army had left the defile, and the Basques waited for the approach of the baggage train which, as it was proved, was protected by a most inadequate rearguard. As soon as the first wagon appeared in the defile, huge rocks were hurled down from above, and the Basques hurried down into the defile, to cut the rearguard off from the main part of the Frankish forces. The Basques fell on the baggage train, looting and killing in the manner of beasts driven by frenzy.[15] A chronicle has preserved a few names from among the fallen: Eghard, one of the King's seneschals, Anselm, Count of the Palace, and one Roland, Governor of the Breton March, whose name is spelt Hruodland by the annalist. That brief mention made, Roland entered into the romantic literature for ever.

There must have been at least one survivor who hurried to reach the main army and the King lost no time in turning back. But night had already fallen, the Basques had vanished into the wooded heights, taking the booty with them, and presently the dawn broke over the narrow defile strewn with

the bodies of the Franks, ransacked and shattered wagons
telling their own story. The bodies given as honourable a burial
as the environment allowed, Charlemagne's men turned their
faces towards Frankland.

* * *

Einhard[16] says that Charlemagne's war against the Northmen was his last military enterprise. It will be rembered that
the Saxon chieftain, Widukind, had Gotfried of Denmark, '*rex
terribilis*', for his friend and ally. Charlemagne knew quite
enough about the Danish onslaught on Scotland, Ireland and
Northumbria. Travellers would have told him about the
imperial bodyguard at Constantinople, the so called Variangy
who left the south of Sweden to sail down the Neva and other
rivers, finally reaching the Dnieper, the Black Sea and the
Bosphorus to enter the Emperor's service. There were many of
them; they were all picked men and unacquainted with fear.
Charlemagne also knew that the terrible Gotfried, 'puffed up
with false hopes' ('*vana spe inflatus*'), had boasted of invading
Frankland and putting Aachen to the sack.

In spite of the subjugation of the Saxons, the murder of
Gotfried, and the accession of a ruler willing to keep peace, the
Northmen remained a menace. They were all pagan as yet,
but a crusade against them was out of the question. They were
supreme on the water, and a fleet built by Charlemagne would
have been no match against their prowess.

They pillaged the Frisian coast in 810. Charlemagne's army
gave a good account of its strength and repulsed their efforts to
advance far inland, but the statesman in the King knew well
that the peril remained. True that he had not travelled much
beyond the Imperial boundaries, but he gave a ready welcome
to many travellers visiting him at Aachen and elsewhere, and
his imagination, continually stirred by curiosity, enabled him
to understand much about the lands he had not seen and the
people he had not met. The threat from the North must have
been far clearer to him than to most of his contemporaries.
Unlike his Merovingian predecessors, he did much to guard
the coasts of Frankland and was deeply interested in the details
of maritime warfare, but his Franks, who had few if any equals

in fighting on land, were not seafarers. Charlemagne, with old age gathering round about him, must have known that the Frankish rivers could prove an open sesame to the Norse ships.

Notker Balbulus was indeed an author of a great many fables, but at least one of his stories[17] need not be rejected out of hand. He tells us how once at dinner at one of his palaces along the Mediterranean coast, Charlemagne looked out of the window and wept at the sight of the Northmen's ships in the distance. 'He left off eating . . . [and] stood by the window . . . nobody dared speak to him.' Then Charlemagne turned to his household and said that he had no personal dread of the pirates, but 'I grieve to think of the evil thay may do to those who will follow me'.

Those words were to prove grimly prophetic.

*   *   *

In all the wars of his long reign Charlemagne never lost sight of a vision of a united Christian Europe. The colour of that vision was borrowed from St Augustine, whose 'City of God' was Charlemagne's favourite book. Unity rather than uniformity was his goal, but he remained a Frank to the end, and all the Christian observances, however faithfully practised, could never oust the leaven of ancient Frankish customs. In the end it was precisely his reverence for those customs which put a seal on the Utopian picture of a united Europe. One son only was living at the time of Charlemagne's death, but Louis the Pious would inherit more than an empire: respect for old customs was part of the legacy bequeathed to him by Charlemagne, and one such custom demanded a division of all the teatator's possessions among his sons, of which Louis the Pious had more than one.

V

THE ARCHITECTURE
OF A VAST HOUSEHOLD

Largely on the witness of Gregory of Tours and his successor, Fredegar, it used to be legitimate to picture the Merovingian Frankland as a vast, shadowy wilderness, its length and breadth torn and scarred by murder, rapine and arson, a land ungoverned rather than misgoverned, the small volume of its trade in alien hands, its foreign policy ignored by other countries, its common folk dragging out an existence scarcely above the animal level, its Church corrupt to the marrow, and its lay officials' integrity sorrily shrivelled.

Some of this is true, but the whole picture is most clumsily exaggerated. Research among sources, not known to contemporary chroniclers, and archeological discoveries have helped to rub out some of the least pleasing colours on the Merovingian canvas. Savagery abounded indeed, but not every Frank was a wild beast clothed in human likeness.

In the first place, not all the Merovingian sovereigns were *rois fainéants*. Secondly, when the latter came in, Mayors of the Palace in Burgundy, Neustria and Austrasia were already holding the reins, and when a great Arnulfing became King of the Franks, he did not have to build on quicksands of administrative chaos. A pattern, however blurred, imperfect and even disturbed, lay ready to his hand. The many decades of internecine wars had not destroyed everything, though admittedly vast reaches of the country still carried scars of many bloody battles. Yet man's brutality and stupidity could never cause an irremediable breach in the law of nature, and the orderly processional of the four seasons was never subject to the chaos of social life. Corn could still be sown and harvested, fruit

trees and wild berry bushes did not deny their yield, there were
fish in the rivers, and the great Frankish forests teemed with
game. Many of the old Roman roads had indeed gone far
beyond repair, but the waters of Frankland afforded an easy
enough means of transport, and there was no lack of timber
for barges and rafts, the Franks not having forgotten the art of
building river craft.

Justice of a kind was still administered in courts in spite of
the extravagant use of palm oil. People of substance could be
certain that their testamentary dispositions would be honoured
in full detail. Fairs and markets were still held, all of them
subject to regulations some among which went back to the
days when Rome was mistress of the world.

Naturally, there was much to uproot and to reform, and some
of the work was carried out by Pippin of Heristal, Charles
Martel and Pippin the Short, but it fell to the lot of Charlemagne to extend, if not to perfect, the stage of accomplishment
reached by the first Carolingians. Any success in that field should
be attributed to the originality of Charlemagne's approach to
the entire problem of governing: the key to it all lay in the use
man made of land.

He did not discard the earlier administrative pattern because
he knew how closely and truly it answered the basic needs of
the country, but he exerted all his energies and his imagination
to clarify the outline where it had grown blurred, and to fill in
such lacunae as had been caused by maladministration.
Whatever his failure, Charlemagne certainly succeeded in
narrowing the gulf between the administrative theory and
practice.

Apart from the frontier districts, perpetually in need of a
close supervision from the centre, Frankland came to be
divided into a number of '*pagus*', or '*Gau*', each being ruled by
a count[1] who was invested with the triple authority of judge,
chief constable and military commander. Each '*Gau*' was sub-
divided into several 'hundreds', and it was the duty of the count
to visit all the hundreds three times a year and to administer
the King's justice at a court known as '*placita*'.

It seems as though any count, his authority considered, held
the office of a monarch in little in his '*Gau*'. In reality, he

wielded no absolute power; even the rank and file were not denied the right of appealing to the crown, and that right was exercised often enough. The Diocesans and immunist landowners, who were mostly abbots and priors, were not subject to the count's authority, but that apparent freedom did little more than add to their burden: the King held them responsible for the maintenance of law and decent living on their demesnes.

A count's authority would be automatically dwarfed every time the grant of immunity was bestowed on a religious house in his *Gau*. Such cases inevitably led to administrative tangles, the unravelling of which sometimes came to the centre. Often enough, abbots and priors would question the validity of orders made by the count just before the bestowal of immunity.

Roughly, administrative authority suggested a triangle: counts and their officials, bishops and the great body of secular clergy and, finally, the members of religious communities fanatically jealous of their prerogative and independence. The involutions of that triangle, once carried into practice, were numberless, and all too often many of them were concerned with trivialities. A count, reaching a 'hundred' to hold his court, might find the calendar crowded with cases which did not properly belong to his jurisdiction. A parish priest was accused of fishing in a river belonging to a lay landowner. The plaintiff, aware that a layman's judgment would find for him, refused to have the case referred to an episcopal court where both compassion and prejudice would be favourable to the defendant.

It was in order to lessen the confusion and waste of time that Charlemagne early on decided that the King's messengers (*missi dominici*), having no axes of their own to grind, would be useful in disentangling those provincial knots. Those officers were chosen by him personally – not so much for their knowledge of the law as for their integrity. They belonged to the King's court and had no narrowly personal interests in provincial matters. Some among them were laymen, others prelates and clerics. Gradually, their office became a recognized state institution, and their duties were clearly codified. It was no longer a matter of a straying pig in someone's orchard, or a sack of nuts brought to a market, no tax having been paid on it.

The '*missi*' paid lengthy annual visits, their clerks busy with pen and ink-horn, and detailed reports were sent to the sovereign. The *missi* were his representatives in a far more intimate sense than a count could ever be, and the theocratic element, so prominent at the centre, began making itself felt in the provinces. The *missi* were able to interpret the King's mind because they knew him personally. They could bring with them more than the directives written in the royal chancery.

By 802 the whole of Frankland had been surveyed by the '*missi*', and divided into so many '*missiatica*', or provinces. Each such '*missiaticum*' was entrusted to two or three '*missi*'. They visited their provinces once a year and they had ample authority to inspect, to pass judgment, and even to reform. Their detailed reports were discussed at the annual general assembly usually held in early spring.

The scope of their work can be learned from the numberless capitularies[1] always issued in Charlemagne's name and some-times drafted by himself. Those instructions were sometimes rich in meticulous detail, sometimes drawn up hastily to clarify and resolve some emergency. The dry-as-dust clerkly formalism is wholly absent in all such documents issued during Charle-magne's reign. They remain, in the words of the late Henri Pirenne, '*le plus beau monument que nous ait conservé l'époque carolin-gienne*'. Their enormous content is inevitably heterogeneous, but all of them are informed by a sense of cohesion and unity.

Capitularies continued to be issued during the reign of Charlemagne's successor, Louis the Pious, but by then the wording became rigidly official. A clerk's mind lacked the elasticity and the imagination evident in earlier documents.

Charlemagne's ideas swept over wide horizons. The dead hand of rigid bureaucracy never fell on his administrative measures, every one of them carrying some reflection of his vision of a perfect state under God's rule. Yet it would be idle to deny that the noblest and purest conception is apt to get soiled among the many pitfalls of the interpretative process. The *missi* were all men of high integrity, but they did not spend all their time in the provinces, and the lesser officials' venality could not always be checked. The very fluidity of the link between the centre and the provincial cells was sometimes a blessing, more often a curse. Access to the sovereign was a right within the reach of every free-born Frank, whatever his social background. We know from Einhard[2] that even during his afternoon rest Charlemagne did not deny himself to petitioners. '. . . he would hear the case and give his judgment on the spot.'

Yet Frankland was vast, and the means of personal communication between the sovereign and an aggrieved subject was a matter wholly under the hammer of chance. How could a commoner reach his lord when the whereabouts of that lord was not always known in the country? As will be seen later, it was not till his latter years that Charlemagne settled himself permanently at his beloved Aachen. Until then he travelled continually even during the winter months when military matters were more or less at a standstill. It was often difficult enough for foreign ambassadors to present their credentials, though such men, possessing much gold in their pouches, were able to command the surest and fastest means of transport available at the time. It was not so easy even for counts and their officials, and virtually impossible for private individuals, who might have put most of their substance to the hazards of travelling from, say, Frankfurt to Salzburg only to find that the court had moved to Ingelsheim.

The capitularies abound in rather sternly worded directives addressed to clergy and to laity.[3] Blood feud was forbidden again and again. Contrary to the prevailing practice, monks were not to dispute a diocesan's authority. All clergy, whether secular or regular, were forbidden to keep hounds, falcons and hawks. The Capitulary of 802[4] throws sharp light on the need of reforming the Frankish Church. '. . . most of all it saddens and disturbs us . . . that it can be proved that an evil should have arisen . . . some monks being sodomites.'

Many such directives had to be repeated more than once. 'Again we say that fealty to the sovereign is due from all men in the Kingdom.'

Frankland at the time was not particularly rich in inns and hospices. Travellers had to depend on what shelter was afforded by religious houses and manors. 'None is to deny hospitality to the rich or to the poor or to pilgrims, that is to say, none shall refuse shelter, fire and water.'[5] Food is not mentioned. Presumably all travellers carried their own provender but the amenities, defined by law, were to be offered without payment.

Beginning with the Frankfurt Assembly in 794, Charlemagne carried on his ideas of fixed prices for grain, wine, all cereals, salt and cattle. The wording of the relevant article in the 794 Capitulary[6] suggests that profiteering flourished on a perilous scale so that fixed prices allowed of no deviation and the least departure from the law involved grim penalties – particularly during 'the times of scarcity'.

Some few years earlier, in the *Admonitio Generalis*[7] Charlemagne all but out-Puritaned the Puritans. Sundays in Frankland were to be wholly dedicated to God. All Sabbath activity fell under the ban, gardening and walking for pleasure included. Only three transport purposes were permitted – the army, food and funerals. Women were not to touch their distaffs, men were not to clean their agricultural implements. No singing was allowed except of canticles which, as one would imagine, could not have been known to the commonalty who had no Latin. Fires might be lit for the purposes of cooking, but no comforts were to be encouraged. Horses could be taken to the river to be watered, but no riding was allowed. The rules applied to the manor as well as to a villein's hut, but it is more than doubtful that any of them were kept. Certainly that pathetically rigid clause in the *Admonitio* was not often, if ever, observed in Charlemagne's household with singing and music accompanying the dinner.

*   *   *

Speculation and hoarding were by no means the only vices Charlemagne fought to uproot. There was the evil of usury, viler in his eyes than other social crimes in that it dug a pit under the poor man's feet.

He considered lending and borrowing as perfectly healthy processes of social life. If a man had, say, some few thousand turnips put away for the winter use, it was in keeping with the law of Christian charity for him to lend a thousand or so to a less fortunate neighbour, the loan to be repaid after the next harvest. If a poor man's daughter was getting married, it seemed perfectly legitimate for her mother to borrow a piece of cloth or some household utensil from a neighbour so that the girl would not have to go undowried to the altar. If a man, needing to increase his holding, borrowed so many pieces of silver from the neighbouring abbey wherewith to purchase the land he needed, where was the harm? But when one thousand borrowed turnips was known to be doubled in repayment, when a bride's mother had to sell a pig or even a cow to pay for a loan not worth one tenth of the sum borrowed, when an abbey demanded twenty pieces of silver to redeem the ten it had lent, then, as Charlemagne saw it, Christian charity was ground to the dust. 'Sir,' said a prior to him, 'we have to take a risk in lending our substance. We must safeguard ourselves.' 'You are worse than the Jews,' Charlemagne is supposed to have retorted.

Usury had been spread widely enough in the Merovingian days – both among clergy and laity. Charlemagne was the first Frankish sovereign to put laity under the ban. In 789, at a council held at Aachen, the very first mention was made of laymen who amassed great fortunes out of usury. Charlemagne's indignation leapt high. He quoted the Holy Writ, the conciliar enactments, the writings of Leo the Great and others. The assembly listened in respectful silence, many of those present aware that their own escutcheons were by no means clean. Nobody dared start an argument, and the King declared all usury to be illegal and its practice subject to grim penalties.

The penalties were duly legalized, but usury was not uprooted. It merely went underground, practised mostly by Jews and by Greek merchants, but the venality of some religious houses and of many minor Frankish officials, who fancied themselves unable to subsist on their salaries, could not but help its continuance in the social life of Frankland.

*   *   *

It has already been said that the fiscal problems in the Merovingian era were something of a Gordian knot,[8] that condition being mainly due to many private mints, some sanctioned by the King and others working independently of any such sanction.

Pippin the Short made the first efforts at a radical monetary reform in 755, hoping that some such measures would restore health to the Frankish trade. But Pippin had not gone very far towards achieving his aim of monometallism. It was left to his son to carry it through – in spite of all the difficulties and prejudices along the way.

Already in 780 a pound of silver was formally declared to be worth twenty sous, each sou equalling twelve deniers. All the coins were to be silver, and little by little gold ceased to be the normal tender. Next, the Royal Mint, attached to the King's household, was ordered to strike coins in great numbers. There was no need to import the raw metal. Frankland had its own silver mines in Poitou, the Harz region, Bohemia and elsewhere. From many contemporary records it is clear that by the end of the eighth century gold was virtually out of circulation. We are, however, unable to translate the actual weight of a Carolingian silver pound into modern terms.

That fiscal measure first and foremost was designed to help the rank and file in their necessarily small financial transactions. One denier, the twelfth part of a sou, fully answered what humble household purchases might be made at a market stall or a fair. None the less, its introduction gave birth to a tumult up and down the country.

In capitulary after capitulary, Charlemagne declared minting to be a royal monopoly. But protests continued almost to the end of the reign. The Capitulary of 808 decreed unequivocally that 'nowhere' ('*in nullo loco*') were coins to be struck except at the Royal Mint. That law was binding everywhere, and the count of every province was to see to its strict observance.[9]

The law did not concern the commonalty to whom it remained a matter of indifference where the coins were struck in which the artisans and others received their meagre wage. The reform was resisted at higher social levels. In the first place, there were many private minters who enjoyed high prestige and were well trained in the art of feathering their nest with the least publicity and the greatest profit. Next, there were the bishops' palaces, the abbeys and even important laity, all of whom had a private mint of their own, a privilege sometimes granted and again wrested in the Merovingian

times. None of them felt great concern about the introduction
of monometallism. All were greedily anxious to preserve their
privilege. The Carolingian reform cut the ground from under
their feet. Private minters found themselves robbed of their
livelihood, and the others resented the humiliation born of a
summarily withdrawn privilege.

That, however, by no means summed up Charlemagne's
troubles. The same people whom he had meant to help took
to sullen murmuring.

The King should have remembered that the mediaeval mind
was insolubly wedded to custom. A silver denier, whatever its
value and provenance, symbolized an abrupt departure from
custom. Now in one place, now in another, the little coin would
be rejected, and the old specie went on circulating among the
high and the low. A count, holding his *placita*, imposed fines
and even harsher penalties for the proved cases of disregard for
the law, but a count's own conscience was not clear, and a
judgment by him delivered was no more and no less than a
grotesque perversion of justice.

At the Frankfurt Assembly of 794, Charlemagne himself
drafted the fifth article which threatened with deposition not
only counts and other lay officials but such among bishops and
abbots who were either guilty of the same offence, or neglected
to deal with proved incidents. The theocratic temper of the
King here came well into the foreground. If the hierarchy
disobeyed him, the hierarchy would have to pay the same
penalty as any lay transgressor. There were murmurs and
uneasily whispered hints that Rome stood for a final court of
appeal. Charlemagne ignored all such insinuations.

It proved a long drawn struggle, and he won at the end. He
saw most clearly the national necessity of possessing a uniform
and *healthily* guaranteed monetary standard. Privately struck
coinage carried no such guarantee. Moreover, it could not be
used as tender in foreign transactions. Charlemagne's imagination, aided and deepened by the expert advice of his councillors,
created a specie which fully answered the needs of the people.[10]
Lot was right when he said that the chief merit of Charlemagne
was to make money do what it was meant to do, within the
framework of the economy he had planned. That economy, as

will shortly be seen, was essentially agricultural, '*où les trans-actions étaient médiocres.*' The humble denier was just the right coin to buy a little meat, bread, salt, or wine. The King's ideas about building the city of God in this world were certainly Utopian. None the less, his fiscal reforms were stamped with realism. He clearly saw the necessity of 'getting value for money', and hence lost no time in passing a law which safeguarded 'the trueness and uniformity of weights and measures' throughout the whole of Frankland. It was the comparatively poor folk who spent their meagre substance at market stalls, and large reaches of Charlemagne's economic policy were shaped to protect those people from the rapacity and dishonesty of the better-moneyed folk.

*   *   *

In broad terms, the Carolingian economy was based on military needs and agriculture, and often enough the former interwove itself into the latter. The iron mines in Styria and Carinthia produced ample raw material for war purposes. The farms in those two regions were expected to supply food for the miners. In Burgundy, great numbers of armourers developed a special technique in making pattern-welded hauberks. There, again, they were to be sustained by the agricultural yield of the neighbourhood. All those labourers worked long hours, and their appetites asked for much more than a hunk of cheese and a turnip for their dinners.

The war economy led to a most minute legislation. No armour or weapons might be exported. Even dirks and knives were included in the list. A traveller crossing to Britain might or might not be allowed to take a knife with him to cut up his victuals, and yet Frankland and Britain were – with one brief exception – on friendly terms. Charlemagne's '*missi*' were given special instructions to prevent any such commerce with enemy countries.

All in all, it could not have been easy to be a Frankish exporter at the time. Many capitularies teem with terse directives to Frankish merchants going abroad on business, and the list of prohibited exports included many more items than weapons. The bans were fluid, and stood subject to the circum-stances of the moment. For instance, during spells of drought or famine, all export of grain and edible roots was forbidden even to Britain and Ireland.

The earliest Frankish exports were timber, undressed hides, salt and slaves. Timber would be floated down the rivers, hides and salt taken by road. Long before the days of the Arnulfings, salt used to be made by incinerating the halophytic peat and leaching the ashes. There were, moreover, rich salt deposits in the Bavarian Alps and in Saxony, particularly along the banks of the Saale. Some abbeys, Prümes for one, worked smaller salt mines on their own lands. The home sales and the export of salt were heavily taxed, and taxation was not easy to avoid. From the mouth of the Elbe down to the Danube, and along south and west coasts, special customs houses were built – strong enough to withstand both the vagaries of climate and the armed assaults of brigands, some of whom would be hired by exporters to create a tumult and engage the official attention away from the taxable merchandise.

Those customs houses were all staffed by men known to the King. Their proved integrity placed them far above the least suspicion of connivance or perjury, and the customs houses were in reality so many keeps, well supplied with weapons. Tax evasion involved harsh penalties, though it cannot be said that the Carolingian legislation succeeded in putting an end to smuggling. The Frankish coasts and inland frontiers were too far flung for official supervision to guard them all, and Frankish hauberks found their way to the Iberian Peninsula, and undressed hides were carried across the Alps, not a penny of tax paid on them.

As has been mentioned before, Frankish home trade got sadly crippled during the eighth century, but it would be wrong to assume that it perished altogether, and the first Carolingians were able to build on the earlier foundations. By far the most important item of export was slavery.

Charlemagne's capitularies go a long way to prove the unease of his conscience about it.[11] He knew the writings of Gregory the Great and held him in deep respect. According to that Pope, any slave, taking sanctuary, was irreclaimable by secular authority. Gregory would not object to slaves entering monasteries once it was proved that they had a true vocation

I

to religious life, but Gregory the Great was not the only pontiff whose writings Charlemagne had studied. There was also Leo the Great who expressly forbade ordination of slaves 'whom their masters refused to set free'.[12] That seemed clear enough, but the King's mind was confused, when he learned that Gregory the Great held that Christ's redemption of mankind meant freedom for all men, and pleaded for a general manu-mission,[13] and yet archbishops and bishops thought nothing of having slaves in their possession and no pontifical thunderbolts were loosed against them. The Salic Law was drawn up by Christian lawyers, and yet it took slavery in the light of a social norm, and even decreed that any free-born men and women, who contracted marriage with slaves, forfeited their own liberty.

His mind confused and his conscience troubled, Charlemagne tried to ease the lot of slaves in Frankland. As early as 779, to quote M.Latouche,[14] a royal decree was issued to the effect that *'les ventes d'esclaves se fissent en présence du comte ou du l'évêque du lieu et, à leur défaut, du celle de leurs représentants autorisés.'* All such sales were girdled by many exacting formalities. According to a capitulary, they were forbidden to be held between sunset and sunrise.

But Charlemagne could not afford to abolish slavery, and it is doubtful if he ever considered such abolition. Prisoners of war were, as a rule, Crown slaves, and the King needed a large labour force to carry out much of the work on the land. They came from among hostile Slavic tribes in the North, from Saxon lands, and from Pannonia. They were clothed, fed and housed but received no wages. They repaired old roads and made new ones, worked in the forests and fields, and the more intelligent among them were trained in some craft or other. In large terms, for all the grim hardihoods of their condition Crown slaves in Frankland had an easier time than those in private ownership who were often exported together with timber and hides.

*   *   *

The main source of revenue was the yield of the land. Once the *Volkerwanderungs* were ended, Europe entered a new econ-omic era – but this did not happen with the suddenness of a

summer storm: it evolved slowly, sometimes faultily and pain-
fully. 'The process was an affair of centuries; it was always
interrupted by the ravages of war and had always to be associated with making them good'.[15] Yet the above applies far
more to the Merovingian than to the early Carolingian epoch
when landownership was, however slowly, growing into the
basis of personal political power, and when land became
heritable not by whim or chance but by legislation. The great
House of Arnulf would never have attained the heights had it
not been for their vast demesnes.

In law and in theory every square foot of the land belonged
to the King. On occasions, that ownership would be translated
into terms of rough practice.[16] Thus in 807, one Godbert, who
held lands near Angers and elsewhere, forfeited them all as
punishment for incest, ('*pro incestuosa*') and other 'detestable and
unlawful acts', and Charlemagne ordered that all those estates
were to be made over to the Abbot and community of Prümes.

First, there were the sovereign's own possessions, and it
should be remembered that the vast Carolingian patrimony
was so scattered as to make centralized administration a matter
of great difficulties. The King's estates lay thickest in the
Ardennes region and in the country between the Meuse, the
Moselle and the Rhine. All those widely separated demesnes,
known as '*fisci*,' were in the care of officials most of whom tended
towards independence, a drift all but impossible to avoid when
we consider the difficulties of contemporary transport and the
distances lying between many '*fisci*' and the centre. There was
an official styled '*provisor villarum*', but the references to his
work and the scope of his authority are rather obscure. It is
difficult to gauge the power he exercised between a particular
domain and the administrative centre.

Every royal estate had a superintendent, known as '*index
major*', and it is pretty clear that he had a free hand in the
management. His subordinates were called '*mayors*' ('*Meier*' in
German). The administrative architecture and the activities of
one such '*villa*' are known to us through the wealth of detail
offered by the '*Capitulare de Villis*'. It is not dated, but the word
'*regina*' occurs four times in the text. Therefore, the Capitulary
must have been drawn up between 770, the year of Charle-

magne's marriage to the Lombard princess[17] and the early summer of 800 when Queen Liutgard, Charlemagne's fourth and last wife, died at Tours. An anonymous author of a life of Louis the Pious chose to give the year 794 as the date, but the statement is conjectural.

Imaginatively speaking, the *Capitulare de Villis* might be considered as a textual version of the Bayeux tapestry. Its seventy chapters paint the structure and the heartbeats of a royal manor in most compelling colours, and they cover a vast field of most varied and minute details. Here and there we come on patently democratic breaths: it is obvious that Charlemagne wished the humblest among his labourers to better his condition. The manor's superintendent had to produce fully itemized annual accounts. So much of the yield was allocated for the use of the court and the army, but the manor folk enjoyed the right of selling the surplus at the nearest market.

The document deals with farm work and produce – cattle yards, kitchen gardens, orchards, workshops. Nor was horticulture forgotten. The very last chapter opens with the words, '*volumus quod in horto omnes herbas habeant*', and the manor gardens must indeed have been rich in herbs and flowers even if only some of the 95 plants, mentioned in the text, found a place there.

We learn how the men worked and spent their leisure, what tools they used, what they ate and wore. The household of a '*villa*', both officials and workmen, formed a unit known as '*familia*'. Charlemagne insisted that his lands were meant to serve his purposes and all those who lived and worked there were to be treated fairly so long as their work was done honestly. The '*villa*' was truly a bee-hive of well-ordered activity – sowing of cereals and vegetables, making various domestic articles, using wood, leather and iron in the workshops, selling the surplus of corn and fish, buying horses, cattle, poultry, undressed hides, and iron ore. But first and foremost, however skilful its workmen in producing harness and trenchers, in weaving cloth and turning a block of well-seasoned timber into tables and trestles, first and foremost, then, the *villa* was a gigantic farm, and the King's main interest lay precisely there.

Every Christmas the chief manager was expected to present a detailed report down to the last sack of spelt, and all the monies due to the exchequer were to be sent yearly on Palm Sunday, rather an odd choice of a day for such a transaction! Yet the *villa* was not a closed shop in the old Merovingian sense. As has been said before, some of the surplus was at the personal disposal of the *familia*, and they enjoyed the privilege of using it as they pleased. This made for a healthy development of markets in the provinces, and by the beginning of the ninth century, quite a number of peasants' sons went into towns there to carry on with what particular craft they had been taught at the *villa*. Nowhere in the Capitulary do we find a clause forbidding a workman to leave the manor.

To Charlemagne, the land and its yield summed up God's care for the material needs of man. The smallest root of rosemary or hearts' ease stood to him for a token of the Maker's bounty. As M. Latouche finely put it:[18] '. . . . *le dirigisme de Charlemagne a exercé sur la vie rurale son influence organisatrice. Charlemagne a compris cette vérité élémentaire que dans une économie encore fruste la terre est la grande nourricière des hommes*'.

Yet the mass of reiterated commands and directives, and wrathful rebukes for inexcusably delayed reports, show the vastness of the gulf between theory and practice. An ideal had been set up, but reality seldom runs in full accord with any ideal, and the agricultural machinery did not work as smoothly as its royal architect had planned. According to the late Marc Bloc,[19] '*certes, le royaume franc était vaste, et les soucis de son chef par la même multiples et souvent poignants, mais l'administration restait rudimentaire: l'exploitation des domaines tenait dans les finances une grande place: la fortune privée du souverain était une de ses forces*'.

Agricultural activities were still based on processes and implements inherited from the past. So much iron ore was needed for military purposes that little of it could be spared for a plough or a harrow. Still, the Carolingian era brought in a few innovations – not always easy to introduce because of the deeply rooted Frankish adherence to ancient usages. In broad terms, the mediaeval mind considered that whatever was customary had to be right *per se*, and conversely. So oxen were still harnessed to carts and ploughs, and wheels were of solid wood, with no spokes. Among the innovations may be mentioned the wheeled plough, the flail, and the three years' rotation of crops, the latter measure accepted more reluctantly than any other.

The administration limped badly. But the yield did not – except whan a bad harvest smote the land. It is clear that unimportant smallholders had an advantage over great estates. Once their crops failed, the crown came to their aid, remitting taxes and supplying free seeds.

Barley, hardiest of all grains, held the pride of place. It was used for porridge, bread, beer, and also as fodder for horses. Rye and oats were sown extensively, but wheat cost so dear that sometimes it would be sown in walled-in gardens. The poorer population sustained themselves on maslin, a rough mixture of rye and barley, sometimes ground into flour, sometimes used as porridge.

Turnips, beans, peas and lentils were often boiled together to make some kind of pottage. Little meat found its way into the labourer's hut except by way of poaching. Fish was plentiful. Butter remained a luxury only the well-to-do could afford. Yet the poorest villein kept a pig or two, and pork lard was a mainstay. So were hens and geese.

The Church concerned herself with the national diet. Her calendar was crowded with fasts, vigils and days of abstinence when no meat might be eaten. Landowners and important abbeys could afford to have fish ponds mostly stocked with carp. The poorer folk went for their fish in legally free waters, but they could not afford to add any seasoning except salt, and that not very often. Goats' milk was used for rough cheese.

All in all, the mediaeval diet was monotonous. Bee-keeping yielded honey, but salt was beyond the reach of many who must eat their porridge and pottage unseasoned. The better-off folk and the rich could afford the imported spices – cinnamon, sage, coriander and others – all used rather indiscriminately with fish, meat, poultry and puddings.

The entire volume of produce, whether consumed at home or sold at markets, stood subject to most minute legislation.

The vine having been brought to Gaul by the Romans, wine had been made at Beaune in Burgundy long before the Mero-

vingian days. Under Charlemagne, who discouraged such
imports, foreign wines were heavily taxed. He abhorred
drunkenness, and his abstemiousness in this particular should
have been an example, but he could not prevent unpleasant
excesses even in his own banqueting hall. None the less, he was
deeply interested in viticulture. At his order, extensive vineyards
were planted in the neighbourhood of Worms and Speyer, in
Schwabia, Franconia and Thuringia. In the *Capitulare de Villis*
minute directions were given such as, for instance, that grapes
were not to be crushed with bare feet 'as had been the custom
in the past'.[20]

Carolingian wines, however, could not have been very
pleasant to the palate. Otherwise, honey would hardly have
been added to sweeten them, or cinnamon and coriander
added to smooth their roughness. Spices were a luxury enjoyed
by a minority, but even the roughest wines remained beyond
the reach of the commonalty. After a grey, wet summer when
grapes could not ripen, they would be turned into verjuice
used in cooking. Spirits being then unknown, a great quantity
of beer was drunk by all social strata. The poorer among the
peasants made beer out of bog myrtle, wild rosemary and
yarrow. Hops began to be cultivated about 768, but it was from
the orchards of Frankland that the rich and the poor alike
gathered enough to make cider, perry and all mannner of
fermented fruit drinks. From forests came wild berries in such
quantities that they fetched almost nothing at a market, but
village women sent their children to gather them. Dried over a
smoking fire, those berries made a refreshing addition to the
monotonous winter fare.

Olives did not grow north of the Alps, and the imported oil
was even more costly than spices: Church and Court alone
could afford it. Otherwise, oil, extracted from rape and poppy
seeds, was used both in cooking and for medicines.

All in all, it was a small-meshed agricultural economy –
wholly dependent on the whims of the weather and the sweat
of man, yet on those simplicities rested Charlemagne's military
efforts. Masses of victuals, particularly flour and salted beef,
were needed for every campaign.

However Utopian his conception of an ideal Christian state,

Charlemagne proved himself a staunch realist in all that concerned the land. Crops were precious, and laws were enforced to protect them from the ravages of wild beasts. All the fields were either deeply ditched or fenced on all sides. Stockades, known as *sepes*, would be made of high thick posts linked by three broad bars. Some fences were constructed of whole trees, put closely together and joined by three or four horizontal bars. Poultry yards were walled whenever possible, and so were cattle enclosures. Grazing was not always safe even by daylight, particularly when a field happened to be in the neighbourhood of a forest: brigandage was rampant, and the theft of a cow or a goat a most frequent occurrence. When caught, the offenders were dealt with most savagely since the law had no mercy on them, but the grimmest penalties did not go very far to uproot the evil.

Out of the four seasons of the year, spring, summer and autumn hummed with outdoor activity, but the winter season might well be compared with the monastic '*clausura*' at its strictest. The lord stayed at his manor. The villein kept to his village. The townspeople ventured abroad only during the hours of daylight. It was not only the climatic rigours which slowed down the daily rhythm, but the increased hazards of travelling, particularly the wild beasts, bear, wolf, wild boar, auroch and pole-cat roaming all over the country, driven by a savage hunger as they were.

Late autumn would be spent in provisioning manor, small farm steading, and hut. At a manor, beeves and pigs were slaughtered and salted, the pork being turned into sausages and ham. The actual killing apart, women had more than their share in all these labours. Tubs of fruit, well soaked in verjuice, would be buried in the courtyard. All manner of poultry would be brought inside the stockade, and great stacks of tree trunks were there for the fuel. Fish was steeped in brine, and the yield of the orchard either dried for future use as garnish for meat and cheese, or else turned into cider and perry. These things done, the women took to spinning, weaving, and embroidering. They had to use the utmost care with their bone needles since, in some cases, it was impossible to replenish the supply within the stockade. The men's occupation consisted in repairing the war gear and harness, exercising the horses, and hunting, though they took care not to ride too far from home. A kill was considered a great triumph because it meant fresh meat at table.

No such extensive preparations could be made on lower social levels. The smallholders did well enough, but the village folk had a sad time of it. They had to be contented with enough meal for porridge to last till the spring, root vegetables, and a small barrel of herrings. The more venturesome hid the fruits of their poaching activities well under the earthen floor of the hut. But there were many cases of bitter hunger in the country.

Life crept rather than ran. The rich had a log fire and sometimes could afford oil for a lamp, but the latter had to be used with amost rigid economy. The poor had to depend on casual supplies of kindling and a rushlight now and again. But, the daily meal eaten, they spent most of their time in sleep.

The well-to-do might have a priest wintering at the manor, and so were able to hear Mass. But many among the poor died unshriven and comfortless, their priest not venturing to face the hazards outside his own hut. It was a curiously blanketed existence, a season when the powers of darkness held their sway over the land, when the dimly remembered examples of demonic wickedness leapt into the mind and peopled every shadowy corner with unspeakably monstrous images.

Christmas and other Church festivals, however, succeeded in breaking through the pagan crust. Songs would be heard, and neither honey nor spices grudged for the making of gingerbread in the shape of a star.

*   *   *

The enormous forests of Frankland played an important part in the land economy. The Saxon wars gave great impetus to land clearing. Timber remained a major export but much of it was needed for the building of keeps and forts along the banks of the Elbe, the Saale, the Rhine and the Main to protect the frontiers. Deforestation was a necessity and, the forest soil being rich, it brought many advantages. Saxon hostages were there in great numbers to provide free labour and Saxon hands were good at wielding an axe, but all the royal decrees on forestry met with sullen resistance and worse. Deforestation limped often and that for other causes than the laziness, incompetence and sometimes dishonesty of officials. Any tree, oaks in particular, wore an aura of hallowed mystery to the Frankish mind. It was the habitation of a god whose pleasure was hard to win and whose anger broke out all too frequently. More than three centuries of Christian preaching and practice had not been able to destroy the ancient beliefs, and the coming of Saxon prisoners could not but lend strength and colour to that deep-buried consciousness. As to the Saxons themselves, the compulsory baptism had not even brushed against their souls' true tissue. Thus many schemes came to shipwreck, many daily stints either wholly neglected or carried out most casually. Charlemagne dealt ruthlessly with all defaulters and trans-gressors, but the most cruel penalties did not bring the scheme to as swift a rhythm as he had hoped for.

Yet that was one detail out of many. Looked upon as a whole, the Carolingian effort was superb in the sweep of its horizons. By what M. Latouche called 'sa politique réaliste',[21] Charlemagne established foreign trade not only with Britain and Byzantium but with the Islamic world. Most of those relations were based on the personal touch: Charlemagne was ready to give audiences not only to accredited ambassadors but to merchants also. The volume of imports increased year by year, but the exchequer, sustained by taxation, continually swelling exports and, after the Avar war, the fabulous booty found in Pannonia, could carry the increase easily. Moreover, only the imports for the sovereign's personal use were exempt from taxation. Large sums were levied on the remainder. Charlemagne, however simple his personal habits, loved luxury. His court at Aachen became the greatest star on the day's horizon, and the wealthier among his vassals certainly imitated his example. Rare stuffs from Baghdad, Damascus and Teheran came to Frankland. Frankish ladies wore veils which could never have been woven on Frankish looms. Trifles of ivory and jade, curiously wrought leather coffers, seeds and plants unknown in Europe, crossed the Frankish frontier.

Travel by sea became more and more costly because of the hazards of piracy. Goods carried in foreign bottoms had to be so highly insured as to threaten the Frankish mercantile health, and Charlemagne encouraged travel by land. At his commands, well-protected inns were raised over the Alps and beyond. Excise dues were to be paid, but a customs officer offered more than shelter from the weather, water for the horses, and rough comfort for the travellers. There was a small armoury attached to every customs house, and men in the King's service were provided with weapons. They would guide a merchant and his companions through some particularly dangerous lap of the journey – to the great dismay of brigands.

The effort was indeed grandiose, but, towards the end of Charlemagne's reign, the very vastness of his possessions came to demand a corresponding increase in bureaucratic ranks. Great numbers of those officials had no other idea of grandeur than that of adding to their own substance, and they did not much care about the colour of the means they used. Charlemagne's ultimate aim of establishing his realm as mistress of Europe meant as much to them as a Greek quotation to an illiterate peasant. The less important fry among the officials had their own ambitions, but those went no further than another pig in the sty, another gown for the wife, well-spiced meat at his dinner, and something hidden away to sweeten the inevitable sourness of old age.

The chief shortcoming of Charlemagne, if it may be given so unpleasant a label, was his proneness to measure other men's energies by his own. He made ample allowances for their hunger for gold, their greed for promotion, their insatiable desire to prove themselves abler, more imaginative and daring than the next man. But Charlemagne had it not in him to understand the narrowness of horizons, the pedestrian aims, the hodden-grey colour of personal purposes, in which lesser men took such a delight.

VI

'DOMINUS ILLUMINATIO MEA'

More than two centuries separate Boëthius from Charlemagne but, for all the virtually unceasing wars in Europe and
the barbarian invasions, lamps of learning were not allowed to
die down altogether in Ireland, Gaul, Northumbria, Spain and
Italy. Man's hunger for knowledge remained a fountain not to
be dried up by the drought brought about by outward
circumstances.

Thus, the two centuries were by no means devoid of great
names – Cassiodorus in Italy, Aldhelm, Bede and Benedict
Biscop in Britain, Isidore of Seville, Julian of Toledo and
Ildefonse in Spain. The Merovingian Frankland bore Gregory
of Tours and Avitus of Vienna, counted as the last great
Latinist of his generation. She also gave hospitality to the
genius of Venantius Fortunatus and to Columbanus, to name
no other name from Ireland. Irish missionaries, whose faith
equalled their learning, went all over Frankland and, crossing
the Alps, shared the wealth of their minds with Italian scholars.

Learning lived on. Yet physical and mental pressures increased in impact and in number. Unrest in Ireland, the
troubles of the Heptarchy in Britain, the Lombard invasion of
Italy, the Arab sweep over Spain, and the gradual approach
of yet another menace from the far North, all these inevitably
darkened the European horizon. With the death of Fortunatus,
the spirit of poetry fled from Frankland. With the passing of
Avitus, classical Latin fell into a grave.

None the less, it would be misleading to talk of a Carolingian
Renaissance in art and letters. The eclipse had not been total.
Even in the so-called little arts the Merovingian era had left a
pleasant imprint. Charlemagne's great merit lies elsewhere.

In broad terms, there were three wide streams of learning under the Christian aegis – Irish, Northumbrian and Iberian. By the time Charlemagne started his efforts towards mental enlightenment, the great schools of Toledo and Seville were no more, Spain having been under the Moslem yoke since the beginning of the eighth century, and the threat of the Northmen was no longer remote from either Ireland or Northumbria. Scholars from those countries would be invited to Aachen or wherever the King of the Franks happened to be. Some came uninvited, unable to carry on their work at home, and all alike were made welcome by the man in whom an intellectual hunger burned with a fierceness hard to match in his day. Those men went to Frankland not only to teach but also to learn one from another. Others, like Theodulf from Spain and Alcuin of York, served Charlemagne in other capacities than those of schoolmasters.

That Palace School was truly international, a most fortunate fusion of four great mediaeval cultures – Irish, Spanish, English and Italian – and little by little the seemingly moribund Frankish genius began stirring from its slumbers. In that field, and probably in no other, did Charlemagne come closest to his grandiose idea of a united Europe, since learning, as he so rightly saw, should submit to no political or national barriers – 'ayant l'univers pour sa patrie' as the French bibliophile, Quérard, would say more than a thousand years later.[1] Here, then, is the true heartbeat of Charlemagne's great service to his generation and to those who came after. He 'resurrected' nothing, and the Palace School was by no means a mediaeval Athens, but he may well be considered as the first mediaeval man to recognize and to give something of a shape to the idea of the intellectual brotherhood of man.

It should be said at the outset that the scholars brought together by Charlemagne were in no position to take pleasure in creative work. They must first salvage what pearls there remained from a wealthier and easier past, and revive the all but forgotten rhythms. They taught, compiled, assimilated. They were not always fortunate when plunging into the waters of original work. With one or two exceptions, the verse of Theodulf can stand no comparison with the poetry of Venantius

Fortunatus. Einhard's deservedly famous biography of Charlemagne was based on Suetonius's 'Lives of the Caesars', and its style cannot be said to improve on the classical pattern. Alcuin's voluminous correspondence certainly justifies his title of a *lettré*, but the claim falls to the ground when we consider the heavy verbiage of his theological works. Only here and there among his verse do we come on a flash of true poetry.[2]

Still, there were moments of sheer splendour such as, for instance, Paul the Deacon's brief epitaph on an infant daughter of Charlemagne,[3] or the poignant lament, its authorship unknown, for Charlemagne himself.[4]

Many of such may seem to be so many rills rather than a wide river and yet their value is by no means belittled by the camparison, – just as the laborious compilations of earlier centuries should not be denied their place in the cultural march of Europe. Not merely an idle and patchy curiosity but a genuine deep hunger of the mediaeval mind was satisfied by the Etymologies of Isidore of Seville, or by the *Liber Scintillarum*, an anthology of Biblical and patristic quotations by Defensor, a monk of Ligugé Abbey near Poitiers. The late Helen Waddell most aptly called the Etymologies 'a mediaeval Encyclopedia Britannica'. Defensor's little book proved a best seller all through the Middle Ages, and answered the need of many unable to possess libraries of their own.[5]

Isidore of Seville's geographical and historical flights of fancy[6] are certainly far more excusable than those of Saxo Grammaticus who, writing more than five centuries after Isidore, had no scruples about weaving an abundance of mythical threads into his facts.[7]

*   *   *

The best introduction to however brief a survey of Charlemagne's work in this sphere is to be found in Einhard's classical biography of his patron.[8] Einhard himself belonged to the Palace School, but his intimacy with the King plumbed far deeper depths than anyone else's at Charlemagne's court. His little book is stamped with an authenticity found but rarely in works of that kind. He neither flattered nor censured. As will be seen below, there was much to censure in Charlemagne. Yet Einhard's reticence invites respect rather than annoyance, and his record is all the more valuable because nothing except what was known to him personally found its way into the book.

Einhard was born about 770 in the valley of the Main. His parents were people of substance as is proved by their gifts of land and of money to the neighbouring Abbey of Fulda. There Einhard went as a boy, not to become a monk but to be educated in the fullest sense of the word. Fulda's teachers were known all over the continent, and Einhard was indeed fortunate in having such men to develop his mind. His studies included the Bible, Patristics, and a few classics – Virgil, Livy, Tacitus, Caesar and Suetonius. But Fulda taught Einhard more than that. They trained him well in the so-called little arts, carving in ivory and wood, gilt tooling, silver-smithing, leatherwork and illuminating. They must also have taught him something of natural sciences and mathematics. In later years, Einhard would be known for his remarkable skill in solving knotty arithmetical problems, and he knew geometry too.

They thought much of Einhard at Fulda. The King is known to have visited the Abbey frequently, and it is rather pleasing to imagine him taking notice of the small youth from the valley of the Main. But there is no record of any such meeting. All we do know is that in 793 Abbot Baugulf, a great friend of Charlemagne's, sent Einhard to Aachen there 'to be of use to the King'. It is permissible to conjecture that Charlemagne had asked for the young man to join the growing fellowship of scholars and poets.

Einhard's beginnings at court were not rose-coloured. Long accustomed as he was to the unbroken tranquillity of the cloister, the tumult of the daily to-and-fro at court, the singing and the laughter, and the ribald jests wholly beyond his comprehension, all of it together confused and frightened Einhard. Again, it does not seem that his many gifts were used much during those first difficult months. He was chiefly employed in fetching and carrying for the important court officials, and frequently laughed at because of his uncommonly small stature. 'A tiny ant' – so Theodulf of Orleans called the newcomer from Fulda in a piece of sharply mordant verse. Yet there was Alcuin with his deep charity, and, presumably aware of Einhard's quality, he took 'the dwarf' under his protection. Theodulf's unkind lines were soon enough answered by the Head of the Palace School. 'The young man's smallness of body should not be despised . . . The bee is small enough and yet it carries a store of honey'. Alcuin went much further than composing those lines of great comfort to Einhard, whose 'honey' was soon brought by Flaccus (Alcuin's nickname at court) to the royal notice. A little later, in a letter to the King gone to fight the Saxons, Alcuin wrote 'Beseleel[9] is always at hand to help you and me.' Thus 'the dwarf' was established and loved.

In his preface to Einhard's biography of Charlemagne,[10] Walafrid Strabo, Abbot of Reichenau, rightly said that there was hardly another man at court to whom the King 'opened his mind so readily, widely and frequently as to Einhard' . . . and that the King was justified in his confidence so amply merited by Einhard (*'et re vera non inmerito'*).

Little by little 'the dwarf' became indispensable to Charlemagne. No official post was ever held by him except that of the surveyor of building work, but we often hear of him as 'being very dear to the King', often acting as his spokesman at the council table, and as frequently accompanying the King on his many expeditions up and down Frankland and even beyond.

In his own preface to the biography Einhard, always careful in his choice of words, says that his task would be to record the deeds (*'gestas'*) of *'Domini et nutritoris mei Karoli'*. Now, the use of the word *'nutritor'* carries much significance. It has a much more intimate ring than would be produced by the word 'patron'. 'Foster-father' would answer much better.[11] We do not know the exact date of the deaths of Einhard's parents, but the passage quoted above rather hints at the King's care for Einhard before his coming to Aachen in 793. Abbot Baugulf and Charlemagne were friends, and the King's visits to the Abbey were rather frequent. It may well be that 'the dwarf's' quality had been noticed by the King at an earlier date than 793.

Einhard was no theologian like Alcuin or Paulinus of Aquileia. He was no historian of Paul the Deacon's calibre, still less a poet like Theodulf and Angilbert. His literary legacy, however, for all its slimness, is very important on account of the *Vita*. As has been said, it is a narrative based on Suetonius's

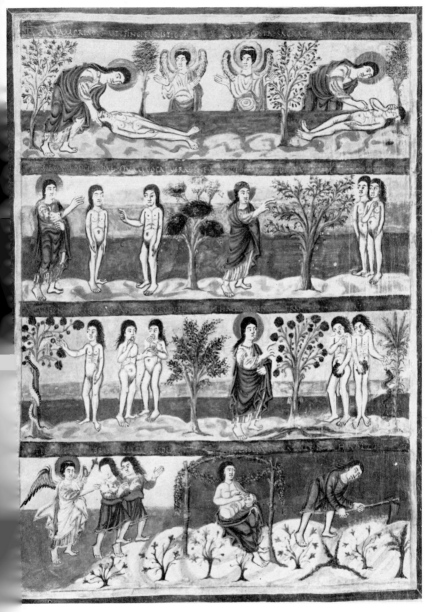

enesis scenes from the Moutier Grandival Bible – Carolingian work (possibly Orléans)
(*British Museum*)

Carolingian ivory book cover
(*Bodleian Library, Oxford*)

'Lives of the Caesars', but the analogy goes no further than the style. It is a warm, intimate narrative, compact and colourful, many of its sentences written from a grateful heart.

We know that Einhard joined the Aachen fellowship later than the others. He knew them all well, but his task was to write the life of Charlemagne and that with the utmost economy of words. So Einhard makes no mention of any other names at Aachen with the exception of Peter of Pisa,[12] an old man who taught grammar. 'For all other subjects (*'in ceteris disciplinis'*) there was Alcuin'.[13] It is a curious contradiction, and it all but quarrels with Einhard's repute as recorded by Alcuin, Walafrid Strabo and others. It is true that Alcuin was the Head of the Palace School until his retirement to St Martin's Abbey at Tours, but Alcuin, whilst at Aachen, stood at the head of a numerous company among whom Peter of Pisa was certainly not the most prominent member. But Einhard mentions no other names, and we cannot tell the reason behind the omission. It may well have been that the old Peter of Pisa followed Alcuin's example in showing kindness to the newcomer from Fulda, and such gestures would be remembered in gratitude. Yet that is no more than a conjecture.

We know from Tacitus that the Germans took delight in poems which told of brave deeds performed by their forefathers. Those epics, never written down, would be learned by heart and transmitted by word of mouth from one generation to another. The first Merovingians would have them either sung or recited, in their banqueting halls. At Charlemagne's court, singing, recitation, music, as well as theological and philosophical debates, accompanied both dinner and supper, filled the none too frequent spells of leisure, and went on even in camp or during a return ride from a hunt.

Too modest to claim his personal share in the work, Einhard mentions[14] that Charlemagne began the collection of those very old songs (*'antiquissima carmina'*) towards the end of his life. The epics were carefully written down and gathered together. All the themes were naturally pagan, and the collection was later destroyed by Charlemagne's successor, the Emperor Louis the Pious. Out of loyalty to the Carolingian dynasty, Einhard makes no mention of the destruction, but later generations knew of the collection and its lamentable fate, and Saxa Poeta, who died in 890, mentioned it.[15]

H. O. Taylor[16] says that Charlemagne ordered 'a book to be made of Germanic poems which till then presumably had been carried in men's memories'. 'Hildebrandslied' is supposed to be the only epic to have escaped the destruction,[17] but the ultimate fate of the collection still remains a problem.

Einhard married, lived happily with his wife, buried her, and ended his own life in peaceable surroundings, his debt to Charlemagne discharged to the full by a biography which alone throws some light on the foremost personality of the day.

*   *   *

The most important figure at the Palace School was Alcuin of York, honest, pedantic, occasionally boring, far more re-nowned as teacher than author – always with the exception of his vast correspondence. Friends in Northumbria, Ireland, Spain, Italy and Frankland enjoyed those letters with their innumerable flashes of irony, humour, delight, censure and anger. Alcuin's correspondence is a veritable chronicle ranging over the huge canvas of his generation. No statesman, he could grasp and approve his patron's statesmanship. He could be charitable and censorious by turn, but even his sharpest 'scoldings' were sometimes seasoned by the salt of humour which raised them above the hodden-grey level of wooden-minded criticism.

He met Charlemagne at Parma in 781. His heart was an-chored in Northumbria, but he accepted the royal invitation to come to Aachen on condition that his joining the Palace School would be approved by his king and his Archbishop. The sanction once gained, Alcuin stayed at Aachen, with a few intermissions, till 796 when, his ill-health increasing, he was compelled to lay down that particular burden, and Charle-magne endowed him with St Martin's Abbey at Tours, the gift accompanied by several other tokens of royal generosity. Retirement, however, did not lead to indolence. Growing more and more frail in body but miraculously active in mind, Alcuin continued teaching, lecturing and writing until his death in 804.

His work at York must have been a high recommendation. In his quest for enlightenment, Charlemagne never wearied of searching for the best, and his search seldom failed. Alcuin came to Aachen as a worthy representative of Northumbrian scholarship. His whole life was a dedication to learning, and he infused that spirit into his colleagues. It is true that his character was a complete antithesis to the King's, but that in no way created a gulf between the two men. Alcuin's austerity must have often amazed Charlemagne, and the Northumbrian's care for his health appeared something of a contradiction in terms to a King who was unacquainted with either fatigue or illness. Alcuin's outlook on 'the things of the world' was admittedly narrow, but the puritansim created no distance between the two friends.

Alcuin taught Charlemagne and many others and, for all the dullness of his teaching methods, he was a genius in that he could inspire others to engage their minds wholly with 'matters of enlightenment'. His own mind as many-sided as that of Isidore of Seville's, Alcuin proved an ideal teacher for Charlemagne, whose curiosity knew no frontiers.

Their friendship deepened. Probably Charlemagne stood on terms of greater intimacy with Einhard and Angilbert, but Alcuin was his necessity. The royal family, beginning with Queen Bertrada, soon learned Alcuin's worth. He praised but never flattered, was respectful but never servile and, at least on one occasion, as will be seen below, he dared to join issue with his royal patron.

His method of teaching answered the needs of the day. It would certainly seem dull today, and dull it was, but its very dullness rang convincingly. In written theses, it took the form of a rather cumbrously contrived dialogue between master and pupil. The idea was by no means original. Others had employed it in earlier days, and there is an interesting precedent in a *Regula* by an anonymous author[18] who must either have been a Frank or lived in Frankland either in the seventh or the first half of the eighth century because references to Mayors of the Palace are found in the text. Questions posed by the pupil are models of brevity. 'What should an abbot be like?' The master's reply takes up a whole page of small print.

Here is an example of Alcuin's dialogue:

'What is speech?'
'The betrayer of the soul.'
'What is sleep?'
'The image of death,' and so on.

Both question and answers are brief, incisive and clear. Presumably the pupils of the Palace School learned them by heart.

Alcuin was not a young man when he came to Aachen, and his tasks were many and hard. To the forefront of everybody stood the King, whom he taught untiringly until his death in 804. To help Charlemagne with the multitude of public speeches and to teach him the rudiments of convincing rhetoric, Alcuin, having studied Cicero's '*De inventione*', composed a small manual of rhetoric for the King's use.

And there was the Palace School for which Charlemagne grudged nothing even when his exchequer was perilously low. Books, parchment, ink and styles were in abundance. The pupils paid no fees, and were lodged, fed and clothed at the King's expense. Many among Alcuin's pupils were to come to full and splendid stature in the ninth century – Abbot Smaragdus, the grammarian, Rabanus of Fulda, who in his turn had Walafrid Strabo of Reichenau for his pupil; Agobard of Lyons, the theologian, Radpert of Corbie, Nithard, Charlemagne's bastard grandson and a historian of note, Sedulius Scotus, the poet, and many others who would transmit their intellectual prowess to the next generations until learning came to be fruitfully established in Paris, Bologna, Montpelier, Salerno and Padua.

But teaching was by no means Alcuin's only task. He took an active part in the debates so beloved by the King, he spoke at synods and other assemblies, and was kept busy in answering endless queries of his royal patron in letters where the formal '*vos*', used to a sovereign, all too often gave way to '*tu*' as to an intimate friend, Alcuin's 'sweetest David' ('*Dulcissime David*'). It is in those letters that Alcuin's personality shines like a sunflower on a bright summer morning.[19] When we consider his work at the Palace School, his voluminous writings and his truly prodigious exercises of piety, it becomes all but incredible that Alcuin found the time to satisfy the King's insatiable curiosity, but he did.

About 797 he wrote to Charlemagne[20] praising him for his efforts 'to disperse the twilight of ignorance' all over Europe. There is no sugared flattery in the letter but heartfelt delight of a master in a promising pupil, who was also demanding in the extreme. The late Helen Waddell called Charlemagne 'that Athenian lover of strange things', and those who served him early learned to expect the unexpected. Now he wished to be instructed about lunar cycles and Alcuin was considered the only person to do so. He warned the King that astronomy was a very difficult but indispensable discipline,[21] and then proceeded to furnish what information was available at the time. Now Charlemagne wished his opinion about the Saxon war, and Alcuin, though a man of peace, admitted that the campaign could be considered a crusade.[22] Far away from his palaces, plunged into the very thick of a war, Charlemagne succeeded in finding time for other inquiries. Etymology stirred his curiosity and Alcuin was apparently the only one to explain the meaning of the word *'amicus'*. Alcuin must have been tired or unwell the day he replied to the King's letter by penning a most laborious explanation of 'friendship', his mind rather heavily leaning on Isidore of Seville's Etymologies. A far lovelier definition of the word and happily remote from all philological allegory can be found in Alcuin's letter to Paulinus, Patriarch of Aquileia:[23] 'True friendship does not suffer from the bodily absence of a friend.'

Alcuin had already begun to work on his revision of the Vulgate when Charlemagne interrupted his concentration by writing to ask what hymn was sung at the end of the Last Supper.[24]

Alcuin took great care with his reply. First of all he pointed out that the entire Psalter was a book of hymns. Then, quoting from Isidore's sixth book of Etymologies, he wrote that any hymn was primarily a song of joy and praise (*'carmen laetitiae et laudis'*) and that according to St Jerome it was an ancient Jewish custom 'to sing praises' after a meal. Alcuin's conclusion is rather remarkable. He reminded the King that St John makes no mention of either bread or wine but, after the washing of the feet, Christ began His prayer, '*Pater, clarifica*' etc. 'That', declared Alcuin, 'is the hymn' ('*Iste est hymnus*').[25]

But liturgies, rhetoric and grammar by no means exhausted the list of themes discussed in that correspondence. Alcuin was no statesman in the strict sense of the word but he knew enough to advise his 'sweetest David' to settle more and more Saxon prisoners in Frankland[26] who, he felt certain, would profit greatly by finding themselves in a Christian environment. 'Those who remained behind [in their own country] would stay riveted in the faith of paganism and other vices.' Evidently, Alcuin set no great store on compulsory baptism.

When the storm of the Adoptionist heresy broke out Charlemagne chose Alcuin, a layman, to enter the lists. His deep-rooted modesty shrank from the inevitable publicity. He admitted that he had Felix of Urgel's book but he urged the King 'to get many learned men together to fight for the honour of the faith'.[27] He suggested that the Pope, Paulinus of Aquileia, Theodulf of Orléans and a few other able theologians were far better equipped for the task than he was, but his 'most beloved lord and friend' proved himself an autocrat in this instance, and Alcuin had no liberty of choice left to him. He set to work – however unwillingly, and his famous seven books '*Contra Felicem*' demolished the fantastic heresy point by fine point.

But Alcuin could be obstinate, too. Charlemagne did not give up his studies even during his campaigns, and it pleased him to have now one, now another member of the Aachen fellowship with him in camp. Letters, however informative, did not always satisfy, and Alcuin was a well of knowledge in the King's eyes. So in the spring of 798 the Northumbrian was urged to join the royal camp during the Saxon campaign of that summer. A King's invitation was tantamount to a command. But Alcuin would not come.[28] It answered far better, he wrote to Charlemagne, to have the bliss of conversing together in the land of peace and gladness than in a country of war and dissensions. His bodily infirmities were great, and he knew nothing about the art of warfare. 'I am but a lamb reared in peace and what could I do if I find myself among ravaging lions?'

The letter was honest, even if somewhat coloured with self-pity, but the King was annoyed. He sent no reply and, apparently wrote no further letters to his 'beloved master' for quite a long time because a little later, Alcuin, writing to a friend[29] begged to be informed about the probable date of the King's return to Frankland since he, Alcuin, 'knew nothing of it'. But Charlemagne came back in late summer, his anger wholly forgotten and his respect for the indefatigable teacher deeper than ever.

Alcuin travelled to Britain on more than one occasion until his bodily frailty made such excursions impossible, but even when absorbed in many labours in Frankland, he kept in touch with 'the friends over the water'. One of those was the Irishman Colchu, teacher at the great monastery of Clonmacnoise.[30] For a time Colchu must have been at York because Alcuin, sending him some money from the King and himself, added a jar of oil 'which is scarce in Britain'.[31]

A layman, Alcuin was far more austere than an anchorite, and the decree forbidding all clerics to occupy themselves with hunting, falconry and gambling[32] gave him much pleasure. His austerity had certainly many repellent streaks in it. He wrote to a friend that it was better 'to care for the poor' than for the jugglers and vagabonds, and there he may well have been moved by charity, but his long letter to Higbald, Bishop of Lindisfarne, might have been written by the most vehement Puritan of the seventeenth century.[33] 'It is better that beggars should be fed at thy table than jugglers, minstrels and such-like . . .The word of God and the sayings of the Fathers should be listened to rather than vulgar songs and worldly music. . .'
In many of the letters Alcuin gave evidence of his deep-rooted abhorrence of all secular amusements. 'Jugglers and suchlike, if hungry, should be given food because they are beggars and not because they were jugglers' (*non quia histriones'*). Alcuin also sent a passionate epistle to the Abbot and community of Fulda, imploring them that the boys in their care should not waste their time 'in stupid games' ('*inanes ludos'*), and his gay colleague, Angilbert, poet and diplomat, caused Alcuin great sorrow because of his love affairs and his passion for worldly amusements. Alcuin complained bitterly to Adalhart of

Corbie that all his efforts to restrain Angilbert proved fruitless. He dared not mention that Angilbert was the acknowledged lover of a daughter of Charlemagne.

Alcuin's friendship with a King whose sexual behaviour certainly defied all the Canons of the Church is rather a phenomenon. 'Jugglers, minstrels and suchlike', the crowd of entertainers whom Alcuin considered damned in eternity, were always welcome at court. Alcuin was in charge of the Palace School and he acquitted himself nobly of the task laid upon him. But when the King was at Aachen, his 'beloved teacher' would join him at dinner. Sometimes there would be debates to please the Northumbrian's mind, but more often than not 'jugglers and suchlike' were summoned to the hall to entertain the King, and women would be present, more than one of them known to enjoy or to have enjoyed the King's caresses. In no single letter of his to Charlemagne did Alcuin allow himself as much as a hint about his pupil's private life. He could indeed teach him rhetoric, grammar, theology, liturgies and etymology. Further he might not go, and in the whole of his voluminous correspondence there is not a word to tell us what he, more austere than an anchorite in the Egyptian desert, must have felt about the immoralities Charlemagne's court took for granted.

Towards the end of the eighth century Alcuin begged to be released from his labours at the Palace School, and asked Charlemagne to let him retire to St Martin's Abbey at Tours.[34] The King gave his consent, and one Fredugis succeeded Alcuin as Head of the School. To him Alcuin, away at Tours, could open his mind[35] in words poignant enough: 'Don't let the crowned doves, who fly all over the palace, come to thy windows, nor wild horses break down the door of thy room. Thou must not pay attention to dancing bears but rather to the chanting of clerks.' 'The crowned doves' were Charlemagne's daughters whom he would not allow to marry but on whose love affairs he looked indulgently. The dancing bears were one of the most common entertainments at court.

Yet such outbursts were rare. None but Alcuin's intimates, and Fredugis was one among them, would have received such a letter. And yet Charlemagne certainly belonged to that circle. All the ugly streaks up and down the canvas of court life were not only known to him but shared by him, drunkenness excepted. That Alcuin lacked courage is evident from his silence on these matters. It might be argued that he considered the King's frequent lapses to be a matter between his conscience and God, and yet Angilbert's immoralities compelled Alcuin to spend himself in bitter reproaches made not only to the sinner himself but to others. The situation was curious in the extreme, and it could hardly be explained by the idea that in Alcuin's eyes the King stood above the judgment of man.

The Northumbrian's relations with the whole royal family were friendly. Charlemagne's fourth and last wife, Queen Liutgard, greatly revered him and often stayed at Tours where she died in June 800. The King's sister, Abbess Gisla of Chelles, and his daughter, Rothrud, who was a nun there, were Alcuin's 'dearest sisters'.

Yet Alcuin was not always a coward. Some time in 802, a cleric from Orléans, accused of a grave trespass, escaped from prison and sought sanctuary at St Martin's at Tours. Alcuin granted it to him. Theodulf of Orléans sent messengers to Tours with the request that the man was to be returned to Orléans. Theodulf and Alcuin had been great friends for many years but in this matter he stood firm: sanctuary could not be broken, was all he said. The men from Orléans stormed their way into the Abbey, but the monks' resistance checked them. Meanwhile, a rumour flamed all over Tours that the men from Orléans had come to steal St Martin's body from its shrine. The result was inevitable: the tumult once started could not be checked, violence lifted its head, and Theodulf's emissaries, together with their retinue, were severely manhandled.

After the quietening, Theodulf and Alcuin wrote to Aachen, each presenting the case from his point of view, and Charlemagne's 'terrible wrath' fell on Alcuin.[36] He had no business to grant sanctuary. The good name of St Martin's Abbey was defamed, and not without reason ('*et non absque re* . . .'). In one bitter sentence after another Charlemagne accused Alcuin of having betrayed the royal trust. He, a stranger and a foreigner, had been invited to teach and to show a good example to all the others. And now alas ('*pro dolor*'), everything was destroyed by his lack of responsibility and good judgment, and the fair name of St Martin's Abbey became a butt for mockery, such brawling and worse having desecrated its walls.

It was a cruel letter to send to an old and ailing man who had done so much to further Charlemagne's 'hopes for enlightenment', but Charlemagne could be cruel on occasions and, though his anger passed as swiftly as it came and the trouble was soon forgotten at Aachen, yet Alcuin wrote rather sadly to his old friend, Arno of Salzburg, that certain as he felt of the Emperor's personal benvolence towards him, yet he knew that there were many among the councillors at Aachen 'who had no clear sense of justice and preferred their private purposes to God's'.

In May 804 Alcuin died at Tours, and none mourned for him as deeply as his 'sweetest David'.

Undoubtedly, he was the outstanding intellect of his day, even though his was no creative genius. As a teacher and an interpreter of available knowledge, Alcuin had no compeers at Aachen, and Charlemagne's debt to him stood above all reckoning. There was more. In Alcuin's work the international leaven of Aachen found its richest and most rewarding expression. Geographical boundaries meant nothing to him. Even when unable to travel, he kept in constant communication with men of letters and of thought in Britain, Italy, Spain and Ireland. We may indeed smile at his censure of worldly amusements. We can have nothing but admiration for his unflagging zeal as a teacher and his wide charity as a friend.

Charlemagne's debt to him covered other than purely personal reaches. From the very start of his work at Aachen Alcuin had grasped the King's purpose 'to disperse the shadows of ignorance' and would not spare himself in carrying out that purpose, with all the strength he commanded. Thus he became a veritable torch-bearer of the century, and his work did not die with his death.

*   *   *

Among Alcuin's many colleagues at Aachen was one Paul Warnefrid, commonly known as Paul the Deacon, a nobly born Lombard and a monk of Monte Cassino, whose scholarship was respected far beyond the Alps.

About 781 Paul went to Frankland to plead with Charlemagne about a grave injustice done to his brother's family.
The case took some time to settle. At the end, the King, always
eager to find fresh talent for the Palace School, persuaded Paul
to stay and become one of the teachers. The abbot and the
community of Monte Cassino lost no time in approving the
King's invitation.

Paul's primary task was to teach history. He formed a few
friendships and joined in many debates, but from the very
beginning the Lombard kept himself aloof from the noise and
the splendour of court occasions. He was fully in accord with
Charlemagne in all educational matters, and he welcomed
the King's efforts to raise the moral and intellectual standards
among the religious in Frankland,[37] but the wide gulf between
the scholarly purposes at Aachen and the noisy and frequently
amoral abandon of the daily life at court saddened and bewildered Paul. His fastidiousness hurt to the utmost, the historian
sent a poignant *cri de coeur* to Theudemar, Abbot of Monte
Cassino.[38]

Scrupulously fair, Paul admitted that he had nothing but
gratitude for the welcome accorded to him. Everybody was
kind and the King's benevolence was like a mantle flung over a
stranger from Lombardy. Yet, whenever he thought of his
remote and beloved cloister, the palace seemed a noisome
prison to him (. . . *'mihi palatium carcer est . . .'*). The work expected of him at the Palace School was certainly most interesting
but, once away from the lecture-rooms and the comparative
seclusion of his own quarters, the erudite Lombard found
himself in a climate his mind abhorred and his senses revolted
from. Rough horseplay, coarse jokes, much drunkenness,
violent quarrels among the lesser official fry in the King's
household, questionable songs, endless gossip about the princesses and their maidens, and all of it to the accompaniment of
deafening noise. The atmosphere did not seem to disturb men
like Theodulf and Angilbert. It certainly disturbed Alcuin but
he kept reticent about his reaction to it.

So Paul the Deacon taught much and taught well, but
remained an outsider for the whole of his stay in Frankland.
For Charlemagne he had a deep affection, and dedicated to the

King his 'Vocabularies' – 'desiring to add something to your library'. In between his lectures Paul, complying with the royal request, wrote a somewhat dull history of the diocese of Metz in honour of St Arnulf, Charlemagne's ancestor.

In spite of all the difficulties, Paul the Deacon must have had his high moments at Aachen. His '*carmina*' are delicate and pleasing, and his epitaphs tender, in particular one on Queen Hildegard, Charlemagne's second wife. 'So wholly joined to him in love, thou alone was found worthy to hold the golden sceptre.' A brief poem on a daughter of Charlemagne's who died in infancy, carries a line as splendid as it is moving:

'So great a grief left by so small a maid'.

But the court atmosphere continued pressing heavily on Paul. In about five or six years he succeeded in persuading his abbot to have him recalled to 'the silent paradise'. Charlemagne let him go reluctantly enough. Yet, in an unofficial sense, the shy scholar remained in the King's service till his death in 800, and the link of affection between the two men was never broken.

The quiet of Monte Cassino enabled Paul to write his *opus major*, the classical 'History of the Lombards'. A little later, at the King's request, Paul compiled a *Homiliarius*, a formidable collection of patristic excerpts to serve as models for sermons throughout the entire calendar,[39] using Origen, Leo the Great, St Augustine and many others. The book was dedicated to Charlemagne, but, curiously enough, the preface was written by the King himself who explained that the collection was made for the purpose of enlarging the mental horizons of clergy both secular and regular. It was his earnest desire to see ignorance swept away from the clerical sky, and his forebears too had desired it. As to himself, said Charlemagne, 'Providence has always been near me, both in the tumults of war and the tranquillity of peace'.

Some of the excerpts are anonymous, and a few of them may well have been composed by Paul himself, his humility forbidding him to have his name appear in such illustrious company. The very fine piece on 'Silence'[40] is undoubtedly his own. It is the work of a poet held in the blessed thraldom of God's love, a thraldom which is the ultimate liberty of the soul.

There are three kinds of silence, Paul says, and the third is the loveliest. It will never end, 'and happy shall he be who lives within it'. The first and the second silences are full of many words spoken and unspoken. Then God's generosity sent The Word to live among men at a time when the last shred of hope seemed gone in the world. Despair fled when The Word was uttered, but it came very, very still, and that was the birthday of the third and greatest silence.

Paul the Deacon won his fame by 'The History of the Lombards' which has remained a classic to this day. His poems are now all but forgotten. The '*Homiliarius*' enjoyed a measure of success for two or three centuries. The piece on 'Silence', however, turned its author into an unconscious forerunner of neo-Platonism.

Charlemagne's generosity to his friends knew no limits. He bestowed bishoprics and abbacies on them, and all too often the exchequer might be temporarily empty because the royal bounty had over-run the royal resources. But neither mitre nor jewellery could be given to Paul the Deacon, who lived and died a humble monk. In the King's eyes, the Lombard stood for a symbol of what a scholarly religious should be. Paul had no use for flattery or half-truths, and Charlemagne knew well the reason for the Lombard's return to Monte Cassino. Yet that created no gulf between the two because Charlemagne could respect motives beyond his comprehension, and in Paul's eyes the King's 'thirst for enlightenment' cancelled out the many unpleasantnesses of his private life.

Comparatively short though it was, Paul's work at the Palace School left an imprint for many generations to come. He had taught history as a master, his immense erudition finely blended with imagination. Rabanus Maurus, later Abbot of Fulda, attended his lectures, and in time followed their pattern at his own Abbey school.

*   *   *

Notker of St Gall is no reliable authority, and some chapters of his incredibly jumbled narrative might well have served as models for a mediaeval humorist. Such, for instance, is the story[41] about Charlemagne's complaint that 'he wished he had

twelve clerks as learned and wise as Jerome and Augustine';
Alcuin, who was supposed to be there, 'dared greatly in the
presence of terrible Charles and said to him: "The Creator
Himself has not many like those two, and do you expect to
have twelve?"'

Some such complaint may or may not have been made by a
sovereign who, always and greedily expecting the best, was
frequently disappointed in his expectations. For that particular
plaint there exists no authority. Notker, writing towards the
end of the ninth century, may well have repeated a piece of
stale gossip which had travelled from one generation to another.
But Alcuin's retort is wholly out of character. In the first place,
he would never have answered in such a vein in the presence
of a witness. Secondly, though Charlemagne's corps of scholars
did not include any giants of St Jerome's and St Augustine's
stature, it was none the less a brilliant galaxy, its light not to be
put out even by the depressing shadows of the tenth century.

Nor were they twelve in number. Alcuin, Paulinus of
Aquileia, theologian and statesman, Peter of Pisa the grammarian, Clement of Ireland who taught the same discipline,
the poet Hibernicus Exul, known by no other name, Dungal,
Durcuil the geographer, Godescalc the Illuminator, to whose
genius we owe the exquisite Aachen Gospels (c. 781), Einhard,
the learned abbots of Corbie, Fulda and Lorsch, Arno of
Salzburg and many more – of such was the erudite company
at the Palace School.

The most elegant poet of the day was Theodulf, a Spaniard,
later Archbishop of Orléans, a self-confessed lover of beauty
and luxury, whose ironical verse sometimes irritated and
wounded, who had something of Swift in his character and
speech, was mordant and sarcastic in debates, and was well
known for his dislike of the Irishmen at Aachen. 'I cannot abide
them because of their levity,' Theodulf is supposed to have
said, but the reason does not accord well with what we know
of his own character. That frequently expressed contempt for
the Irish, doubtless born of jealousy because of their learning,
was a thin unlovely streak in Theodulf. Yet his classical
erudition was great, he used noble models for his lectures on
poetry, and Charlemagne valued him for that and for his

statesmanship. One of Theodulf's longer poems is 'an admonition to the King's judges' written after he had been as '*missus dominici*' to Southern Frankland in 798. He loved and revered Alcuin, had a bitter quarrel with him in 802, was soon enough reconciled to his old friend, and came to Tours in 804 to shed genuine tears at Alcuin's funeral. To the English-speaking world of today Theodulf is best known as the author of the Palm Sunday hymn 'All glory, laud and honour'.

And there was Angilbert, Charlemagne's councillor and life-long friend, debonair and gay, poet and diplomat, who had the King's daughter, Bertha, for his mistress, with the King's consent. He was the Adonis of Aachen, and Bertha was by no means alone in sharing his bed. Angilbert wrote Latin verse, much lighter and more polished than Theodulf's, begot a son, Nithard, the future historian of Frankland, was loved by the King for his wit in argument and his gaiety, and caused much sorrow to Alcuin by his unending moral lapses. To Angilbert, the matter of sex was but a detail of life. He took it all as casually as he ate his roast venison at dinner, and was in that particular in full accord with his unacknowledged father-in-law. His Latin lectures certainly bore their fruit, but Angilbert was a poet first and last. Not interested in matters of fire and sword, he began a long poem, almost an epic, to interpret his own vision of a dedicated crusade, something of the nature of the future '*Chanson de Roland*'. Alcuin loved him, called him 'Homer', sorrowed over him and prayed for him unceasingly. Alcuin's prayers must have been heard. Angilbert died in the sanctified quiet of St Riguiers Abbey on the same day as Charlemagne in January 814, 'the caresses of mistresses and the antics of dancing bears' remote from his daily life for many a year.

There, at Aachen, and certainly not in the background, were the brilliant scholars from Ireland who brought with them, over and above their prodigious learning, their own peculiar leaven of gaiety blended with gravity, of humour wholly divorced from malice, and a passion for learning. There was the venerable Dungal who taught astronomy, Clement, the most famous grammarian of the century, Dicuil the geographer, whose finely tempered conscience forbade

him to mention tides in his book. He left the task 'to such
scholars who had their home by the sea-shore, and I live far
from the sea and have no opportunity of studying the tides'.
Finally, there was Fredugis, a Frank, Alcuin's pupil and his
successor as head of the Palace School, whose tender lament for
Alcuin[42] is the finest monument raised to a great teacher's
memory.

The teaching genius of Alcuin, Paul the Deacon's great
learning, the freshness of Einhard's mind, the gifts of Theodulf,
Angilbert, Paulinus and of those Irish scholars, whose ability
both to absorb and to transmit learning was never conquered
by the most untoward circumstances, all of it together would
not be ended with the days of their flesh because they had
taught young men who were to reach their full mental stature
after the death of Charlemagne.

*   *   *

In the words of H. O. Taylor[43] 'the whole period was at
school where it needed to be: at school to the Church Fathers,
at school to the transmitters of antique culture, and the school
prospered all the more happily because its crowned "*Nutritor*"
himself sat on a school bench, and thus caused a revival of
sacred and profane studies, with Alcuin as his chief luminary'.

Two-thirds of the above paragraph describe the situation
with a brilliant clarity, but we may be excused for qualifying
the last two lines to some slight degree. Charlemagne's educational reforms might be compared with the vigorous use of
bellows over an apparently dead fire. Life, however hidden,
had not altogether gone from the hearth. A spark here and a
spark there did their work until the united and wholly dedicated
energies of Charlemagne's team turned those sparks into a
column of brave flame.

That fire burned all the more brightly because of the
absolute liberty of action given them by their royal patron and
pupil. No single scholar invited to the Palace School found
himself yoked to a rigid curriculum. In generously fluid terms
they could all follow the traditional framework of the seven
liberal arts, with its classical division into the Trivium (grammar, rhetoric, and dialectic) and the Quadrivium (arithmetic,

Charlemagne's Coronation, from the Chroniques de St Denis (fourteenth century)
(*Radio Times Hulton Picture Library*)

Charlemagne – a bronze statuette in the Musée Carnavalet, Paris
(*Radio Times Hulton Picture Library*)

geometry, music and cosmography), but they taught other disciplines as well – logic, geography and natural sciences. Among all the masters, Alcuin alone kept to a method of his own. The others preferred to teach after their own individual fashion, but all the masters together had one common aim in view: the Palace School was a university in little in that its primary purpose was to teach its pupils how to use their minds. All else was subsidiary to it.

Naturally, they had tools for the work, and Charlemagne, ceaselessly collecting manuscripts for his own library, spent much on purchasing books for the School. The diplomats he employed on many missions had secretaries one of whose duties was to search for manuscripts wherever they went, and to engage skilled copyists without grudging the expense. They had Isidore of Seville's twenty books of Etymologies with their marvellous blending of fact and fable covering every known facet of life – from anatomy and zoology to gemmology and botany. They had Boëthius, Bede and Aldhelm. They had fine copies of patristics – Origen, Tertullian, Clement of Alexandria, St Augustine, Leo the Great and Gregory the Great, to name but a few of the Fathers. They had Martianus Capella, Donatus and Priscian. Beautifully copied books of the early Christian poets had a place of honour on their shelves, Paulinus of Nola and Prudentius among others. The great classics were their pattern – Livy, Sallust, Cicero, Virgil, Horace, Martial, Tacitus, Caesar and Suetonius. They taught their pupils to model their versification on Virgil and Horace and their prose essays on Tacitus and Caesar. Their Bible was the Vulgate, and Charlemagne charged Alcuin to make a revision of it, so many mistakes having crept in through the carelessness of copyists.

What few Greek books were in the School library wore a Latin garb. There were no outstanding Greek scholars at Aachen. Charlemagne himself, though able to follow the speeches of Byzantine ambassadors, could hardly speak the language. The Palace School was wholly western, absorbing the classic heritage from the wealth left by Rome, not by Hellas. As has already been said, the ablest Frankish theologians made a sorry muddle when they translated a Council's findings from Greek into Latin.

L

But theology alone could not be held accountable for the deepening gulf between East and West. The Franks, having once settled in Gaul, made the Gallo-Roman matter their own. In prose and in poetry and in law also they recognized themselves as inheritors of the antique culture. Greek to them remained an alien tongue, mastered with difficulty and never reaching the inmost sanctuary of the mind. That, no doubt, is regrettable, but it remains a fact. Not a theological squabble alone led to the final rupture of Rome and Constantinople in 1054.

At Aachen they delighted in classical poetry, more especially men like Theodulf and Angilbert. Though their own Latin could not recapture much of the genuine classical flavour, still their grammar and spelling stood far above the standard employed by the Merovingian clerks, an example of which is given in a footnote.[44]

The whole volume of that mental activity lay within the climate of acceptance rather than interpretation, still less creativeness. Here and there (but not too often) came flashes of true poetry in what is left of the work of Angilbert, Theodulf and Paul the Deacon. Einhard's biography of Charlemagne, whatever its indebtedness to Suetonius, and Paul's 'History of the Lombards' take a high place indeed, otherwise the long list includes many patristic compilations, Bible commentaries, much colourless hagiography, mathematical and cosmographic treatises and suchlike. The content, however, is of secondary importance. What mattered was the impetus given to the mind, the search for form, the hunger for learning *per se*.

When we turn aside from the disciplines so ably taught at the Palace School, we remember that Charlemagne's reign witnessed the birth of the Romanesque movement. As King and Emperor, Charlemagne had a passion for building on a gigantic scale until the innumerable splendours of Aachen alone became the cynosure of all Europe. Einhard and Godescalc, masters of the so called 'little arts', had many pupils of promise. Ivories and enamels often stressed the Byzantine impact on the Frankish imagination, and many exquisite trifles from Ravenna were copied in colour and in design and lent beauty to the erstwhile grim and barren interiors. In the scriptoria of Corbie, St Martin of Tours, Fulda, Lorsch, St Gall and Reichenau, the exquisitely clear Carolingian minuscule was reaching its perfection.

Incessant wars notwithstanding, grace began breathing in Frankland, a happy and fruitful blending of the antique culture with the zest and freshness of the Teutonic contribution, and much of it would carry a permanent imprint on the moulding of both France and Germany.

*   *   *

All of it was certainly not the work of one man, but it was one man who most clearly realized the day's immediate needs, met most of them and forestalled the rest. It is true that Charlemagne's primary purpose was to raise the intellectual standards among the clergy. Yet it was during his reign that enlightened laymen first moved into the foreground and were enabled both to teach and to pursue their own studies.

Charlemagne wanted the best, did not always get it, and was on occasions dissatisfied with the best when he got it. Alcuin's letters alone throw a sharp light on that many-faceted mind. 'The dearest master' had to answer questions on grammar and rhetoric, on bibliology and liturgics, on astronomy and the idea of time, on law and on semantics. Everything was grist to the mill of Charlemagne's mind. With a philosopher born centuries after him, he might have said: '*Homo sum et nihil humanum a me alienum puto*'.

Charlemagne was no forerunner but a man of his day. Therefore, the Catholic faith was his point of departure in all things. Not a single educational effort of his but was made to enable his people to understand the tenets of the Faith. Such is the burden of many capitularies and of his 'open letters' – 'that you may more easily and rightly penetrate the mysteries of the Holy Scriptures' ('*ut facilius et rectius divinarum scripturarum mysteria valeatis penetrare*'). Such was the key which in Charlemagne's eyes was to open the door not only to mental enlightenment but to prosperity and ultimate peace in all his dominions, and though, freely mixing among the humblest of his subjects, he was at home in his native Teutonic tongue, his spiritual language was Latin. He could follow the speeches of the Emperor's ambassadors but his own spoken Greek was very halting.

We know from Einhard that the King revered and richly rewarded all those who taught the liberal arts and the natural sciences, and his own Will tells us that he had collected a large library of his own at Aachen.[45] Social antecedents of the masters and pupils at the Palace School carried no weight with Charlemagne. A keenly bladed brain, a live imagination and hard work were the only credentials to win his favour. On one occasion he enabled two young sons of a miller in the service of Luxeuil Abbey to continue with their studies long after they should have started to earn their livelihood as field labourers. Charlemagne's learnings towards a true democracy may appear out of accord with the autocratic hammer he wielded so often, and yet, in a subtly satisfying fashion, the one complements the other.

Many of Notker Balbulus's stories about Charlemagne are either fantastic or insignificant, but a few do carry seeds of authenticity.[46]

He was in the habit of paying frequent visits to the Palace School whenever he stayed at Aachen. On one occasion, when, according to Notker, 'one Clement the Irishman was master', the King came in to assure himself that the pupils had not been idle during his absence. Poems and various essays were read aloud, and it happened that the boys 'of lowly birth' were able to account for 'far finer work than the King had hoped for'. Scions of noble houses failed most dismally. Having listened to their clumsy efforts at versification, Charlemagne first turned towards the boys 'on his right side, and said, "I promise you great honours in the future. Well done!"' Then, 'his eyes aflame with anger', he looked at the nobly born sprigs and thundered at them: '"Relying on your high birth and great wealth, you have dared to neglect my orders made for your advancement, and wasted your time most shamefully. You can be sure that you will never receive any favour from me unless you atone for your idleness by hard study."'

Thus Notker, and the story is in character: Charlemagne held idleness in deep abhorrence.

Metaphorically, he sat on a school bench of his own, and

that wherever he happened to be – in his private rooms at one of his many palaces or in camp, in a banqueting hall, or riding back from a hunt, with a lively debate born out of a casual remark, a debate on statesmanship, fiscal matters, Latin prosody, astronomy, the art of computation, history, law, horticulture, the Byzantine arrogance, a Pope's difficulties, or the problem of crushing the Crescent. All helped to enlarge his own horizons and to sharpen his appetite for more and more knowledge.

Alcuin's letters to him are most rewardingly illuminating. Very few of Charlemagne's own letters have come to us, and yet the picture is clear enough. In Alcuin's correspondence and in the pages of Einhard's biography we find ourselves facing a man whose curiosity swept far beyond the horizons known in his time, who counted a day ill spent when he retired not having learned something he did not know at his rising from his bed in the morning.

Yet Charlemagne ruled over a vast dominion. The business of governing absorbed much of his time. There were the endless capitularies, quite a few of them drafted by himself, his duties of piety, diplomatic matters and all but incessant campaigns, one or two sports he delighted in and, finally, sleep. Where, one can but ask, was the time for him to engage in the travail of the mind?

There is only one answer: a superb physique in full accord with a widely windowed mind, an iron will which jettisoned the very idea of fatigue, a conception of life as a stream of activity in Time until the waters reached the shoreless sea of Eternity, a boy's keenness which barred the way to the least staleness in the thought, and a rock-like conviction that even his questions about tides, lunar cycles and viticultural details were at one with his hope of establishing his Lord's Kingdom in Europe.

VII

THE MAN

The remarkably curious paragraph at the end of Einhard's preface to Charlemagne's biography has given rise to endless conjectures. The Emperor had died in 814 at the age of 72 and at least some of his contemporaries would have been alive at the time when 'the dwarf' began his work, which is supposed to be between 820 and 825. Moreover, Einhard, having spent more than twenty years at court, could not but have known many men able to furnish him with important details about his hero's beginnings.

Yet not only does he say that he could find nothing about his patron's boyhood and youth,[1] but he even amplifies the statement by an assertion that nobody was then living who had any personal knowledge of such things.

At first glance, such words are puzzling indeed, and later more than one historian thought that Einhard was carrying out Charlemagne's own wishes, the latter being supposed to dislike any allusions to his early years because of his being born out of wedlock. It is quite true that the date of Pippin the Short's marriage to Bertrada is unknown, and that many sources vary about the date and the place of Charlemagne's own birth. But the conjecture falls to the ground once it is remembered that bastardy carried no slur at the time. It has further been suggested that Einhard's reticence was due to the fact of his knowing something about Charlemagne's allegedly unhappy childhood, that Pippin the Short had been a harsh if not a cruel parent, and that Charlemagne would not have those sable-coloured memories shared by posterity.

Here again we face a blank wall because nothing is known of Pippin's character, and Charlemagne's later relations with his mother and sister certainly do not suggest an earlier landscape of misery. The most that can be said is that a Frankish father of the day would hardly have permitted himself to indulge in tenderness towards a son, and that Charlemagne and his younger brother, Carloman, were brought up in the customary hardy fashion, early taught not to complain about climatic vagaries, well-versed in the iron discipline of palace and camp, early at home in the saddle and early, too, inured to the unpredictable perils of a wild-boar hunt. Charlemagne, in particular, would have been early accustomed to carry himself well in the presence of strangers as befitted a king's son and heir.

Certain traits very much to the fore when he came to manhood may well have been there in childhood and youth: his passion for swimming and hunting, love of good food and hatred of fasting, quick temper, great simplicity and, above all, his hunger for knowledge.

Now Einhard's refusal to lend his pen to any of it may be explained by a streak of unconscious vanity. Born in 770, he was about twenty years younger than his patron, and in the biography he emphasized that he would touch on nothing except what was known to him personally, such knowledge being considered to offer enough material for a book. Second- and third-hand stories and tittle-tattle were wholly beneath his notice. The vanity does not raise its voice, but its whispers are audible enough. In his own preface to the Biography, Walafrid Strabo repeated what he must have heard from his master, Rabanus Maurus of Fulda, himself an old pupil at Aachen, i.e., that no one at court had won Charlemagne's confidence as much as Einhard. That may well have been so, and Einhard would have been justly proud of it. So he decided to deal with matters known either from personal observation or shared with him by his patron, and Charlemagne's early years did not belong there.[2]

In one sense, it is a regrettable vanity. In another, it enlarges the value of the book.

Pippin the Short had a small family – two sons, and a daughter, Gisla, who became a nun and later the Abbess of Chelles. Charlemagne loved her devotedly, and the parlour of Chelles, to say nothing of its chapel, brought him the refreshment of spirit he needed so often. Gisla, herself no mean scholar and a friend of Alcuin, understood her brother's aims and hopes better than some of his councillors.

There was the younger brother, Carloman, whose promises to amend his way of life were like so many spent breaths, who often provoked Charlemagne to the very edge of a quarrel. But he would not quarrel with him, not even after Carloman's shabbily broken word in the Aquitanian matter when he refused to go to the elder brother's help. It was fortunate for Frankland that Carloman died in his early twenties.

Of Pippin's private life very little is known. Charlemagne's mother, Bertrada, had been a mistress before becoming a wife, and it is more than likely that Pippin had many other women in his life.

Canonically, marriage was sacrosanct and indissoluble, though the latter condition did not come to be observed in the case of Charlemagne's brief union with the Lombard princess. In loose terms, however, the sacrament of marriage was considered in the light of a legalized concession to human fraility. From the viewpoint of the early Fathers of the Church, the state of virginity stood much higher. Married life, for all its hallowing, was hedged about with many canonical regulations, and intercourse was forbidden during Advent, Lent and vigils of great feasts.

Yet to the mediaeval man, the whole matter of sex remained apart from all such subtleties. The approach to it was brutally simple: it was an appetite which demanded satisfaction, and that summed up everything.

As H. O. Taylor remarked,[3] 'from the time of the barbarian inroads and all through the Carolingian period . . . there was enough barbarism and brutality to impede the development of a high standard of marriage . . . his own lustful heart led Charlemagne to marry and re-marry at will and have many mistresses besides.'

No names of any concubines are recorded before 770 when the unfortunate Hilmentrud, mother of a hunchback son, was set aside, Queen Bertrada having decided that a daughter of the King of the Lombards would make a fitting bride for her eldest son. Bertrada's motives are rather obscure; she was returning to Frankland after many pious exercises in Rome, and her stay at Pavia caused much astonishment. We know enough of Charlemagne's devotion to his mother and of their mutual confidence to allow that the Queen-Mother's matrimonial scheme would have been known to and approved by him before she set out for Italy. But it was a state secret until the arrival of the Lombard girl.

Pope Stephen, ignoring Bertrada, thundered against Charlemagne and called Hilmentrud his 'wife' whom he might not lawfully put away. But to Einhard, the hunchback's mother remained a nameless concubine,[4] and in his own turn Notker called her the King's mistress.[5] Pope Stephen's vehement protests against the Lombard marriage rested not on canonical reasons but on his anxiety about the possible consequences of such union in what concerned the safety of St Peter's patrimony. It is highly improbable that the Pope would have entered the lists on Hilmentrud's behalf if the princess chosen by Queen Bertrada had not been an enemy's daughter but belonged to some notable Frankish stock. Pope Stephen's mind was wholly engaged by the formidable menace of an alliance between Frankland, Lombardy and Bavaria where Duke Tassilo had another of King Desiderius's daughters for his wife.

The Pope's angry tirades achieved nothing. Frankish bishops had no scruples in performing the rite. Once again, as so often before and later, too, the sacrament of marriage became a tool of expediency in high dynastic matters. According to Notker[6] '. . . the alliance was formed . . . to prevent [the Lombards] from ever again fighting against [the Franks]'. If Queen Bertrada had some such purpose in view, her short-sightedness and imprudence are indeed remarkable: no ties of kinship would have prevented Desiderius from starting a war if the moment and the circumstances were favourable.

Charlemagne's own behaviour was odd. Not having objected to his mother's choice, he duly married the bride in 770. Less than a year later he sent her back to Pavia, the marriage contract being annulled at an assembly of clerics and laymen. Rumour had it that the girl suffered from a disability which would have prevented her from bearing children, but nobody knew it as a certainty. 'She was,' as Notker says, 'by the counsel of the clergy put aside as though she were dead.' Einhard merely mentions the divorce 'for a reason unknown'. The episode is as sad as it seems futile. The rumour about the girl's physical disabilities rested on nothing but common tittle-tattle. Had the princess been really unfit, Queen Bertrada would have heard of it in Italy.

The girl was even denied a name by the annalists. She appears merely as 'a daughter of King Desiderius' (*'filia Desiderii regis'*). The Lombards enjoyed no great popularity in Frankland; Tassilo's wife was already known for her intrigues, and Charlemagne's unfortunate bride may well have been returned to Pavia not only 'by the counsel of the clergy' but on the advice of his ministers and intimate friends.

That shipwrecked marriage, however, led to many family dissensions, some pious cousins of Charlemagne's being outraged by the mere idea of a divorce. It also led to the first and only quarrel between the King and his mother. Queen Bertrada used all her skill to dissuade her son from such a decision, but he stood firm, and back to Pavia the girl went, her royal rank of no account to the Franks, nameless and rejected, a mere pale wraith against the rich and varied colours of the King's court. No voice from Rome was lifted to protest against the divorce. The Frankish hierarchy having counselled the King to follow his own way, Charlemagne's hold on theocracy was strengthened. The quarrel with his mother soon came to be forgotten, and no great astonishment broke out among the Franks on learning that they had a new queen, one Hildegard of noble Schwabian origins, who was duly married and crowned in splendour. Her reign lasted till 783. She bore her husband three sons and three daughters; the succession was amply assured and the Pavian interlude vanished from the people's memory. At Hildegard's death Charlemagne wept bitterly – such a good wife, mother and queen she had been.

Yet his affection did not mean fidelity to his marriage vows, nor did he stoop to the shoddy level of meaningless excuses. Hildegard was not always able to accompany her lord on his unceasing travels and campaigns, and Charlemagne was no celibate. His mistresses were not kept in remote corners. They shared his bed. They shared what splendours fell to their

moment, and they were dismissed with honour and gifts, due
provision being made for any children they might have borne
during the liaison. The annalists seldom mention their names.
Only four are noticed by Einhard, but those were undoubtedly
maîtresses en chef who occupied the stage after the death of the
fourth and last queen in 800. By those four women Charlemagne had seven sons and two daughters. A certain Regina,
her origins unknown, was the mother of two sons. One Hugo,
later Abbot of St Quentin, ended as chancellor to his father's
successor, the Emperor Louis the Pious. The other, Drogo,
became Archbishop of Metz. Illegitimacy barred the way to
succession but not to promotion up the ecclesiastical ladder.

There must have been countless others whose names never
found their way into any chronicle, and Einhard is particularly
reticent on the subject. There would have been Saxon and
Slav girls brought to the royal tent for a casual embrace and as
casual a dismissal, sweetened by the gift of some beads, a bangle,
or a parcel of food. When we remember that Charlemagne's
martial discipline laid a ban on camp followers, we can
assume that either such encounters were arranged in secrecy
or that the ban was not really observed in all its strictness. It
seems rather like a sauce enjoyed both by the gander and the
goose. Any warrior in the Frankish host was as virile as his
sovereign and it is difficult to believe that a wholesome self-
restraint could have been practised through an entire summer.

The only species of womankind they all avoided were the
Avar girls, 'that bestial and inferior race,' who fed on horseflesh
and drank mares' milk. For a Frank to lie with an Avar girl
was tantamount to a betrayal of his birthright.

In bald terms, Charlemagne was amoral rather than im-
moral, like most people of his generation. The commandments
and the Church canons certainly spoke a language he could
well understand. So did the Gospels, and that curious halvedness in him came out most strongly when at assemblies and
synods he would extol chastity and inflict grim penalties on
both clerical and lay adulterers always so long as the trespass
was dragged into the open.

Yet the halvedness, however repellent it may seem, was only
apparent. There were two distinct selves in Charlemagne; one

was the symbol of sovereignty and power, which lent grace and meaning to his reforms and made him what he was from the European point of view – the first ruler whose words were listened to and whose policy was respected. The other self was a man, always sexually hungry, almost childlike in his enjoyment of simple pleasures, a keen pupil, a good soldier, a fearless hunter, a good husband, an indulgent father and a generous lover.

We know that Queen Hildegard's death all but felled him, and that year, 783, was all the sadder because of the passing of his mother. Charlemagne had them both buried with high honours at St Denys, and he mourned for them in all sincerity.

None the less, he needed a queen if but as a figurehead for his splendid court, and towards the end of 783 he was married once again.

It was a most unfortunate choice of a bride. Fastrada was nobly born but not nobly minded. The beautiful face was but a mask of a jealous, cruel, small-horizoned nature. Frankland heard of the marriage and sighed because the lady's qualities were too well known. They whispered about her meanness: she was supposed to be capable of haggling about the price of eggs from her father's farmyard. They whispered about her cruelty to the maids who served her, and of her incredible pride. People came to believe that Queen Fastrada's intrigues were responsible for the wrecking of the betrothal between Princess Rothrud and the Emperor Constantine VI. Fastrada was known to be jealous of her own rank, and those nearest to the court alleged that she had said, 'I am a queen, and how could I endure to see a stepdaughter become an empress?' That may have been idle gossip, but the engagement was broken off, Princess Rothrud hid herself at the Abbey of Chelles, and it was common knowledge that Fastrada loathed and maltreated her other stepdaughters, though she took care not to show her malice in the King's presence. She bore him two daughters, Hiltrud and Theoderada, and reigned for twelve years. Her death in 795 greatly lightened the Frankish skies.

It is not court gossip but a proved fact that the two conspiracies against Charlemagne happened during those twelve years, and even Einhard ascribed them to Fastrada's cruelty

and her unfortunate influence over her husband. It is true that
Charlemagne's third queen hated her hunchback son even
though, owing to his deformity, he lived in retirement and
never appeared at court. The conspiracy of 792 was rather
obscurely traced to him. Many people were involved and
punished in accordance with the cruel standards of the age.
Fastrada is supposed to have urged the prince's execution, but
Charlemagne refused to shed a son's blood. The young man
was sent to the Abbey of Prümes and forced to become a monk.

Few, if any, had anything to say in favour of a woman whose
capacity for hatred was like a shoreless sea. Yet Charlemagne
loved her. One of the very few extant letters written by him
was addressed to her from his camp on the banks of the Danube.
It was not a very long letter but it breathed with affection and
concern.

Fastrada died early in 795, and before that year was out,
Charlemagne had led yet another woman to the altar, his
fourth and last queen, one Liutgard of noble Allemannian stock.
She was gentle and pious, with a leaning towards books;
Alcuin had a deep regard for her, and she would often come
to St Martin's Abbey for the quiet and refreshment she could
not find at court. It was at Tours that she died in June 800,
and Charlemagne's court would never know another queen.

Yet '*maîtresses en titre*' and many others followed the path
none but a wife should have walked.[7] Einhard mentions four
names only, but there may well have been many more. One
of them was Gerswinda, a Saxon. Between them they bore
several children, and ample provision was made for a family
all but suggesting a clan.

The climate at court was anything but healthy. Until his
death[8] Charlemagne kept his daughters at home saying 'that he
could not bear to be parted from them', and there his honest
biographer saw the root of the evil at court, though he wrote of
it with a well-nigh exaggerated reticence. '. . . hence the high
fortune that was his in all other respects was here broken by a
touch of scandal', an understatement which, however in accord
with Einhard's loyalty, carries no conviction at all. 'A touch of
scandal' was like a giant's mantle thrown all over the immensity
of the palace at Aachen. The *palatium*, with few exceptions,

took the cue from the sovereign and restraint became a butt for mockery.

Charlemagne's sons were all married, and he welcomed his legitimate grandchildren who assured a safe future for the Arnulfing House. But he wished to have no sons-in-law. Princess Rothrud's betrothal to the Emperor was an event so exceptional that many people refused to believe it. It was freely rumoured that though Charlemagne felt humiliated by its rupture, it brought no personal grief to him. A daughter of King Offa of Mercia was suggested as bride for one of Charlemagne's three sons, and the King welcomed the proposal but all the preliminaries came to an end when Offa wanted one of the Frankish princesses to marry his heir. Charlemagne's refusal was unequivocal.

So his daughters, forced to remain unwed, chose to have lovers. Their father pretended to know nothing about those affairs, but the pretence could not carry any weight because of the princesses' pregnancies. Half-royal babies were born in the palace, and Angilbert, the poet, was one of the unrecognized sons-in-law. Alcuin's poignant complaint about 'the crowned doves' at the palace was indeed the voice of a man crying in the wilderness – but it was no isolated voice. Paulinus of Aquileia and Paul the Deacon, to name no others, felt all but stifled in that climate of unending licentiousness, but none, not even Alcuin, dared risk Charlemagne's anger by breaching a matter he had no wish to hear about.

The *palatium* was no brothel in the narrowly technical sense. Love was neither bought nor sold under its roof. Rather, it suggested a liberty hall of the worst, most deeply stained kind where women from princesses down to the least attractive kitchen wench enjoyed their lovers' embraces. In Aquitania, King Louis, one day to be Emperor known as the Pious, spent many hours praying for his father and sisters. Yet not until 814 would the gay princesses and their no less dissolute female attendants be exiled from Aachen to the gloom of such convents as Charlemagne's successor considered to stand highest in the observance of a harsh rule.

Yet Charlemagne was devoted to all his daughters and he denied them nothing except their marriage lines, and the

Carolingian dichotomy, so lamentably apparent in his forebears, was not lacking in him. According to Einhard[9], Charlemagne had all his children, both legitimate and not, well
grounded in the liberal arts. He was proud of his sons' military
exploits, and had poets celebrate their victories. He never
complained about Louis's grotesquely exaggerated piety. The
deaths of his two sons, Charles and Pippin, all but shattered
him.

The princesses shared their brothers' early lessons, and were
also instructed in all manner of needlework – 'so to avoid idleness and to have high principles fostered in them'. It would
be pleasant to believe that Einhard's irony may have been
unconscious.

Whenever Charlemagne was at home, they had free access
to him. They joined him at dinner and supper, and he took a
keen interest in their studies. On some occasions they would
accompany him on his travels. They rode in the rear, their
beautiful faces unveiled.

The King's palace, wherever it happened to be, had a chapel
as well as conveniently remote bedrooms, and Charlemagne
never missed his daily Mass and other services.

Presumably, the princesses would often leave their lovers'
arms to join their father at his devotions. The incongruity of
such a pattern did not seem to disturb them. Alone among
them, Princess Rothrud seems to have possessed a genuine lien
on the spirit.[10]

All those girls were educated far above the average. They had
the advantage of a high example set by their aunt at Chelles,
of two queens, Hildegard and Luitgard, of Alcuin and others
whose repute was never stained by a single scandal. But they
had a great Arnulfing for their father, and consistency had
never been a family trait among them. Again, for all his
affection and intimacy, that father stood on a high pinnacle,
the foremost sovereign in Europe. The crown and the sceptre
were a delight to wear and to hold.

The contradictions in his character seem well-nigh insoluble.
He loathed all manner of cheating and dishonesty, and yet he
refused to see that the dazzling stage of his court screened
intrigues, moral shabbiness and downright dishonesty. He had

all the details of his daily life governed by Church rules and acknowledged himself to be her humble servant; and yet his very obvious theocratic practices warred against all such submission. On occasions, such contradictions suggest the plight of an actor trying to learn the lines in a wholly unfamiliar language.

Yet Charlemagne was a genius, and all those contradictions became dwarfed to the very edge of insignificance once we realize that to govern his country and to heighten her honour came first and last with him.

*   *   *

Very much in the manner of his Merovingian predecessors, Charlemagne was incessantly 'on the move' all through the peace spells and in his wars. Wintry inclemencies never debarred him and the court had no choice but to follow their sovereign all over Frankland. Yet, at total variance with the Merovingian past, Charlemagne's comings and goings could not be compared with the onslaught of locusts.

For one thing, his domestic economy rested on a pattern which did not denude any part of the kingdom he visited. Ample supplies reached the royal household wherever it happened to be. For another, Charlemagne's passion for building led to many a grim keep or an uncomfortable farmhouse of the earlier days being turned into a palace. He had architects and other experts to carry out his wishes, but local labour had to be employed and paid sometimes in specie and sometimes in kind. Thus a villein's wife had something to put into her dinner pot and her children could enjoy some warmth through the winter months.

Not until the end of his life did Charlemagne settle down at Aachen, but he had loved it for years chiefly on account of its warm springs. By the beginning of the ninth century Aachen was the wonder city of Europe. Still, he had many other roofs to call his own and to delight in: Ingelheim on the Rhine, Quérzy-sur-Oise near Lâon, Paderborn in the conquered Saxon lands, Attigny in the Ardennes, Heristal near the Meuse, the cherished home of the early Arnulfings, Nijmegen on the Waal and others. Some palaces stood there when Charlemagne came into his own. Others were built by local labour, out of local materials. Any site chosen by him must be near a river or a lake because he loved swimming and bathing as much as, if not more than, hunting.

So the King came and went, his enormous household and his library following him, but the building of a new palace or the enlargement of an old one led to no urban development in the neighbourhood. Not even markets were held near the palace gates, and the hunger for city walls was not yet born.

Charlemagne's many palaces had to be immense not only because of the household. Ambassadors, officials, friends and the King's numerous kin had to find the sovereign wherever he happened to be. None of them could have been given shelter in a barn, and thus any palace of his must grow and expand to afford adequate room for all.

The two focal points of every palace were the chapel and the great hall. In the former, Charlemagne performed his daily duties of piety. In the hall he fed, dictated to his secretaries, heard his ministers' reports, entertained his friends, and gave formal audiences. At dinner and at supper, books were read aloud to him.

The great hall did not resemble the hall of the early Merovingian days when swords and axes were used at the least provocation, the flagged floor would run crimson with blood, and dogs howl and quarrel over the bones flung from the high table. The Carolingians had learned their manners. Knives and spoons were used to a purpose, dishes were brought ceremonially and, if there were no reading, music and singing were offered to the company.

The tapestries and mosaics of the hall were as nothing compared with the beauty lavished on the chapel. Home-bred talent and foreign genius were called upon to work all the details of gold, silver and brass, of cunningly woven hangings and multicoloured marble. There Charlemagne heard his daily Mass and assisted at the services, never failing to criticize the least shortcoming of the choir. For the rest, any palace of his had numberless bedrooms, passages, kitchens, store-rooms and pantries. In spite of the size, there could be little privacy

M

and much noise up and down the flagged passages. Great candles burnt in the hall, the chapel, and the King's private rooms. Elsewhere, the smoke from the rushlights mingled with the acrid smoke from great hearths.

A certain etiquette was followed, but it had nothing elaborate, and ambassadors from the East wondered at its simplicity. The Franks bowed to their King but did not bend their knees before him, and Charlemagne was known to detest the least sign of servility. 'You kneel to your Maker and none else.' Yet the simplicity of demeanour, inherited from their proud forebears, was now surrounded by grandeur and splendour.

The *Palatium* formed the enormous household. The head of the King's private chancery was always an ecclesiastic. There followed a crowd of secretaries, chamberlains, marshals, seneschals, counts of the Palace and butlers whose functions were far more important than those suggested by the modern use of the word. A Carolingian butler did not concern himself solely with table service. He trained the men newly entered on the King's service; he brought stuffs for hangings and bed-curtains, directed the work of the palace carpenters, kept an eye on what structural repairs were necessary and saw to it that the household and the King's guests were properly boarded and bedded.

Then there was the endless to and fro of the royal '*missi*', most of them men chosen by Charlemagne for loyalty, intelligence and honesty rather than high birth. Finally there came crowds of lesser serving fry – cooks, scullions, kitchen wenches, farmhands, grooms and errand boys.

The palace also had rooms for treasury officials who – with their coffers and rolls of parchment – had to follow the King all over the place. They received the taxes both in specie and in kind and the revenues from the royal demesnes. Their work could not have been particularly rewarding. The largest landowner in Europe, Charlemagne should have been the richest man of his day. He was not. Expenditure invariably galloped far ahead of the revenues – chiefly because of a generosity run mad. According to the contemporary sources the immense booty after the Avar war enriched Frankland in a

superficial sense only. It ended by depreciating the Frankish
specie and led to a sharp rise in prices.

Among all the palaces, Aachen stood to the forefront, a town
rather than a palace with its magnificent basilica, its colonnade,
its immense hunting grounds, its pleasances laid out by the
best horticulturists of the time. It was one palace after another
linked by galleries and courtyards, the tremendous roofage
sheltering thousands of people. Its warm medicinal springs
had attracted Charlemagne early enough, and towards the end
Aachen grew to be a home of his inmost heart.

The great hall, its floor of rare marble, its walls laid out with
bronze and gold, finely woven hangings in between, excited
the admiration of all visitors to Aachen, including the Greeks,
accustomed though they were to the splendours of Byzantine
palaces. The basilica, its dome crowned by an immense golden
ball,[11] had doors of solid brass, exquisitely carved choir stalls,
a cunningly patterned marble floor, and mosaics on its walls in
between tall candelabra of gold and silver studded with semi-
precious stones. There were no marble quarries in Frankland,
and the marble came from Italy at huge expense and labour.
Every square foot of the great building was cherished by
Charlemagne, who insisted that 'nothing dirty' was ever to be
brought in. With his faithful Einhard being [director of the
royal works, Charlemagne watched the flowering of his favourite
palace with the jealous eyes of a lover, and it pleased him to
hear that stories of its splendours were winged far beyond the
borders of Frankland. In North Africa and Asia Minor, to say
nothing of the neighbouring countries of Europe, men wove a
veritable Arabian Nights' story from the magnificence of the
environment created by a crowned giant who probably deserved
the title of *Stupor Mundi* to a higher degree than the Emperor
Frederick II.

Charlemagne lived in splendour, but the latter was no wall
separating him from his people. He was approachable to all,
but he never forgot what was due not to himself but to his high
office. On one occasion, when invited to dinner with a bishop,
Charlemagne saw that his host was being served first. The King
reined in his temper since, according to an ancient Frankish
usage, a guest should never appear dissatisfied, let alone angry.

But when a dish was set before him, Charlemagne would not eat and, the meal over, he bowed to his host and left the hall without waiting for the bishop's blessing.

*   *   *

It is again to Einhard that we are indebted for Charlemagne's portrait as well as for a graphic description of his ordinary day.[12]

Unlike his father, Pippin the Short, Charlemagne was immensely tall, heavy and strong, but his dignity of demeanour served him well in that it helped to lessen his bulk. He had an exceptionally clear voice but rather of too small a volume for so big a man. He loved its sound a little too much so that occasionally he lapsed into garrulity (*'ut etiam dicaculus appareret'*). In private he spoke his native German of Austrasia, but he was equally at home in the Neustrian Romance and in Latin, and could follow the speeches of Byzantine ambassadors, though his own spoken Greek was anything but fluent. His hair, delicately golden in his younger days, was silver-white by the time Einhard came to Aachen. Charlemagne was most particular about his hair and beard – always well-combed, flowing, beautiful, and even scented when some great moment asked for it.

He had a most winning smile and normally his expression was cheerful and happy (*'facie laeta et hilari'*). It was left to others to describe Charlemagne's temper. It flared up with the suddenness of summer lightning; he could not shout, but the stamping of his great foot brought terror even to his closest intimates, and the large blue eyes darkened to black and looked terrible.

All his life Charlemagne seems to have enjoyed an iron constitution, well-hardened by his habit of riding in all weathers hunting and swimming. About the only branch of knowledge he had no use for was medicine, and his court physicians could not have had a comfortable time when, towards the end, his health took to failing and he would refuse all their carefully prepared concoctions. His one panacea for all the known ailments of man was a very simple one: an empty stomach, he argued, was the surest means towards a quick recovery.

Except for ceremonial occasions, Charlemagne wore the ordinary Frankish clothes, such as were worn by the humblest

among his subjects; a shirt and drawers of linen, a brief red
tunic, linen hose cross-gartered by red leather thongs and rough
square-toed shoes. In winter, he would put on a fur jerkin over
the tunic. At other times the tunic would be covered by a
blue square-shaped cloak which all but reached his ankles in
front and behind and hung just above the knees at the sides.
When walking about the immense grounds of Aachen, Charlemagne like to carry a short stick of pear or apple wood heavily
knobbed with silver and gold. Winter and summer alike, he
slept naked as was the custom of the age. Einhard mentions
that the King preferred to take off his clothes even for a brief
rest after a meal.

All that simplicity vanished whenever ambassadors or foreign
guests came to Aachen. Then Charlemagne's plain oaken chair
was replaced by a golden throne with a crimson canopy. Gold
and silver platters and cups were set out on the tables draped
with fine white silk. Charlemagne appeared in a tunic of cloth
of gold, and the collar and hem of his rich mantle were studded
with gems. His shoes of soft green leather were embroidered
with pearls, and a broad golden girdle carried a bejewelled
sword. The golden crown set off his silver-white hair to
perfection. A great emerald buckle clasped his mantle on the
right shoulder, and there gleamed bracelets and rings on his
wrists and fingers. But the great occasion finished and the
guests gone, the first gentleman of Frankland found relief in
putting on his everyday clothes.

There were few things Charlemagne disliked as much as
outlandish fashions. Nothing except his courtesy to the Pope –
and that twice only – could persuade him to wear the long
Roman tunic, a flowing cloak and sandals.

In sharp contrast to his ancestors, he was most temperate in
drinking. He loathed drunkenness and though at his own table
wine and beer would be served in abundance few were the
members of the household who dared to get tipsy in his
presence. It goes without saying that drunkenness was a sore
on the body of Frankland, and Charlemagne tried to fight it as
zealously as he fought against ignorance, but his efforts were
hardly rewarded. The poor folk, whose means forbade the
purchase of wine, were content to get thoroughly inebriated on

home-made beer, cider and perry, whilst away from the great hall, the Palace of Aachen was certainly no temple of temperance.

As ran the custom in his generation, Charlemagne fed twice a day – dinner in the morning and supper at sunset with a light collation of fruit and bread served during his brief afternoon rest. At first glance, it might appear a meagre daily diet; but one dinner eaten by Charlemagne would have more than satisfied several people today. He was no glutton in the strict sense of the word, but his physique coupled with the enormous daily expenditure of energy demanded much. Einhard says that his ordinary dinner consisted of 'four courses, excluding the roast', which the King preferred to any other food, but each of the 'four courses' might well have meant several dishes – some of it eaten together. The Carolingian palate was not too fastidious about the mixing of flavours, and a fruit pasty, sweetened with honey and sharpened by spices, might well have been served and eaten together with a stuffed goose.

Yet, however prodigious Charlemagne's appetite, eating and drinking were not the only business at table. Whilst his body was being refreshed, his mind received its own nourishment. Many lectors were on duty during the meal, and books were read aloud, more often than not St Augustine's 'City of God', which to Charlemagne stood next to Holy Writ. Or again the Aachen minstrels would be summoned to sing the old, old lays handed down from a pagan past, or else a master of the Palace School might start a debate on theology, astronomy, or any other discipline taught at the school. Even a traveller of no particular standing might be invited to share his impressions of the wonders seen in alien lands – strange beasts who swam in the water and galloped on land, dragons with fiery tongues and flaming tails, the alarming colour of a wintry sky, a woman capable of chattering in several languages and unable to understand a single word said to her, and a prodigy of a year old infant who could discourse on the Grace of God. All those wonders were grist to the mediaeval imagination in the day when credulity knew no barriers.

But Advent, Lent and vigils of great feasts brought much annoyance to Charlemagne because of the rigours of fasting,

when one meal only was allowed and meat could not be eaten
every day. Charlemagne's cooks exercised their ingenuity to
the utmost by turning out attractive messes of pulse, fish and
vegetables, but he needed meat and argued that fasting
injured his health. There is no recorded evidence in any
sources, but Charlemagne, known to break more than one
commandment, could hardly be expected to keep the fasts.
True that neither boiled beef nor venison might then appear
in the great hall, but it is permissible to suppose that he might
have enjoyed some such liberty in his private rooms. There
were so many days of fasting, and it is rather incredible that
Charlemagne could have got through a day's work on a bowl of
porridge and some baked fish. Einhard is dutifully silent about
such very likely transgressions, and Notker[13] says that during
Lent the King's only meal was served at seven in the morning
after he had heard Mass and Lauds. A certain bishop once
took the King to task for dining so early. The unfortunate
prelate did not know that whether a strict fast was kept or not,
the royal temper usually got frayed towards the end of Lent.

For once Charlemagne reined in his anger and replied 'in
all humility' that, perhaps, the bishop's words were spoken
sensibly. Now he, the King, wondered if he might offer some
advice to the bishop, namely, that on a certain day he should
stay fasting until the very last member of the royal household
had been fed. The prelate had no choice but to agree.

Now Charlemagne and his immediate kin dined by themselves, the highest in the land waiting upon them. However
meagre and dull the Lenten fare, the meal took some time.
Once the King and his family had finished, those who had
served them sat down to their own dinner and, according to
the protocol, they were served by the counts of the Palace.
Next came the turn of army officers, masters and scholars of
the Palace School who were followed by the chief members of
the household. Finally, the lesser domestic fry came in for their
turn and often enough they did not break their fast until late
afternoon or evening. At the end, the unhappy bishop was all
but dying of hunger. On Easter Day Charlemagne said to him,
'Now perhaps you will understand that it is neither greed nor
whim making me dine at an early hour; but my care for all the

others. I must be the first at table, and were I to dine any later in Lent, my servants might have to wait for their food till midnight.'

Many of the stories related by Notker are sheer fantasy. Some few ring true, and that is one of them.

Charlemagne, used to crowds since his early years, loved the companionship of some few chosen friends, but purely social duties bored him exceedingly. He did not give frequent banquets, but so lavish was he both with the good cheer and the costly presents that the gentlemen of the exchequer were often anxious about the expenditure. Many others grumbled and argued that taxation would not be such a burden if the sovereign could learn to restrain his generosity. But nobody dared to complain in the open – the King's temper was known but too well.

If Charlemagne's presents were stupendous both in frequency and in value, so were his charities. He spent far more than he could afford on relieving the distress of the Christians in Syria, Palestine and Egypt. He was also in the habit of sending constant and costly gifts to the Pope personally and to St Peter's Basilica, because he nursed a deep devotion for the Apostle's shrine. Constantinople was not forgotten: King Offa of Mercia and King Alfonso of the Asturias were among those who often benefited by the Frank's generosity. The famous Harun-al-Raschid at Baghdad was in no need of succour but *his* presents had to be acknowledged in a manner best answering the dignity of the first sovereign in Europe.

Nearer at home there were Charlemagne's army commanders and their families, the scholars invited by him to Aachen, and his numerous '*missi*'. Finally, nobody who served him well but was amply rewarded. Smaller abbeys and priories finding themselves in straits could always count on royal assistance. And there were many purely private gestures of bounty – ranging from a turquoise ring or a silver goblet to a parcel of land or a few head of cattle.

Giving was a necessity to Charlemagne, and, childlike, he delighted in the many gifts made to him. Those were sent from all parts of the then known world.[14] He and his forebears had vowed to crush the iniquity of Islam, but Harun-al-Raschid and he were close friends – though the two men would never meet. From the East came unguents, spices, scents, fine silken stuffs and jewels in such profusion that it looked as though the East had been left bare for the enrichment of the West. There were also animals – housed in great cages all over the pleasure-grounds of Aachen – lions, bears, monkeys, and rarely coloured birds never before seen by the Franks. The very first elephant to come to Europe reached Aachen sometime in 802, a gift from Harun-al-Raschid, and the elephant, greatly cared for, lived for quite a few years in that incongenial climate. Such was his renown that his death came to be recorded by annalists.

Harun-al-Raschid was a genius in his choice of gifts. He sent tents of rainbow-coloured silk which, once they were set up, brought glory to the greyest autumn day; there were candelabra of finely chased silver inlaid with almandine and amethyst, and scents so delicate they might have been made in Paradise. There were exquisite trifles of jade, ivory and porphyry, and boxes and coffers of fragrant woods unknown in Europe. On one occasion the gentleman at Baghdad surpassed himself by sending Charlemagne a present voted by everybody to be a marvel of Eastern workmanship: it was a clock which rang out the hours. There were twelve tiny doors, each with a miniature platform in front, all round about the dial. As the clock struck the hour, the doors opened and twelve tiny, fully armoured men appeared, turned round, and vanished as soon as the clock had done striking, the doors closing on them. No human agency controlled those movements, it was pure magic and, though fierily pious prelates might frown at such a present from 'an infidel', Charlemagne delighted in it.

He had his own gifted goldsmiths and silversmiths, whose work was very fine, but they could not copy such oriental contrivances. However, there was one present that could be sent to Baghdad and greatly admired there: bolts of Frisian cloth, the weave never before seen in the East, blue, white, red, green and a soft pearly grey.

*　　*　　*

Charlemagne's temper has already been mentioned, and he did not always succeed in checking it. He lived in a cruel age, and there was a streak of cruelty in him, but it was his flaming temper which – on occasions – made him turn his back on common justice. Someone having told him that a certain count 'was indulging in immorality and kindred vices'. Charlemagne did not summon the man or have the case proved in any court. The count was immediately dispossessed of all his lands which were turned over to a neighbouring abbey.

Notker[15] tells a story about one Liutfrid, the foreman of builders at Aachen. The man had been suspected of defalcations, but nothing had ever been proved against him. He died suddenly and one of the marshals of the court ordered his home to be searched. Some gold was found, and Liutfrid's kin argued that it was the money he had hoarded for masses and candles for the repose of his own soul. In the end, the case came to Charlemagne, whose decision was swift and ruthless. The gold was to be distributed among the poor. 'No ill-gotten gains must be used to help his soul out of Purgatory.' To arrive at such a judgment on the feather-thin weight of suspicion alone argues an instability both of mind and heart.

In all truth, Charlemagne suggested a 'bundle of contradictions' so far as his private life was concerned – cruel and merciful, arrogant and humble, patient and impatient, wise and imprudent. Einhard[16] attributed the cruelty to Queen Fastrada's baneful influence, but the Verden massacre, Charlemagne's worst crime against his own kind, had taken place some years before his marriage to Fastrada. Moreover, had she exercised any influence over him, Charlemagne would certainly have ordered the execution of Pippin the Hunchback after the discovery of the conspiracy. Fastrada hated that unfortunate stepson of hers and she could not have been pleased when Charlemagne spared his life. Again, no other Saxon leader had caused him as much trouble as Widukind but, the surrender once made, all the trespasses were blotted out. He bore no grudge against his widowed sister-in-law for spreading calumnies against him in Lombardy, and yet he was capable of dictating a most cruel letter to Alcuin, his 'beloved master'. All in all, Charlemagne's private behaviour carries a stamp of the enigmatic.

*   *   *

Charlemagne's need for mistresses was purely physical. His need for friends possessed him wholly,[17] and Einhard did not exaggerate when he spoke of his patron's 'constancy' once anyone was 'joined to him by the link of friendship'. There was nothing he would deny them, and he 'wept bitterly' on learning about the death of Pope Adrian I.

Adalard and Wala, both grandsons of Charles Martel and Charlemagne's first cousins, were particularly close to him. Nor were they afraid of opening their minds to him, and there was a quarrel over the Lombard divorce, Adalard arguing that marriage was insoluble to any true Catholic. But the estrangement lasted for less than a year: by 772 the three men returned to the warmth of their earlier intimacy. When, at a later date, Charlemagne's second son, Pippin, was made King of Italy, his father chose the two brothers as tutors and counsellors of the boy.

Another great friend was Hildebald, Archbishop of Cologne, whom Charlemagne appointed Arch-chaplain at Aachen and who remained the royal confessor to the very end. Hugo, Count of Tours, of no high antecedents but an upright and gifted man, enjoyed Charlemagne's confidence to the full and was often employed on delicate diplomatic missions, particularly to Byzantium. Rarely enough would Charlemagne spare Hildebald who, in crude terms, so often proved a wall between the royal sinner and the anger of God, and Hildebald, accompanied by the able and patient Jesse, Bishop of Amiens, left Aachen in 811 on a long and hazardous journey to Byzantium there to argue the Western Emperor's case with Nicephorus, Emperor of the East.

At the Palace School Charlemagne's closest intimates were Alcuin, whose death in 804 brought a sharp grief, Theodulf of Orléans, the debonair Angilbert, Paul the Deacon, whose departure from Frankland in no way interfered with the affection Charlemagne had for him, and, finally, 'the dwarf', Einhard, whose loyalty was like a shoreless sea.

Those friendships were his daily bread and wine, enlarging his horizons and deepening his mind.

Charlemagne had many others, whose way of life did not permit frequent or lengthy sojourns at his palace, because they had great abbeys to rule. Yet he visited them, sought their counsel, and was gladdened by their letters. At the Abbey of Fulda, Sturm, who died in 779, Baugulf, who succeeded him and lived long enough to see his friend crowned Emperor, and, finally, Ratgart, who outlived him, were all intimates – not so much because of their piety but because of their learning. So was the venerable Archbishop of Lyons, Leidrad, who survived Charlemagne by two years, Wald and Haito, the two abbots of Reichenau, and Wizo, Archbishop of Trier.

All those and many more gave Charlemagne of their best, and he paid back in the same shining coin. They could follow the workings of his mind, shared his longing for a reformed Frankland, and did not consider as Utopian his vision of a united Christendom, all the forbidding frontiers vanishing into the shadowy past. Of course, there were many disagreements and acrid arguments. Charlemagne's terrible temper could not but break out on many occasions, but no friendship was ever irrevocably fragmented because of his anger. In broad terms, he considered friendship as a continuous and fruitful exchange of impressions, confidences, points of view and gifts.

In a sense, Charlemagne's circle of friends was a corollary to the Palace School. Most of the men closest to him were either scholars or soldiers, and it is hard to imagine that any among them would have wasted their time on telling their royal friend that rain was wet and honey sweet.

Charlemagne gave much, but he demanded just as much, if not more. His curiosity was a bottomless well. It was an insatiable curiosity of a Christian with a good deal of pagan leaven in him.

He was hungry to learn a little of just anything, no matter how small or even irrelevant it was to the high office he held. Theology was by no means the only stream to fill Charlemagne's pitcher. He was interested in all the disciplines known in his day. Astronomy and geography excited him. Among the treasures at Aachen were two tables of silver, their tops engraved with maps, and many were the moments of leisure Charlemagne devoted to their study. Ducuil, that Irish genius of geography and cosmography, taught him much.

The purely secular learning absorbed by Charlemagne fed

and deepened his faith. The great Creed he so ably defended at the Frankfurt Assembly of 794 was to him something of a plinth securely supporting the pillar of secular knowledge. The more he learned, the more fervently he believed. No more than anyone else among his contemporaries Charlemagne was capable of explaining why the faintest glimmer of light glancing over a concrete fact should have confirmed his faith in the great Abstract – the awful mystery of a Triune God and the unceasing Providence in the world. Frankland, together with other coutries, was cancered with many evils; life was a knotty hard business ribbed through and through with distress, hunger, injustice and disease, and one of the petitions in the Lord's Prayer seemed all too often unanswered since few people were delivered from one or other of the evils rampant in the world. The Devil was as real as God to the mediaeval man. Prompted by the Devil, Charlemagne kept stumbling into a multitude of trespasses, but in his better moments he knew them for such, and he felt certain that payment would be required of him after his death. Being an honourable debtor, he never belittled what penalties awaited him in Purgatory.

It is odd to think that, a convinced Christian as Charlemagne was, the pagan in him never died. Persecuting the heathen Saxons, felling their sacred trees, and trampling down their sanctuaries – Charlemagne none the less accorded all of it a reluctant recognition and felt a sneaking affection for the beliefs upheld by his remote forebears. Hence came his conviction that the German past should not be forgotten among his people. He saw it as a cradle which had once sheltered them and which must not fall into dust and decay. From this came his command for a collection of ancient epics and lays,[18] a command which was an unconscious recognition of ancestral claims far, far older than the Merovingian epoch. Those ancient songs lauded chieftains reared in grim forests, acquainted with peril and hardship from infancy, and waging fierce war on any neighbour and on nature. Later, they decided to leave the impenetrable forest fastnesses for the liberty of open spaces, and swept down, so many savages, to kill, burn and ravage whatever stood in their unmapped path. Still later, the wild movement over, they settled down and took to learning the bounty of the soil, and used their axes for other purposes than that of cleaving an enemy's head. Little by little they became reconciled to the land that nurtured them, but they guarded their sanctuaries from the least alien encroachment, and by their coming they brought refreshment to a stale and tired Europe.

Deep-seated ancestral memories must have stirred in Charlemagne when he sat listening to the minstrels. His son's foolish decision to have that collection destroyed was more than a gesture of piety – it was an absurdity and worse.

Taken all in all, Charlemagne's character remains an enigma. His occasional cruelty certainly answered the harsh temper of his day, but his gentleness did not belong to his century. His sexual backslidings were of little account at the time. From a larger point of view, all his qualities seem grounded within an integrity rare to find in his generation, a hatred of deceit, and a vision never betrayed by him. His sins of the flesh were many and grievous – but none of them had the strength to screen the light shining through all the years of his reign.

VIII

CAROLUS IMPERATOR

Since AD 446 the centre of imperial power had been on the shores of the Bosphorus, the great might and the immense wealth of Byzantium in ample accord with the highest dignity known to that day. Yet within less than three centuries the Byzantine power waned and her link with the West grew more and more tenuous. She was no longer able to afford adequate protection to her large possessions on the Italian peninsula, and the authority of the Exarch of Ravenna could hardly offset the depredations of the Lombards. From Rome plea after piteous plea for help against the aggressions from the North were all but left unanswered. The Empire failed to protect the *Imperium*.

The Arab sweep over land and sea dealt grievous wounds to the body of the Byzantine trade. The Bulgarian onslaughts grew in frequency and ferocity, and various nomadic tribes began menacing the northern borders of Byzantium. Her arm was too weak to deal with a single danger, let alone many. At home, conditions worsened from year to year. Corruption was cancering every tissue of public life, there were venal favourites crowding round about the throne, the army began dictating both to Church and to State, and, finally, violence, which included murder, became a common-place, until the iconoclastic storm cleft the country in two.

Now, all of it, however indirectly, prepared the way for the great and puzzling event of Christmas morning 800. The iconoclastic tumult had been stilled but not quelled. In Constantinople, violence, however cloaked by piety, still trod its apparently uncontrollable measure, and the situation, its coil and curve all but incomprehensible to the Western mind, still further deepened the already existing alienation of West from East. In 754, under the Isaurian's successor, the Emperor Constantine V, a synod was summoned to settle the matter of images. At the Patriarch's wish, invitations were sent out to the Pope and other bishops in the West, and all of them refused to come, conscious as they were that the matter so inflaming the Greek thought was not of the least concern to them. The synod ended by condemning the images and statues, its findings rather heavily leaning towards the ancient Hebraic idea, i.e., that God and His servants should never be subjected to pictorial representation. The Western Church refused to commit herself, and the Greeks labelled the Western hierarchy as idol-worshippers unfit to teach the pure doctrine to their people.

Little by little, the ecclesiastical divergences came to join the purely secular disagreements, so much so that at the end not even an able theologian could distinguish between the two.

The power of the Lombards was broken for good, and the Byzantine overlordship was tottering up and down the Italian peninsula. The papal territories grew in size and importance. The link between Rome and Frankland gained in vigour and in colour, and Charlemagne's victories as well as his achievements at home caused him to be acclaimed the first sovereign in Europe.

Most adroitly did he labour to avoid the least gesture of enmity towards Byzantium, its golden throne remaining a symbol to him. His eldest daughter was promised as bride to Constantine VI, the Isaurian's great-grandson and the son of a beautiful Athenian lady rather ironically called Irene, because matters of peace were never part of her covenant. Her son being a minor at his succession, the Empress-Mother became regent. Under her, a professed icon-worshipper, the icono-clastic fires were dampened down.

The Franco-Greek betrothal was in the end broken off for a multitude of obscure reasons. There was no open rupture between East and West, but a gulf began yawning more and more widely. Already in 781 the Papal See severed all relations with Byzantium. The humiliating treaty the Greeks signed with the Bulgarians led to much contempt in the West. The Greeks, who attended the Frankfurt Assembly in 794, created a disturbance about the double procession of the Holy Ghost and accused Western theologians of ignorance as well as heresy. So hot-tempered were the Byzantine delegates that the Franks felt there was no ground left for a single sound argument, and the Western sense of logic, a legacy from the great Roman past, was outraged by its lack among the Greeks.

Gradually, with one disagreement giving birth to another, a climate was created where it became perilously easy to believe that the matter of Europe meant very little to the inheritors of the ancient imperial dignity. The angry scenes at Frankfurt were not wholly forgotten in 797 when the West received the shattering news from Byzantium: the Empress Irene, jealous of her son's popularity, had had him blinded, and had seized the imperial sceptre for herself.

The age was cruel enough. Cruelty, as such, was more or less taken for granted all over Europe, but for a mother to have thus mutilated her first-born, purposely commanding the executioners to carry out the horror in the very room in the palace where she had borne him, stirred the most hardened conscience into revulsion. Again, it warred against all decency and tradition for a woman to style herself 'Basileus'.

From one end of Europe to another people were asking themselves whether any honest recognition could be given to a female usurper of the ancient title.

Unfortunately, the one voice which might have helped to resolve the problem was by then stilled for ever. Pope Adrian I had died at Christmas 795; his successor was Leo III, a man of obscure origins but of noted saintliness, and his voice would not have impressed anyone. Moreover, he enjoyed but little popularity even in Rome. His election was in perfect conformity with the Church Canons, but it did not please some of the high-born kin of Adrian I who had rather hoped to see a nominee of their own ascend the papal throne.

Adrian I would have been the first to rebuke his cousins for the scandal they created. A conspiracy against Leo was shaped quickly enough but no opportunity for action came until the spring of 799 when Leo III, riding to make his devotions at an ancient sanctuary, was attacked – and that in broad daylight – by hired ruffians, pulled off his horse, most roughly manhandled,

N

menaced with mutilation, and cast into prison to await his trial, the Roman nobility accusing him of perjury, venality and adultery. It was fortunate for Leo III that some emissaries from Aachen happened to be in Rome at the time. They succeeded in rescuing the pontiff and eventually brought him to Charlemagne, then staying to his palace at Paderborn in the Saxon lands.

A tumult broke all over Rome once they learned of the Pope's escape. Throwing all law and precedent to the winds, they declared St Peter's throne to be vacant, though nobody dared to open the preliminaries of an election. Meanwhile, the charges against Leo III were repeated again and again until even a humble fishmonger clamoured for the Pope to be brought back and face his trial.

Far away, first at Paderborn and then at Aaxhen, Leo III stayed as the King's guest. Charlemagne, having heard the pitiful story from the Pontiff himself, reflected upon it together with his councillors and then told the Pope that the matter could not rest there but that he, the King of the Franks, would see to it that no injustice was done to the Pope. It was rather an ambiguous answer to make, but Leo III, aware that he could trust the King, seemed satisfied.

That happened in the late summer of 799.

*   *   *

One of the most repellent women in history might occupy the Imperial throne and give audiences, her fearfully stained hands holding the jewelled sceptre and the glittering globe surmounted by a golden cross, but Irene's usurpation of sovereignty, however horrible its manner, in no way interfered with the concept of '*imperium*'. Though greatly changed since the days of ancient Rome, the idea was still alive in the European mind. It was something like a warmth coming from an apparently cold hearth, a star of justice and strength perceived however dimly on a winter's night, a remote vision of safety and protection which had been and might come again. The imperial writ ran no longer in Italy, and Spain and Britain did not know it either. Many roads and forts constructed by the genius of Roman engineers had fallen into decay all but beyond repair. The very language once heard in the Forum had grown clumsy and debased. But much remained in the thought and in the memory. Breaths of the Roman Law informed many modern codes, and from the ruined grandeur of Provincia, to give but one example, came reminders of a legacy no barbarian influx could engulf. An emperor holding his court in remote Byzantium was little more than an outlandish name to an ordinary man in the West. The office he held still kept its magic.

In Charlemagne's own mind, richly and continuously nourished by Augustine's 'City of God', *imperium* stood as an image of a united body of the faithful in this world, in somewhat cruder forms something of a preparatory school for the infinitely wider marches of Eternity.

Of course, such an idea was wholly Utopian. In the first place, no *imperium* could include the whole of Europe geographically. Charlemagne had indeed hoped to conquer Spain and had failed. Neither Britain nor Ireland ever came within his compass, still less so Scandinavia, unknown except for the southern borders of Denmark. Charlemagne was in no position to command the allegiance of such Christians as lived in Muslim countries, and he must have been aware that his image lacked universality.

In modern terms, his authority included no more than France, the Low Countries and Luxembourg, East and West Germany, Switzerland, Austria, Hungry and Italy, the latter with the exception of imperial and papal possessions.

Yet, however incomplete and even fantastic the image, the fact remained that Charlemagne stood out as the first sovereign in the eighth century world and the only one to desire unity and to pray for it. Neither the Heptarchy in Britain nor the tangled relationships of the Muslim rulers on the Iberian Peninsula created a climate likely to foster the mere beginnings of such a scheme, though it should be admitted that the event of Christmas morning 800 ended by giving Charlemagne a misnomer. He could never be truly considered Emperor of the West.

The contemporaries, however, refused to be troubled by geographical and national subtleties. In their eyes, Charlemagne alone stood out among all the other rulers, and it was unfair to withhold the supreme dignity from him.

Pope Leo III's stay in Frankland proved most opportune. Little by little, discussions on 'the papal case' began yielding pride of place to a different scheme, and a school of thought came into being, with Alcuin for its chief exponent. The sources are silent on the point, but it is difficult to believe that the King knew nothing of such discussions, particularly as the subject soon enough found its way into Alcuin's correspondence.

Arno of Salzburg, Candidus, pupil and close friend of Alcuin, Hildebald of Cologne, Fridugis, now Head of the Palace School, to name but a few, travelled from Aachen to Tours and back again. Inevitably, their discussions reached a point where '*imperium*' and Frankland would be welded together. Here, theocracy became so interwoven with autocracy as to seem one with it, an aspect which could not have appeared pleasant to the exiled Pope and, most likely, it would have been avoided in his presence.

But to Charlemagne such an idea would come clothed in a familiar language. Nobody round about him at Aachen had the least doubt that the imperial sceptre should have been held by him, the power of Byzantium all but a reed to the sturdy oak of his own right. But the King would not commit himself even when Alcuin's letters began striking a note of sheer lyricism.[1]

'Happy is the nation rejoicing in such a ruler . . . your right hand holding the sword of piety, you purify and protect the Church of God . . . with the sword held in your left hand, you defend [her] from the onslaughts of infidels . . . [for] there is the authority of the Vicar of Christ . . . [and] there is the lay power in Constantinople . . . [and] there is the third authority – your sovereignty by which the Lord . . . has appointed you ruler of Christian people, your strength . . . more exalted in dignity and more renowned in wisdom . . . all the hopes of Christ's Church rest upon you alone . . .'

If Charlemagne ever answered that letter, the reply has not come down to us, but it must have given him food for thought – 'there is the lay power in Constantinople'. Irene was an usurper; she might die of some fever, or be poisoned, or merely deposed, and the Greek church, statesmen and army would lose no time in electing her successor . . .

Many shared Alcuin's conviction. Still, there rang not a few dissenting voices. Among them, Adalard, Abbot of Corbie and Charlemagne's cousin, argued that, once there were two holders of the supreme title, the essential idea of *'imperium'* would be corrupted and probably vanish in the end. In principle, Adalard and those who shared his view certainly had a case, but the moment was not very happily chosen since in 799 Irene still sat on the throne and, though the Western mind refused to admit her to be *'basileus'*, yet nobody could ignore her occupation of the imperial seat, and Charlemagne may well have endorsed his cousin's opinion.

Meanwhile, Pope Leo III, having discussed his own affairs with the King, decided that it was time for him to return and discover if there were any change in the Roman pulse. Precautions were taken: the Pope left Frankland in the company of Count Hugo of Tours and surrounded by a formidable Frankish contingent of men under arms.

They entered Rome, no hostile mob greeting them. The rebellion against Leo had been quelled, but the slanderous stories about him still travelled from street to street, from village to village, the Pope's ill-wishers alleging that he had committed both perjury and adultery and been guilty of much venality. Yet the presence of a big Frankish escort checked the least expression of hostility, and there was no longer any talk about the papal throne being vacant, through people had not given up discussing the trial to come.

From his cell at Tours, Alcuin argued most vehemently that nobody was qualified to sit in judgment on the Vicar of Christ,[2] but all his vehemence went for nothing. The majority of Charlemagne's counsellors maintained that, after so terrible a scandal, the Pope should not be denied an opportunity of refuting all the charges laid at his door, and such was the decision reached in the end.

Leo III remained in Rome, adequately guarded by his Frankish escort, but there were no more attempts to kidnap him. The common folk thought it wiser to keep aloof from all conspiratorial rumours. The nobility and members of the

Curia were looking forward to the King's arrival when, with all due observance of law and ceremonial, the charges made against the Pope would undergo a thorough investigation. The chief conspirators and their adherents were in prison.

Rome waited; the tension heightened, but Charlemagne did not appear. In the spring of that year, 800, he made an extensive tour of his dominions, glad to take ample advantage of there being no summer campaign: Frankland was cradled in peace all through that year.

His travels over, Charlemagne made a short stay at Aachen and then joined his wife, Liutgard, at St Martin's Abbey in Tours. His three sons followed him there. So did Hildebald of Cologne, Arno of Salzburg, Theodulf, Jesse of Amiens, and many others, all welcomed by Alcuin. St Martin's became a court in little. The Queen was ill. Ostensibly, Charlemagne stayed on because she needed him. There were many conferences, their resolutions and findings left unrecorded by secretaries, but it was an open secret that once the Queen was recovered, the King would go to Rome there to settle the Pope's case. The second and far more important purpose of the journey was known to all Charlemagne's intimates, but nobody mentioned it.

Queen Liutgard did not recover. Many Masses were said for her, many relics brought to her bedside, many candles burnt at St Martin's shrine for her release from the illness which left the physicians bewildered. Released she was indeed from all the burdens of weary, ailing flesh. She died at the beginning of June 800, the best loved of her husband's four queens.[3]

A hush fell over the lovely gay city. The appointed requiems sung, preparations were started to take Liutgard to St Denys for burial. Now nobody mentioned the journey to Rome. The King lingered at St Martin's until everything was ready, and he succeeded in making Alcuin come with him on the sad pilgrimage. They left Tours for Orléans, and then reached Paris where the Abbot and community of St Denys were awaiting them. The funeral over, Charlemagne went to Aachen, Alcuin glad to be his companion.[4]

It was a dark and apparently aimless summer for the once

again widowed King. They expected him to choose some nobly born Frankish girl for his fifth wife, but he never again led a woman to the altar. The death of Liutgard had smitten him hard, and Alcuin forgot his own weariness in trying to ease his friend's desolation.

Charlemagne was grief-held but he remembered that he did not belong to himself and that the business of governing must go on, whatever the ravages of one's heart. Since 800 was a year of peace, the National Assembly, usually held in early spring, was summoned in the late summer at Mainz.

There the King told his people that he was about to go to Rome – to settle the case of the Pope, to punish the conspirators and, finally, to quell a revolt started by Grimoald, Duke of Beneventum. A mutiny in Beneventum, earlier considered as an expensive nuisance, was this time regarded as a gift from heaven in that it lent a good reason for an immense Frankish host, led by Pippin, Charlemagne's second son, being sent ahead of the King. In the rear of the army came several wagons laden with gifts and victuals for the journey.

August was nearly over; Pippin and his host had gone, but Charlemagne still lingered in Frankland. Louis, the King of Aquitania, had returned to his own country, and Alcuin was back at St Martin's at Tours. Charles, the King's eldest son, stayed on at Aachen, ready to cross the Alps with his father, and there was much excitement in the female quarters of the Palace, Charlemagne having declared that his four daughters were to accompany him to Rome.

He wished for yet another companion, but the wish was denied him.[5] Alcuin, all but worn out by his journey to Paris, Aachen and back to Tours, pleaded his age and lack of competence to deal with the papal case. He, Alcuin, would much rather stay at Tours there to pray for St Martin's help in prospering the King's journey (. . . *apud sanctum Martinum vestrum iter adiuvare* . . .). Some of Alcuin's pupils, however, went to Rome, Candidus among them, and Charlemagne, unable to enjoy the companionship of his 'dearest teacher', insisted on Einhard joining him. To that circumstance we owe one of the most hotly disputed paragraphs in Einhard's biography.

Everything was ready, but the King seemed in no hurry to start on what would prove to be his last visit to Rome. Even when at last they had crossed the Alps and reached Ravenna, Charlemagne lingered there, to engage a few mosaicists to come and work at Aachen. He also stopped at Monte Cassino, though Paul the Deacon was no longer alive. All along the journey, the Frankish theologians, who were with the King, discussed the various aspects of the papal case. The matter of 'imperium' seemed to have been dropped into limbo.

Not till the end of November 800 did Charlemagne and his retinue reach the Campagna, Leo III meeting them at Nomentum (modern Mentana) some 15 miles north of Rome. It was a moment of great honour, surrounded by the customary Roman ceremonial, the Pope and the King conferring for some time in the privacy of a tent, all their intimates being excluded.

The affair of the accusations against Leo III took about a month to settle. Nearly all the noted theologians of the day, Ruculf and Theodulf of Orléans among them, were gathered together. The conspirators against the Pope were formally charged with slander, sacrilege and violence. They repeated their accusations of perjury, venality and adultery. The law demanded that several witnesses should be brought to confirm the charges, but the conspirators were unable to produce one. More was not expected of them. They were ready to unsay all the slanders and to make fit reparation for sacrilege and violence, but they were given no chance. The vast hierarchical assembly unanimously declared that none could sit in judgment on the Vicar of Christ.[6]

On the 23rd December, in St Peter's Basilica, crowded from the narthex to the sanctuary, the Pope, holding a book of the Gospels in his right hand, mounted the pulpit – but not for the purpose of preaching. He solemnly swore 'before God, the angels and Saint Peter' that he was entirely innocent of all the charges laid at his door, adding that nobody had compelled him to give that oath.

Charlemagne was present, and he may well have thought that the scene was somewhat in the nature of an anticlimax since a great hierarchical body had already delivered its opinion about the case.

Anyway, the apparent purpose of the King's visit to Rome was over. Naturally, nobody expected him to start on the homeward journey on Christmas Eve, and it heightened the people's festive sense to know that their overlord would for once keep his Christmas among them. The revolt in Beneventum was crushed, and Pippin, flushed with yet another triumph, could join his father in Rome.

The sources are silent, but the Roman grape-vine must have been kept very busy through those winter months. A coronation is not a matter of a meal to be prepared at a moment's notice as it were. Its details must have occupied the Roman clerics and lay officials for many weeks before Charlemagne's arrival, and the matter would have involved many labouring folk as well. Aachen would have heard of it, and Charlemagne must have given his consent to receive the imperial title.

There had been much reluctance. Adalard of Corbie was by no means the only Frank to argue that, the imperial throne being occupied, his cousin had no right to the dignity. Charlemagne's own reluctance was chiefly fostered by his anxiety lest the mere architecture of a Western '*imperium*' would lead to a breach and worse with Byzantium. Theodulf and Alcuin would argue that Constantinople was in no position to declare war on the West, but the argument did not lessen Charlemagne's apprehensions. To be at war with Byzantium was by no means the only evil he strove to avoid. There might be indignities falling upon his fair and honourable repute, and accusations of choosing to wear an impostor's clothes.

*   *   *

St Peter's Basilica of the Carolingian era was certainly not the one of today. None the less, it was enormous, and most lavishly decorated with multicoloured marbles and mosaics, and many precious gifts of kings and queens 'left to the honour of St Peter' at the end of each pious pilgrimage. The apostle's shrine and the great sanctuary dazzled the eye with their profusion of gold and silver candelabra, fine silken stuffs studded with pearls and other gems. Much of that splendour had come from Frankland. The Merovingians had been lavish enough, but Charlemagne's largesse surpassed them all.

That Christmas morning in 800 the Basilica was crowded with the biggest congregation ever assembled in its walls. Cleric and layman, waiting for Mass to begin, talked about a marvellous event of the previous day, when one Zacharias, a priest in Charlemagne's service, newly returned from Jerusalem, had presented the King with the keys of the Holy Sepulchre as a gift from the Patriarch, together with a most significant message – the King of the Franks was to be known as 'the Protector of the Holy Places'.

The news spread joy, pride and contentment, and that not only among the Franks. The Romans lost no time in claiming their share in the honour. Once again, the great bulwark of 'Pax Romana' seemed a reality, and the pleasure of the Romans was deepened at the sight of Charlemagne dressed in the traditional Roman garb – a wide, flowing cloak worn over a long tunic, and begemmed sandals.

The entire city was caught into a mood of rejoicing and feverish expectancy, and long before dawn, crowds of common folk, aware they would never get admittance into the Basilica, milled up and down in the neighbourhood, hoping for a glimpse of the King, his two sons and four daughters.

By daybreak, there would hardly have been room for a snowflake to fall on St Peter's floor, so full were the huge nave and four aisles. There were Lombards, Romans, Franks, Spaniards and Sicilians. There were some English and Irish worshippers too, and a number of Greeks, but members of the Roman nobility and all the officials of the city attracted most attention by the richness of their jewels and the assured pride of their manner. Rome was indeed 'Mater omnium Christianorum'. Equally, Rome was their very own city, her beginnings infinitely older than Christianity.

The Mass began, Charlemagne, with his family behind him, kneeling in the sanctuary.

The service over and the blessing given, the Pope lifting a gold crown from the altar, turned, and placed it on the King's head, the entire congregation shouting three times: 'life and victory to Charles Augustus, crowned by God, peace-loving and great Emperor of the Romans' ('Carolo Augusto a Deo coronato, magno et pacifico, Imperatori Romanorum, vita et victoria').

The shouting over, Leo III prostrated himself at Charlemagne's feet and kissed the hem of his cloak in accordance with the Byzantine ceremonial.

Einhard was present, and his words, however often misunderstood and misinterpreted, carry no ambiguity[7] '. . . he received the title of Emperor, which he so disliked at first that he affirmed (*'ut affirmaret'*) he would not have entered the church that day . . . if he could have foreseen what the Pope meant to do', and many years later Notker Balbulus[8] wrote that ' . . . [the Pope] declared [Charlemagne] to be Emperor . . . Now [he] had no thought of what was coming and though he could not reject [it] . . . he shewed no gratitude on receiving the new title'.

The idea that Charlemagne knew nothing about his coming coronation is as likely as a walnut growing on an apple tree. The concept of *'imperium'* had been discussed both with the Pope and with his Aachen councillors. The key to Einhard's narrative lies in the words, ' . . . if he could have foreseen what the Pope meant to do' ('. . . *si pontificis consilium praescire potuisset'*). It was just the fact of *him* being crowned by Leo III which struck Charlemagne as an unwarranted encroachment upon his theocratic stand. To have the imperial crown given to him was something bordering on an insult because his own hands should have placed it on his head.

That on its own came as a challenge to Charlemagne's pride, but there were many other reasons to explain his reluctance. He knew that Europe was ready to acclaim his new dignity, but Europe was not the entire world, and Charlemagne's firm grasp on logical issues would have prevented him from accepting the title 'Emperor of the West' as a reality. Byzantium refused to recognize a dignity bestowed by a bishop of Rome, and Irene still sat on the imperial throne. To quote the late Previté-Orton,[9] '. . . surely the method and the illegality of the act . . . displeased [Charlemagne]. It is clear . . . that Byzantine ceremonial was anxiously observed and Byzantine recognition persistently sought by him. He wished to be Roman Emperor as far as legal forms could make him, not a barbaric usurper of another's title.'

Not for eleven years would Byzantium concede the right for

Charlemagne to be called '*Basileus*'. Irene was gone, but her successors stood firm and addressed him as '*Rex*'. From Einhard we know that Charlemagne bore it all very patiently and avoided all friction.[10] Einhard's editor, Jaffé, quotes two of Charlemagne's letters, one to the Emperor Nicephorus and the other to Michael Rangabe, calling them each in turn 'beloved brother',[11] and sending legates with costly presents, but Charlemagne's 'beloved brothers' showed neither affection nor understanding, and stubbornly continued calling him '*Rex Francorum*', and not till the end of 811 did Byzantium's obduracy shew signs of weakening, and that for no other reason than that the Emperor Michael Rangabe stood in sharp need of Frankish help against the Bulgarians. Even so the recognition had to be paid for by Charlemagne abandoning his claims on the Venetian archipelago and some cities along the Dalmatian coast.

On the first Sunday in January 812, the Litany being sung at St Sophia's, Charlemagne was prayed for as '*Basileus*', and his legates were treated with the deference and ceremonial due to imperial ambassadors.

Yet the Greek recognition did not wipe out the initial illegality, whatever the contemporary jurists might say or think about it. Charlemagne had been '*primus inter reges*' for many years, and the coronation did not add anything to his stature. In territorial terms, his '*regnum*' equalled his '*imperium*', but the importance of his coronation had nothing to do with geographical boundaries. It was at once a return and a step forward; a return to the great reaches of imperishable culture left by Rome and a step towards a deeper acceptance of a Western way of life. The cleft between East and West, widening year by year and century by century, was by no means limited to a theological divergence. There were differences in every sphere of public and private life. Such differences between East and West occasionally met one another, borrowed here a line, there a point of view, a term pertaining to any discipline known to the Middle Ages, and those were indeed happily coloured occasions, but the essence of life in the West remained true to its cradle. The very structure of the latter was unknown to the East.

There is a deep significance in Einhard's remark[12] that soon after his assumption of the imperial title, Charlemagne became aware of a multitude of defects in the national legislature. He had already done something towards achieving a semblance of uniformity, and that had not been enough. Now he decided to reconcile all the differences ('. . . *discrepantia unire*') and ordered that all the different laws should be duly collated and written down. That work, however, was not finished at his death.

And it is equally significant that he encouraged the study of the great Roman jurists.

'*Ius*' was to him the true heartbeat of an empire and, Teuton as he was, Charlemagne dreamt of the several rills of ancient tribal laws and customs flowing into the deep sea of the Roman legislation. That, however, would have meant a life-time of work, and he had neither an Ulpian nor a Cicero at Aachen.

In larger terms, the imperial dignity meant a step forward towards a united Europe where the Byzantine writ ran no longer. The recognition accorded by the Emperor Michael Rangabe carried the sense of an anticlimax. More than two centuries were to pass before the rupture of 1054 would establish two different identities of East and West – not only in church matters but through all the social strata, but '*Carolus Imperator*' stood for a bulwark and a banner, an answer to many a question asked during his reign.

IX

THE SUNSET

The Empress Irene was deposed by the army in 802, and one Nicephorus, a man of no high beginnings, succeeded her, but no change of heart came with the change of rulers. Byzantium continued to ignore the coronation of Charlemagne, and for many years all the official documents continued to address him as 'King of the Franks' ('*Rex Francorum*').

It was, however, different in Europe and in the Muslim world, too. Italy felt particularly triumphant. Britain and Ireland welcomed an *Imperium* far less remote than Byzantium and far stronger both in arms and in influence. From Baghdad, Harun-al-Raschid sent an embassy carrying congratulations and rare costly presents. Charlemagne had been crowned in Rome, but the focal point of Europe was Aachen, and nobody dreamt of disrupting its right to pre-eminence.

The imperial dignity had been assumed by Charlemagne quietly enough, but from now on diplomats – not excluding the Greeks – received in audience could hardly escape the consciousness of a heightened rhythm at Aachen, a more pronounced and detailed emphasis on the splendour of such occasions, and a slightly more complicated protocol. Yet, though he had been crowned Emperor in strict accordance with the Byzantine observance, Charlemagne had no use for the exaggerated servilities of the court in Constantinople where the etiquette was well-nigh oriental with its numberless obeisances and prostrations, and where the duty paid to the Emperor all but raised him to the level of a god, a conception not only alien but revolting to the Frankish mind.

Charlemagne was there wholly at one with his people. He loved and understood the Byzantine art. He invited Greek

artists and scholars, too, to work at Aachen, and it greatly
pleased him to see the Frankish imagination assimilating and
interpreting Byzantine motifs in ivory, silver, gold and rare
wood. Beyond that he did not go. He regarded the imperial
title not as a stepping stone to global domination but rather
as a responsibility and a lessened distance between the many
imperfections of life upon earth and the shining gates of a city
not built by hands.

That particular viewpoint explains the heightened tempo of
his activities in the field of legislation. We have already seen[1]
that, on assuming the imperial crown, Charlemagne 'became
aware of several defects in the legal systems in use among his
people . . .', but Einhard might have added that Charlemagne
had been conscious of it all through his reign, and it is something of an understatement for his biographer to say that 'nothing was done except a few capitularies and even those were
incomplete'.[2] It would have been more in accord with reality
to admit that Charlemagne and his advisers were all too often
hampered in their efforts by the greed, venality and laziness of
local officials. To quote Previté-Orton, '. . . in nothing is
Charlemagne's resolve to civilize his government and people . . .
shewn more clearly than in his perpetual legislative activity . . .'[3]
and the use of the word 'perpetual' is no exaggeration.

The focal point of all those measures was the absorption of
the old Teutonic law into the *Lex Romana*, the study of the latter
being greatly encouraged by Charlemagne both at Aachen and
at Orléans where it was taught by Theodulf, the most capable
jurist in the Emperor's service, yet the ancient Teutonic law
could not be assimilated in its entirety. For one thing there
were too many varieties of it, with custom being considered as
binding as law. For another, all the separate systems regarded
an individual only in so far as he happened to be within
the '*Sippe*' (Blood relationship), the ethnological heart-beat of a
tribe. The Salic Law, introduced by Clovis in AD 500, was not
really concerned with uniformity. In Charlemagne's own day
there remained the Bavarian, Riparian, Belgic and Allemannian codes. In the South, the old *Provincia* of the Roman days,
a certain *Breviarium Alarici* was in force, a somewhat untidy
abridgment of the Theodosian Code.

To modify and finally to work all these different systems into a unity of theory and practice was no easy task. The sense of the *Sippe* had by no means gone from Frankland. She was now part of an Empire – but she was also pledged to a far older dispensation, its comprehension all the more demanding for having been delivered by word of mouth from one generation to another. The imperial idea was certainly dazzling, but its very splendours created a distance in the Frankish mind. The tribal idea, however inarticulate they might be about it, was as familiar as the hearth stone. It had found its way into the least important detail of daily life, and four centuries of Christian observance had not dislodged it.

Charlemagne knew that well, and he was determined that the uniformity he had so much at heart should not be purchased by a wholesale abandonment of ancient Teutonic laws. Sometime before 800, a commission headed by Theodulf had begun the work. The National Assembly held in the autumn of 802 proved that Theodulf of Orléans and his helpers had not wasted the years.

A number of customaries, hitherto handed down orally were written down, collated, and subjected to a rigorous revision. The available text of the Salic Law was edited authoritatively and brought closer to the social drifts of the ninth century. True that a great many capitularies were left 'imperfect', but the volume of legislation was so massive that lacunae could hardly be avoided, and it should be remembered that the work produced at the Assembly dealt not only with crime but with every detail of the national economy – the upkeep and repair of bridges and roads, testamentary laws, customs dues, tolls and taxes, harbour and market dues, licences to sell grain, cloth and wine, and the law governing a bride's dowry. The sale of slaves, horses and cattle was hedged about with many regulations. Prices were legally determined, and nobody, with the exception of inn-keepers, was allowed to trade at night. No exports of grain were now permitted during spells of shortage, let alone famine, and no wine might be sold before vintage time.

Two details should here be emphasized. The first was the introduction of Poor Law into Frankland. Almsgiving had always been practised, particularly by religious houses. Now relief of the poor and the dispossessed ceased to depend on charity and became obligatory. All men of substance, both cleric and lay, had to contribute to the poor rate, the amount of the latter to be determined by the count.

The second point could hardly have pleased the important lawyers who wrested a livelihood out of testamentary disputes. Quarrels over wills were as commonplace as snow in December. A dispute could arise and continue for many years to fill a pettifogging lawyer's pouch because of a misspelt word, an ambiguous expression, an abruptly broken off enumeration of a testator's goods and chattels. Sometimes a will would be rejected by the next of kin on the very convenient pretext that the testator did not really mean what he had put in. There were many cases of forgeries, and two testaments by one and the same man meant a veritable gold mine to the jurists.

It was Charlemagne who asked for Alcuin's advice on the general validity of testamentary dispositions. Alcuin could hardly be called a trained jurist, but he worked at the problem most conscientiously. In the end, his findings carried no ambiguity:[4] on a testator's death, his will must stand (*'omnimodo firmitatem obtinuit'*).

802 meant a great step forward, the chief architect of all the legal reforms being Theodulf of Orléans, and the landscape certainly suggests as orderly and rewarding a pattern as could be expected at the time. Yet Theodulf's letters, reports and satirical verses[5] afford ample evidence that the Emperor's judges all over Frankland had small use of directives set out in the capitularies, and lesser officials misinterpreted the law as it pleased them. Inn-keepers being allowed to sell wine and food after sunset, what was to prevent a smith entering a tavern and offering his wares to the inn-keeper's customers – always so long as a certain share of the profit travelled down the official channel? Theodulf and others like him called it venality, bribery and worse. Unimportant officials would be dismissed here and there, but such dismissals failed to eradicate the anomaly of a law being broken in its very enforcement.

* * *

It was in 806 that Charlemagne committed one of the greatest anomalies of his reign. Unity had been his principle, gospel and banner from the beginning, but now the inbred loyalty to the Frankish tradition made him betray the policy to which he had once dedicated himself so wholly and fervently. He divided his dominions among his three legitimate sons born of Queen Hildegard – Charles the Younger, Pippin, King of Italy since his infancy, and Louis of Aquitania. The instrument of inheritance gave Charles Frankland and the Saxon lands; to Pippin's share fell Bavaria and Schwabia, and Louis was to be ruler of Burgundy and of the Spanish Mark. No single clause of that remarkably odd document made even a remote allusion to the question of imperial succession. Logically speaking, Charles the Younger, being the first born, should have been named as Emperor on his father's death, but logic was nowhere when compared with the loyalty to tradition. It is doubtful that Charlemagne would have followed anyone's counsel in the matter. His dearest teacher, Alcuin, was dead by that time, and Alcuin reverenced autocracy to an extent forbidding him to question a decision of importance taken by an autocrat.

Charlemagne certainly had a vast and fair inheritance to bequeath to his sons. The southern Frankland stood firmly defended from all further Arab encroachments. To the South-West, the Spanish Mark reached to the very banks of the Ebro. To the East, the Ostmark commanded the entire Danubian plain. Christianity had spread far Eastwards, and two new bishoprics were established, one at Salzburg and the other at Würzburg. The Avar menace was a thing forgotten and the Saxon lands were conquered in perpetuity.

There was indeed much for heartening. Equally, there remained dangers – particularly to the North and South-East. Comparatively few Slav tribes were under Charlemagne's hand, and quite a number among them still led a nomadic life, adding to the complications of Frankish economic reconstruction and military defence. Finally, in the far North, there loomed the threat of a piracy savage enough to disturb a good soldier's courage: the Northmen, at home on the sea, had already ravaged parts of Britain, Scotland, Ireland, and the Frisian coast.

Still, in larger terms, Charlemagne's empire was cradled in peace. The accession of King Wemming in Denmark led to a lessened tension in the North. In Italy, the tumult-loving duchies of Spoleto and Beneventum seemed to have settled down to a spell of unfamiliar quiet.

Yet those were not years of personal happiness for Charlemagne. Many of his great friends had gone, including Paul the Deacon and Alcuin. Between 810 – 811 he lost both Charles the Younger and Pippin, as well as his eldest daughter, Rothrud, once betrothed to the Emperor Constantine VI. 'He bore the deaths [of his children] with far less patience than might have been expected from his usual stoutness of heart . . . His affection for his family was of a quality equal to his courage [and] it compelled him to weep.'[6] Thus wrote Einhard, by then the Emperor's closest intimate, who may well have witnessed more than one outburst of his master's grief.

Those personal losses drew Charlemagne closer and closer to Hildebald, the Palace Arch-chaplain and his confessor, to Angilbert, his illegitimate son-in-law, and even more particularly to Theodulf of Orleans, whose great hymn for Palm Sunday[7] never failed to move Charlemagne; but Theodulf's statesmanship was not of a quality to reassure the Emperor. His dominions were at peace but he was unable to feel sure about the North. He had a fleet built,[8] and the ships were kept moored along the rivers running into the North Sea. Many forts, stoutly built, well manned and supplied with arms and victuals, were now standing at the mouths of all the navigable rivers. Yet even all those precautions had not prevented the Northmen from ravaging some of the reaches of the Frisian coast.

Those enemies remained a darkly etched question mark in Charlemagne's mind. It looked as though piracy alone did not determine their depredations, and there was nothing in all his earlier military experiences to fit as a comparison with a foe who had no use for a battlefield. Charlemagne was conscious that his faithful Franks were not really bred to the sea, and could be no match for the Northmen who took to seafaring as naturally as a sturdy child took to walking, who laughed in the teeth of a storm, and had no peers in the art of naval warfare.

Travellers came to Aachen and told incredible stories about the Northmen who, not content with their piratical thrusts in the West, penetrated Eastwards, their narrow ships flying down from river to lake, from lake to river until they reached the Euxine, sold what loot they brought in Constantinople, and even entered the imperial service as a specially picked body-guard. They were not the Danes Charlemagne used to meet during his Saxon campaigns, but another Scandinavian tribe from further up in the North. Some travellers said they were Gothlanders, others called them Svyars. In Byzantium, how-ever, they were called Variangy, famous for their courage and universally feared for their cruelty, and that in an age when any manner of cruelty was more or less taken for granted.

*   *   *

It would be idle to conjecture about the probable fate of the Carolingian dynasty if Charlemagne's elder sons had survived him. Both were gifted enough, but neither Charles the Younger nor Pippin equalled their father in mental stature or vision.

Now the ageing Emperor was left with the third son Hildegard had borne him. Louis had been King of Aquitania since 781 when he was precisely three years old. He still lived at his palace of Chasseneuil, very much subjected to the whims of his wife, Ermengard, and the pious counsels of prelates and monks who crowded the palace. Pious to a ludicrous extreme, incapable of sharing his father's ideas, blind to the splendour of his vision, and grieving for his moral lapses, Louis might have made a passably good monk. Even the comparatively un-important crown of Aquitania was too heavy for him.

Not only the recurring palace scandals kept him away from Aachen but his father's closest counsellors, in particular Adalard and Wala, roused both fear and anxiety in Louis. All their ideas ran contrary to his own. Charlemagne's reforms could say little, if anything, to a man whose mental and emotional horizons were firmly pillared on one petition of the Lord's Prayer: 'Thy Will be done.' It was, to Louis, a Divine dispensation that the poor should be poor, the ignorant left in their mental obscurity, and the sick endure the burdens of ailing flesh, and Louis looked upon the latter as the bourne of all evils. The sins of the flesh were to him far more grievous than any others, with the sole exception of non-Christian religions. His father's friendship with Harun-al-Raschid appalled him.

Disastrously enough, Louis remained a well-meaning man and, in spite of all the divergences of opinion and habit, Charlemagne loved him, and Louis's unbreakable gravity of demeanour afforded scope for joking rather than censure. Louis was never heard to laugh, or seen to smile.

Still, after 811, he remained Charlemagne's sole heir. Sometime in 813,[9] the Emperor held 'council in the palace [of Aachen] with all his army, bishops and abbots, his dukes and his cousins. There he told them to promise loyalty to his son . . . [and] asked them if it was their pleasure that a share in the imperial dignity should be given to King Louis . . .', and all those present gave their consent since they could have done no other: the Emperor had legitimate grandsons, but Louis alone remained the heir apparent. That consent, however, could hardly have been given light-heartedly.

The council over, messengers were at once sent to Aquitania to invite Louis to Aachen. Apparently, Charlemagne's invitation did not include the Queen of Aquitania.

Louis wasted no time. He reached Aachen, was welcomed by his father and lodged at the palace in great splendour, but nothing contrived for his delight and comfort led to a single expression of pleasure. On the very next Sunday following Louis's arrival, the Emperor and the King went to Mass in the chapel, Charlemagne wearing his imperial robes and the golden crown. On the high altar, at the Epistle end, another golden crown lay on a crimson cushion.

Hildebald, the Palace Arch-chaplain, was to sing Mass that morning, but he and his assistants did not move forward at the Emperor's entry. Father and son reached the sanctuary and knelt for some time in prayer. Then Charlemagne rose and spoke to his son[10] '. . . in the hearing of a great congregation . . . asking [Louis] to swear that he would obey the command to serve God and the Church, and to defend it, to be kind to his kinsfolk, to show reverence to the clergy, to protect the poor, to turn the stubborn evil-doers into the right way.'

Louis gave the required oath, and Charlemagne told him to

take the golden crown off the altar and to put it on his head.[11]
The great sanctuary was crowded with archbishops, bishops
and abbots, but not one among them was invited to take the
least part in that curious coronation. Louis's own hands
removed the crown off the altar. It was Charlemagne's very
last gesture of consummate theocracy. Pope Leo III would be
duly informed of a *fait accompli*. Charlemagne, Emperor and
King, imparted to his heir that authority and signature which
God had impressed upon himself. In his thought, 'the kingly
character here approached that of the priest.'[12]

The Mass over, the two Emperors went in procession to the
banqueting hall. The festive meal with its several courses,
singing and music could not have pleased Louis's austerity.
Other festivities followed, endured rather than enjoyed by
Charlemagne's son, and then he left for Aquitania. Father and
son were never to meet again.

*   *   *

That great occasion happened in the autumn of 813, but the
years preceding it had prepared the climate. Charlemagne
knew that his sands were running out. The entire household
had been anxious, and its most frustrated members were surely
the Emperor's physicians, whose advice he ignored and whose
very presence often angered him. They were so many cogs in
the complicated machinery of his court, but he denied that
they were essential cogs, and never tired of maintaining that
nature was the best healer of all. In particular, the doctors'
insistence on diet all but maddened Charlemagne. All his life
long he had liked fresh meat roasted on the spit, fish grilled
in hot ashes, venison and other game baked in batter, every
dish lavishly seasoned with spices, and whatever fruit happened
to be ripe. His physicians approved of the fruit and condemned
the rest. They had enough tact not to interfere with the work
of the cooks but they found support among many of the
Emperor's intimates. Messes of plain boiled meat and fish
appeared at dinner to be instantly rejected. His daughters
wept. So did his mistresses. Charlemagne kept frowning until
a dish to his taste was served to him, and the cooks were
triumphant.

Yet food was just one detail out of many. All in all, the giant's physique was hollowed out by a life of many hardihoods, and sexual excesses played their part in the disintegration. Queen Liutgard's death in 800 had not brought Charlemagne to spend lonely nights. Einhard[13] mentions four mistresses by name, but there may well have been others.

Climatic vagaries had never before troubled Charlemagne, trained as he was to endure both cold and heat in the uncomplaining manner of a hardened soldier. But in 811, he was caught in a storm riding home after a hunt, and was drenched to the skin long before he reached the palace. That night, fever gripped him hard, and he treated it in his usual way by rigorous fasting and drinking nothing except water.

It proved the first of many such, and it was a humiliation to realise that a wetting could pull him down. But it was a fact Charlemagne could not escape. He recovered rapidly, to the great amazement of his physicians, but a shadow had fallen across a sunlit wall, and the business genius in him stirred to the necessity of immediate action. Several bishops and others were summoned to Aachen to witness the will the Emperor was having drawn up.

In the end,[14] fourteen bishops, four abbots and fifteen counts appended their signature to the document. It is rather odd that the name of Adalard, Abbot of Corbie, should be missing among the signatures. The list of counts is headed by one Walath[15] which may or may not have been Wala, Adalard's brother and Charlemagne's cousin.

The will was a lengthy and complicated document. The Emperor had immense possessions, not only in land and in specie, but in silver and gold plate, jewellery, furs, uncut gems and books. The main purpose of the will was to make ample provision for the poor who benefited by a whole third of the Emperor's possessions. The balance went to his heir, his numerous kin, and all his servants, both men and women, on the staff of the several palaces.[16]

As was usual with most arrangements made by an Arnulfing the will carried a very curious detail. Charlemagne had collected books since his youth, and one would have expected that immense and valuable library to be bequeathed either to the

Palace School or to some abbey known for the number and quality of its scholars such as Reichenau, St Gall, Lorsch or Fulda. But the Carolingian leaning towards the grotesque and the unusual here came out with all its force. Charlemagne directed that his entire library[17] should be sold at 'a reasonable price' ('*iusto pretio*') and the money used for the relief of the poor already lavishly provided for in the testament.

Four only of his great treasures found a specific mention. The square silver table engraved with a map of Byzantium was to be sent to St Peter's in Rome, and the round silver table was bequeathed to the See of Ravenna. The other two tables, one of silver and one of gold, were to be sold, and the proceeds divided equally between his heirs and the poor.

All those wishes would be carried out most faithfully by the Emperor Louis.[18]

*　　*　　*

In an age of fervent faith and no less deep-rooted superstition, all recorded happenings of the next three years came to be rather loudly coloured by the nearness of Charlemagne's death. Some warnings dealt directly with him. Other portents were taken to foretell a dark future for Frankland. A meteor, flashing across the skies of spring, would have been a subject of terror at any time, but now its threat was intensified by the panic of the Emperor's horse. The animal reared so violently that Charlemagne, for all his wondrous horsemanship, was thrown with such force that the fall broke his girdle of thick leather and silver and his sword went hurtling through the air. So stunned by the fall was the Emperor that he could not raise himself without help. Those who accompanied him looked at one another, all sharing a thought to which none dared give utterance: that meteor had indeed been horrible in its suddenness, but no other horse had thrown its rider, and the Emperor's mounts were the best trained in all Frankland.

Such portents increased.[19] The household at Aachen dared not discuss them in Charlemagne's presence, but everybody knew that their lord, though refusing to be influenced by many unpredicted eclipses of the sun and moon, was sharply aware of their meaning as it concerned himself.

The signs did not come from the skies only. The winged

gallery, built with much care and great labour by Frankish and Italian architects to join the palace to the great chapel, was utterly destroyed in a storm. The wooden bridge over the Rhine at Mainz, which had taken ten years to build, was burned down within three hours. The Palace at Aachen was frequently shaken without any apparent reason – and there were many other portents all to be recorded later by Einhard and by annalists. The damage to the palace buildings and the destruction of the bridge were certainly facts. So were the eclipses seen not only in Frankland but elsewhere. The rest stemmed out of the mediaeval conviction that elements had their part to play in the approaching end of a great life.

Charlemagne paid no attention to such interpretations. He needed no portents to tell him that he would never see another spring. He spent those months at Aachen, permitting himself much more leisure than in the past, and using the time for work at a German grammar, on the emended text of the Vulgate left unfinished by Alcuin, amusing himself by inventing native names for winds, months and days, and often listening to the minstrels singing or reciting old Germanic epics and songs. Fatigue, an earlier unknown guest, now came to him, but he would not change his way of life.

13th January 814 broke so fine that the Emperor decided to go hunting in the environs of Aachen. The morning's promise had not been true. Before long the skies darkened and sleety rain all but blotted out the landscape. By the time Charlemagne rode back to the Palace, he was shivering in spite of his fur cloak, and went to bed. Physicians were summoned but he would have none of them, and began applying his usual treatment of rigorous fasting. This time, however, the fever changed into a discomfort never before experienced by him: he found himself almost unable to breathe, and soon after midnight, on 20th January 814, such weakness swept over him that Hildebald of Cologne gave him the last Sacraments.

Tradition says that Charlemagne murmured '*In manus tuas, Domine, commendo spiritum meum*' before consciousness left him, but there is nothing to tell us if those were indeed his last words. About nine in the morning his breathing ceased. Einhard gave the illness the Greek name of 'pleurisy', but the haste with which they buried him – towards sunset on the same day – suggests that Charlemagne was smitten by the same complaint as his father, Pippin the Short – dropsy.

Night had not yet fallen when messengers were riding to Aquitania to bring the news to the Emperor Louis, who lost no time in claiming his inheritance.

A monk, unknown by name, wrote a moving lament for the dead Emperor.[20] Chroniclers would duly record the overwhelming sorrow of the people, but a heart's grief could hardly be expressed in the dry entry of a chronicle. A poet alone could do so.

> 'Frankland, by many deep griefs wounded,
> Had never borne so sharp a loss
> As on the day when she surrendered
> Charles the Great to the soil of Aix.'[21]

*   *   *

It was a surrender of the tired flesh and no more, even though the sun did set not only for Frankland but for the whole of Europe. It was, too, the knell of a dynasty since no other member of the Arnulfing House brought even a semblance of genius to the throne so matchlessly exalted by Charlemagne. Yet, in a different, far more enduring sense it was the dawn of a continuity though the contemporaries could not understand that Charlemagne had not died in his death.

W. P. Ker[22] caught up the splendour of that reign in one line '*Aurea Roma iterum renovata renascitur orbi*,' and Previté-Orton hardly exaggerated when he wrote that 'in all parts, in law and judgment, in administration and war, [Charlemagne's] inspiring and irresistible personality kept control . . .'[23] There were mistakes and curiously coiled deviations from principle, honoured custom, justice and plain morality, but the balance remained in spite of them: he understood the age and its promise, he understood man and his hunger both of the body and the mind, and he was fully conscious of the bounty of the earth.

More than that. Henri Pirenne was right in maintaining[24] that the core of Charlemagne's genius lay in '*d'avoir fait du neuf*', and that on a scale earlier unknown to man. Newness of the approach to every problem he faced – from practical theology to viticulture, was the hallmark of the reign, a freshness, even if born of a day dream, was enriched by a practical application.

That long reign had created a climate strong enough not to perish utterly in the bloody chaos, the frustrations and griefs of the ninth and tenth centuries, and to carry a few seeds of enlightenment from one age to another. It pleased the makers of legends to imagine Charlemagne as the founder of the Paris University. The fable is informed with the flavour of a prophecy since in his reign it is possible to discern the outline of some such beginning. Universities could not (and cannot) be established by the technical method of erecting a building, drawing up a curriculum and enrolling numbers of young people, whose only goal is a degree enabling them to earn a livelihood. Universities, to use Helen Waddell's happy analogy about liturgies, 'grew', their chief purpose contained in being 'places of learning for learning's sake'. In some such sense did Charlemagne and his circle of scholars at Aachen understand the meaning of '*studium*'. However uncreative and even repetitive their efforts, they left an indestructible imprint on the ages to come.

France claims him as her own, and so does Germany. He belongs to both and to neither. 'Charlemagne' is the Frenchified variant of 'Carolus Magnus'. 'Charles le Grand' would have rung too false a note. 'Karl der Grosse' again does not quite fit. Long before AD 800 he considered the entire Europe as his bourne, but the idea of '*imperium*' never quite engulfed the tribal conception inherited from a brutal but proud past. He was a Frank before the matter of France came to be shaped. By language, custom and heritage he was a Teuton, a descendant of barbarians who had known all the perils, hazards and surprises of a Westward journey. In mid-nineteenth century, Quérard, the French bibliographer, said that humanities had the entire world for their motherland. That idea, greatly enlarged, was reflected in Charlemagne's policy, and the faith he professed stamped a compelling image of unity upon his dominions.

W. E. H. Lecky[25] said that at the particular time it was

necessary for certain tendencies 'to be united in one person who, by the splendour and beauty of his career, could fascinate the imaginations of men . . . Of all the great rulers . . . there has probably been no other who was so truly many-sided, whose influence pervaded so completely all the religious, intellectual and political modes of thought existing in his time. . .'

The epithet 'Great' had, with justice, been used most sparingly in History. Even so it seldom fits those to whom it was given either by contemporaries or by posterity. To take but three examples, Alexander's greatness was determined by his conquests, and Frederick's a blatant misnomer. Catherine II of Russia has a slightly better claim on the strength of the reforms planned at the beginning of her reign. Not one of those three reaches up to Charlemagne's stature: with all his blunders, contradictions and moral lapses, he was *'Magnus'* indeed – far greater than the sum of his qualities, primarily so in his conviction that the mind of man meant immeasurably more than blood, race, or worldly substance. He may with justice be called the first fully integrated European, but he had neither a Homer or a Virgil to tell his story.

EPILOGUE: THE LEGEND

Many variants of mythical stories flashed like lightning all through the Middle Ages but, unlike lightning, they stayed, grew, assumed bolder and still bolder colours, and finally entered the realm of the fantastic to remain there for all time.

It is hardly a matter for wonder that a personality like Charlemagne's should have invited the very particular attention of legend makers and of poets as well. At every point he had stirred the imagination of his contemporaries, and the canon of the Carolingian legendary lore would fill far more than one sizeable volume. It is true that some of the stories are utterly grotesque, and F. McCullough[1] gives one of them, its provenance unknown.

That piece of fantasy tells us about Charlemagne having a fairy for his mistress at Aachen. 'She lived when he approached her, and died at his departure. Once, as the sun's rays fell on her open mouth, [Charlemagne] saw a grain of gold on her tongue. He removed it; she died and never came to life again.'

By AD 1000 the common folk in Europe were staunchly convinced that the great Emperor was not dead but asleep. In 1085, when Pope Urban summoned the first Crusade, many of those who took the Cross were certain that their host was being led by Charlemagne, his great sword, Joyeuse, flashing in the sun, because within far less than a century he had become the chief protagonist in the combat between Cross and Crescent, and it did not much matter to anyone that such an identity was unknown in history.

Soon enough poetic imagination was on fire with the theme. Ballads, songs and fragmentary epics began appearing as early as the middle of the ninth century and continued to be so all through the tenth. Some time at the beginning of the eleventh century came the so-called Chronicle of Turpin, its author unknown. It painted a fantastic landscape of Charlemagne conquering the entire Iberian Peninsula: 'at the prayer of Monseigneur Jacques [Iago of Compostela], our Lord gave this boon to [Charlemagne] that men should speak of him as long as the world endures.'

East of the Rhine, in Guddesberg in Hesse, lay a cave where the Emperor was believed to be sleeping, and waking up at the least sign of danger in the country. Many travellers said they had heard him riding furiously through the lonely mountain passes.

At the end of the eleventh century an anonymous poet of great vision and splendid vocabulary gave the world an epic of no fewer than four thousand lines, the immortal *Chanson de Roland*. The poem envisaged Charlemagne's whole life dedicated to a heroic struggle against Islam. In the story, Charles Martel's great victories were attributed to his descendant, and not only was Spain cleared of the Arabs but Charlemagne crossed the sea, freed the Holy Land, reached Jerusalem, and offered his prayers at the Sepulchre. The Astronomer of Limousin[2] said that all those stories had been current long before the close of the ninth century. But they had to wait for a poet of genius to be gathered up together into a sequence of images, each reflecting a fragment of abiding beauty.

It is not really difficult to understand how the background of the great epic came to be shaped. Charlemagne's reforms at home and his foreign policy had no place there. Mediaeval Europe's imagination could hardly be enflamed by anything except the Emperor's military exploits which alone lent themselves to an imaginative interpretation. Now nobody at the time cared much, if anything, about the Lombard expedition, unpopular enough among the Franks who had had to share in it. And what theme could possibly be hammered out of the drawn-out monotony of the Saxon campaigns? The admittedly dramatic element of the Avar war soon enough came to be forgotten in spite of all the laudatory doggerel written in its honour at the time.

Alone, the brief and disastrous Spanish expedition of 778 offered rewarding material: the dark, narrow and perilous pass in the Pyrenees, the sudden assault of an unseen enemy, the spirit of pure chivalry (albeit ante-dated by some three centuries), the heroic courage of a few in their struggle against the many and, finally, a blood-drenched defeat which had the echoes of a triumph in it since the fallen had surrendered their lives but not their honour. The basic theme of the *Chanson* was chivalry, not the delicately coloured chivalry of a court tournament, but the stern chivalry of a war fought with pure hearts and clean hands. It was pre-eminently a crusading epic and in its lines Charlemagne belonged not to the Frankland which had bred him but to '*la doulce France*', unknown in his generation.

The epic was conceived in an age demanding a brilliant and compelling focal point, an image not only to admire but to worship, a great and flawless mirror reflecting all the knightly virtues. The hero was to be lusty, pious, courageous and handsome. Out of all the military ventures undertaken by Charlemagne none fitted into the frame so well as the Roncevalles disaster.

Yet even the latter suggested too small a canvas. Europe, inebriated with the crusading spirit, desired to see Charlemagne join the great company, free the whole Iberian Peninsula from the Saracen yoke, cross the sea, fight and crush the infidel on his own soil, ride on in triumph and restore all the ancient liberties of the Holy Land to those who followed Christ.

Such a theme, however extravagant in detail, enriched the mediaeval literature beyond all measure, and the undeniable extravagances of detail did not interfere with the central idea. The *Chanson de Roland* had for its protagonist a governor of the Breton March about whom History knows nothing except his variedly spelt baptismal name, his official status, and the fact that he was killed on the homeward march across a pass in the Pyrenees.

'*Le Chanson*,' written by a Frenchman, supposes Charlemagne to be French by his '*courtoisie*'. Except for Saragossa, the whole of Spain is under his hand. Indeed, his imaginary conquests stretch far afield. They include Poland, Scotland, Ireland and Britain, and they were all achieved by the help of Roland and his great sword Durendal.

Betrayed by one in his own host and fighting against impossible odds, Roland would not sound his horn, and no rescue reached him in time. It is a story of a stark and bloody defeat. It is also a triumph of genuine chivalry: Roland and his men laid down their lives '*pour la doulce France*', and, in dying, Roland turned his face towards Spain so that the world might think of him meeting his death as befitted a dedicated knight: with his face towards the enemy.

It was evening when Charlemagne and his paladins reached Roncevalles. They dismounted, and the Emperor knelt in prayer, and heard the angels' voices promising him that daylight would return and not vanish again. So it happened, and the Frenchmen chased the Saracens to the very banks of the Ebro, with neither barge nor bridge to be seen. The Saracens prayed 'to their gods, Mahomet, Tervagant and Apollo', and plunged into the river, but their armour was so heavy that they all perished, and, watching them drown, the Frenchmen shouted: 'You looked on Roland to your own undoing!'

Then they rested on the river bank, and the Emperor with them, still in his full armour – 'his white-fringed hauberk, the helmet studded with jewels, and his great sword *Joyeuse*'.

'We have heard of the lance which pierced our Saviour's side as He hung upon the Cross. A fragment of that lance', says the unknown poet, 'was sealed inside the golden pounce of the Emperor's sword . . . Such were the honour and the virtue whereby the good sword Joyeuse received its name, a fact never to be forgotten by the French because their battle-cry – "*Montjoie*" came from it,' and 'that is the reason why no enemy can prevail against them in battle.'

*   *   *

Those who lived on the East bank of the Rhine chose a different theme. They did not send Charlemagne into Spain or the Holy Land. They did not much mourn over Roland. Instead, they clothed the Emperor with most fantastic immortality, and a little later the German ethos rejected the Latin '*magnus*'. He became '*Karl der Grosse*' in perpetuity. Men like him, said all the epics and the ballads, were so rare that they could not leave the world at their death. They lived in their sleep, and they woke whenever the peril of an hour caused them to spring into action and help their country. As centuries drew on, Charlemagne's policy and achievement became inevitably blurred in the minds of lesser men, but the warmth of his personality and his qualities as leader and hero continued setting on fire the national imagination.

The legendary lore winged its way far beyond Frankland. Towards the end of the twelfth century the Karlamagnus Saga appeared in Scandinavia. Echoes of it were rung in Poland. Spain, as was to be expected, built an image of Charlemagne as a bandit ingloriously routed and chased back from the Pyrenean heights.

So the legends grew apace, but the heart of the reality stayed: a man great enough to understand all the smallnesses of his kind.

He, who appointed and dismissed bishops at his will, would surely have sided with the Emperor Henry IV against Gregory VII in the great investiture clash, and would have despised his successor for going to Canossa. He, whose thirst for the new and the original was never slaked, would have welcomed Roger Bacon, Gutenberg, and not refused help to Columbus.

To follow the liberty of legendary conjecture still further, the present century would have at once excited and angered Charlemagne, in whose thought all knowledge, of however mechanical a nature, came from a source which, using matter, never permitted itself to be used by it. From that point of view, when all the legends and stories have been told, Charlemagne stands out as a challenge to our generation.

He believed in man independently of his origin, merit, achievement, still less his substance. He believed in man and his ability to do the right thing simply because, as he believed, 'The Word became flesh and dwelt among us'. Therefore man was God's brother by the flesh, inheritor of God's dignity, which was never to be lessened by even a single gesture of worship towards the purely material side of life.

It was a simple faith, and Charlemagne's personal behaviour did not always follow it, but the stream of it ran all through his life and his achievements. Within that faith he lived and worked because it was as much a necessity in his day as it is in ours.

P

NOTES

I

1. Caesar, *De Bello Gall.*, III, 8. *"sunt Gallorum subita et repentina consilia"*
2. Cf. Silius Italicus, *Punica*, VIII, 16.
3. Duchesne, *L'Eglise au VIème siècle*, p. 482.
4. The exact beginnings of Christianity in Gaul are obscure. By about AD 177 (the date is rather conjectural), there was a Christian community at Lyons, with one Pothinus for its bishop. Said to have been a disciple of St Polycarp of Smyrna, Pothinus may well have come to Gaul from Asia Minor. (Cf. Duchesne, op. cit.)
5. Socrates, *Hist. Eccl.*, I. V. Quoted in Bettenson, *Documents of the Early Christian Church*, p. 57.
6. Dr Joan Evans, *Magical Jewels*, p. 110.
7. Migne, *Patrologia Latina*, Vol. 71. *'Prosternebat enim quotidie Deus hostes eius sub manu ipsius, et augebat regnum eius quod ambularet recto corde eo, et faceret quae placita erant in oculis eius.'*
8. Cf., Gregory of Tours, *Historia Francorum*. Bk. V.
9. Henri Pirenne, *Mahomet et Charlemagne*.
10. Slave traffic did not cease with the coming of Christianity to Gaul. Even bishops and lesser clerics owned them. Cf. the Will of Bishop Perpetuus, late fifth century.
    'In primis itaque ego, Perpetuus, volo liberos esse liberasque homines et feminas quotquot habeo in Villa Saponaria, quos emi de mea pecunia, ut et pueros quos in die discessus mei non manumisero in Ecclesia; ita tamen ut libere serviant, quamdiu vixerint, Ecclesiae meae, sed absque servitutis ad haeredes transmissibili et glebatica.' Migne, *Patrologia Latina*, Vol. 71, p. 1149.
11. Migne, *Patrologia Latina*, Vol. 71.
12. Latouche, *'Les Origines de l'Economie Occidentale'* p. 66.
13. Cf. Migne, *Patrologia Latina*, Vol. 71, p. 1154 et seq.
14. Ibid.
15. Duchesne, op. cit.
16. Gregory of Tours, *'Historia Francorum'*. Migne, *Patrologia Latina*, Vol. 71.
17. Venantius Fortunatus, *Opera*. Migne, *Patrologia Latina*, Vol. 88.

18. Gregory of Tours, op. cit.
19. Duchesne, *L'Eglise au VIème siècle*. p. 594.
20. Fredegarius, op. cit. In the second quotation, the word in the text is '*aegrotans*' which, according to Freund (*Latin-English Lexicon*, p. 48) means mental as well as physical disorder. He quotes Cicero, and Fredegarius's acquaintance with the classics included the latter.
21. Cf. 'Continuator' of Fredegarius. Text in Migne, *Patrologia Latina*, Vol. 71.
22. Einhard, '*Vita Caroli Magni*,' ed. P. Jaffé, 1867. pp. 26–27.
23. Latouche, op. cit., p. 67.
24. Cf. Migne, *Patrologia Latina*, Vol. 88, p. 1074, et seq.
25. Text from the edition of Baluze in Migne, *Patrologia Latina*, Vol. 53, pp. 25–238. An English translation by Eva M. Sandford, New York, 1930.
26. *Opera*, Migne, *Patrologia Latina*, Vol. 53.
27. 'O Christ, Who art the light and day,' No. 81 in the English Hymnal.

II

1. See the Genealogical Table on page 12.
2. Hodgkin, T., *Charles the Great*, p. 64.
3. Freeman, E. A., *Western Europe in the Eighth Century*, p. 151.
4. Quoted by T. Hodgkin, op. cit., p. 78.
5. Einhard, '*Vita Caroli Magni*,' chap. III. Ed. Jaffé, 1867.
6. Cf. Breysig, T., '*Jahrbücher des frankischen Reiches*' 714–741 (1869), pp. 109–115.
7. Cf. Einhard, op. cit., Preface.
8. Einhard, op. cit., chap. IV.
9. Cf. Einhard, op. cit., chap. XVIII. '*colebat enim eam [i.e. the Queen] cum summa reverentia, ita ut nulla umquam invicem sit exerta discordia, praeter in divortio filiae Desiderii regis . . .*'
10. Hodgkin, op. cit., p. 64.
11. Duchesne, *Liber Pontificalis*, I, 441 f.
12. The year of his birth is uncertain. It was either 741 or 742. The latter date was recorded on his tomb: '*Decessit septuagenarius anno Domini 814.*' Einhard, op. cit., chap. 31.
13. M.G.H., *Diplomata Karolinorum I*, 1906.
14. Freeman, *Western Europe in the Eighth Century*, 1904, p. 151.
15. Einhard, op. cit., chap. III.
16. Einhard. Ibid. '*Mansitque ista quamvis cum summa difficultate concordia*' etc.

17. Einhard. Ibid. *'morbo decessit.'* The word had many connotations in the Middle Ages. It may have been plague, jaundice, or fever. In Carloman's case it may well have been some sharp disorder brought about by intemperance.

18. Cf. Walafrid Strabo's preface to Einhard's *Vita*. (Ed. Jaffé, 1867.) Walafrid vouches for his high character and notes that Einhard was an eye-witness of practically all the events he described. That lent the greatest possible accuracy to his record.

19. Six popes occupied the see of St Peter during Charlemagne's life. He was born in the reign of Zachary (741–752); he made his first 'diplomatic' appearance on Stephen II visiting Frankland (752–757). The others were Paul I (757–67), Stephen III (768–72), and Adrian I (772–795). Leo III (795–816) outlived Charlemagne by two years.

III

1. Notker Balbulus (c. 840–912). *'Gesta Caroli Magni,'* ed. P. Jaffé, *Monumenta Carolina*, Bibliotheca Rerum Germanicarum, Berlin, 1867, Vol. IV. chap. 25.

2. Cf. Paul the Deacon. Charlemagne's preface to his collection of sermons, Migne, *Patrologia Latina*, Vol. 95, pp. 1159–1160.

3. Taylor, *Mediaeval Mind*, Vol. II, p. 302.

4. Einhard, op. cit., chap. 7 . . . *'aliquotes ita domiti et emolliti, ut etiam cultum daemonum dimittere et christianae religione se subdere velle promitterent . . .'*

5. Cf. Charlemagne's letter to Bishop Arno of Salzburg, early 800. (*Monumenta Carolina*, Vol. IV, p. 349).

6. Full text in *Monumenta Carolina*, Vol. IV, p. 351.

7. Full text in *Monumenta Carolina*, Vol. IV, p. 357.

8. M.G.H., *Diplomatum Karolinorum*, ed. Mühlbacher, Berlin, 1956, Vol. I, p. 95 et seq. The full story of Abbot Gudeland's visit to the palace of Heristal, his grievance, and Charlemagne's decision is given there.

9. Ibid., pp. 222–24.

10. Ibid., p. 315.

11. Ibid., pp. 261–262. *'Idcirco suprascriptus Alcuinus abba serenitatem regni nostri petiit, ut in ipsum roborandum bonitatis beneficium largire deberemus.'*

12. *Isidori Hispalensi Episcopi Etymologiarum* . . . Libri XX. Ed. W. M. Lindsay, Oxford, 1966. Vol. II, 3. *'Unde et arbores vitam habere dicuntur, quia gignuntur et crescunt.'*

13. Most of the information in the next two paragraphs is taken from M.G.H., *Concilia Aevi Carolini*, ed. A. Werminghoff, Berlin, 1906, Vol. I.

14. In spite of all the bans and penalties, the clerical standards of morality failed to rise. Towards the very end of Charlemagne's reign, a synod held at Mainz in the spring of 813 banned drunkenness, dice, and all secular pleasures. Gluttony was mentioned, too, and usury. Cf. Ibid, p. 264.

15. Ibid. Cf. articles VI, XI, XII, XIII, XVI, XVIII, XXX, XXXIII, XLI, XLII, XLVIII, LII, LVI.

16. Ibid., article XXXIII.

17. Ibid., article XLII. '. . . *sed hic soli in ecclesia veneranda sint qui ex auctoritate passionum aut vitae merito electi sint.*'

18. Cf. *Monumenta Carolina*, Vol. IV, p. 369.

19. Cf. Ibid, Vol. IV, p. 388.

20. Cf. Flodoard, '*Historia Remensis*,' chap. 18. Migne, *Patrologia Latina*, Vol. 135.

21. The word derives from the division of each such report into several chapters or articles.

22. Cf. *Concilia Aevi Carolini*, Vol. I. ed. A. Werminghoff, 1906.

23. According to Einhard, Notker Balbulus and others, the Pope was wrong. Hilmentrud, the mother of Pippin the Hunchback, was a concubine, not a wife.

24. The text of the letter is in *Monumenta Carolina*, ed. Jaffé, 1867, Vol. IV, pp. 269–70.

25. Einhard, op. cit., chap. 18.

26. Einhard, op. cit., chap. 6.

27. A legend, supposed to have started in the fifth century, alleged that Constantine the Great was baptized in Rome by Pope Sylvester I. The legend gave colour to the so-called Donation of Constantine by virtue of which Constantine was supposed to confer on the Pope the primacy over other patriarchs and absolute authority all over Italy. It is probable that the document was produced in the ninth century though its definite date is not known. First used in 1054 by Pope Leo IX, its falseness was proved some four hundred years later. The Donation was embodied in the volume of the so-called False Decretals, a collection of documents, many of them spurious and written to prove papal supremacy.

28. *Concilia Aevi Carolini*, Vol. I, p. 158. '. . . *et melius est discipulum esse veritatis, quam doctorem existere falsitatis.*'

29. The word derives from 'iconoclast', literally 'the image-breaker'.

30. Cf. the Nicene Creed: 'And I believe in the Holy Ghost . . . who proceedeth from the Father *and the Son.*' ('*Et in Spiritum Sanctum . . . qui ex Patre* Filioque *procedit . . .*') The Eastern Church never accepted the addition.
31. Cf. *Monumenta Carolina*, Vol. IV, pp. 374–75.
32. The third verse of the Athanasian Creed; Common Prayer Book version.
33. Cf. Charlemagne's letter to Baugulf of Fulda, *Monumenta Carolina*, Vol. IV, p. 344.

IV

1. M.G.H., *Monumenta Carolina*, ed. Jaffé, 1867, Vol. IV, pp. 203–205.
2. Einhard, op. cit., 8.
3. Ibid.
4. '*Mansus*' (plural '*mansi*'), a mediaeval land measure, approximately just over an acre.
5. Cf. Notker Balbulus, *Gesta Caroli Magni*.
6. Einhard, op. cit. 6.
7. Idem, 6 and 7.
8. Idem. 7. '*Poterat siquidem citius finiri, si Saxonum hoc perfidia pateretur.*'
9. *Capitularium de Partibus Saxoniae*, ed. von Richthofen, M.G.H., *Leges*, Vol. V. 1889.
10. Einhard, op. cit. 13.
11. Cf. Isidore of Seville, *Etymologiarum Libri XX*, ed. W. M. Lindsay, Clarendon Press, 1966. *Lib. XVI.*
12. Notker Balbulus, op. cit. Book II, 2.
13. Einhard, op. cit., 13.
14. Hodgkin, op. cit., p. 145.
15. Einhard, op. cit., 9.
16. Ibid., 14.
17. Notker Balbulus, op., cit. Book II, 14.

V

1. The word denoted office, not nobility rank. Counts were known in the Merovingian days; so were the so-called '*missi dominici*', i.e., 'the King's messengers', but their services were employed much more energetically by Charlemagne than by his predecessors. By the end of the eighth century, the messengers' status stood above that of the counts. A little later Charlemagne decreed that the messengers were to be chosen from among '*optimatibus*

suis': and they had authority over clerical as well as lay officials·
Cf. Capitulary 802. *Capitularie Regum Francorum.* ed. A. Boretius,
1883. (*Legum Sectio* 2).
2. Einhard, op. cit., chap. 24.
3. Cf. in footnote 1.
4. Cf. Capitulary 802, chap. 17.
5. Ibid, chap. 27.
6. Cf. Concilia Aevi Karolini, ed. A. Wermingoff, 1906. chap. III.
7. Cf. Article 81.
8. Cf. Parts I and II.
9. Cf. *Capitularie Regum Francorum*, ed. A. Boretius. *Legum Sectio* II.
10. Cf. Lot, Ferdinand, *Naissance de la France.* 1948. p. 175.
11. Cf. F. H. Dudden, *Gregory the Great*, 1905. II, pp. 157 and 158.
12. Ibid., II, p. 181, f. 2.
13. Ibid., II, p. 340, f. 4.
14. Latouche, *Les Origines de L'Economie Occidentale*, p. 188.
15. *Shorter Cambridge Mediaeval History*, by C. W. Previté-Orton, ed.
by Philip Grierson, 1952. I, p. 3.
16. M.G.H., *Diplomatum Karolinorum.* Ed. Mühlbacher, 1956, p. 274.
17. Cf. Bloch, Marc, *Mélanges Historiques.* I, chap. V. With reference
to that marriage, Bloch follows Einhard and Notker Balbulus,
and calls the Lombard princess '*sa première femme*'.
18. Latouche, op. cit., p. 207.
19. Bloch, op. cit., I, 152.
20. Cf. *Capit. de Villis*, chap. 48. '. . . *ut vendemia nostra nullus pedibus
praemere praesumat sed omnia nitida et honesta sint*'.
21. Latouche, op. cit., p. 197. '*Elle a été celle de la présence.*'

VI

1. Querard, *L'Histoire Littéraire de la France*, Vol. 22.
2. Such as, for instance, 'the Conflict between Spring and Winter.'
(Text in Dümmler, *Poet. Lat. Car.*, I). Its authorship has been
disputed because of a line 'the goats come to the milking, udders
full' being reminiscent of Horace, unknown in Frankland till the
middle of the ninth century, but the late Helen Waddell destroyed that argument by a far more convincing one of her own,
(Cf. H. Waddell, *Mediaeval Latin Lyrics*, p. 310).
3. See below. M.P.L., 88.
4. See below. Ibid.
5. The text of the '*Liber Scintillarum*' is to be found in Migne,

Patrologia Latina, Vol. 88. It proved to be one of the favourite mediaeval anthologies. Over 300 MSS are known to be extant.

6. Cf. Isidore's Etymologies. Latin text ed. by W. M. Lindsay, 2 Vols. Clarendon Press, 1966.

7. Saxo Grammaticus, Bk. VIII, 'Swedes and Norwegians should . . . consider how far the population of the North has always surpassed the Germans and the Slavs. [The Northmen] should . . . despise an army . . . composed more of a mass of fickle off-scourings than of firm and stout soldiers.' (transl. by O. Elton.)

8. Einhard, op. cit., chaps. 25, 26, and the end of chap. 29, from which much of the information that follows has been taken.

9. It was a habit of Alcuin's to give pet names to his friends and pupils. Thus Charlemagne was 'David'; the Bishop of Arno 'the Venerable Fowl', and Einhard 'Beseleel'. Alcuin himself was 'Flaccus'. 'Bezeleel' comes from Exodus, chap. 31. '(a man) filled with the spirit of God, in wisdom and in understanding, and in knowledge, and in all manner of workmanship, to devise cunning works . . . in brass . . . in cutting of stones . . . in carving of timber.'

10. Einhard, op. cit., Preface.

11 Such is the meaning given by the *Revised Mediaeval Latin Word-list*. Oxford University Press, 1965. p. 317. '*nutritor* – foster-father, c. 700.'

12. Einhard, op. cit., chap. 25. '. . . *in discenda grammatica Petrum Pisanum diaconem senem audivit*' i.e., Charlemagne was taught grammar by Peter of Pisa.

13. That statement is, of course, inaccurate, since Alcuin, though Head of the Palace School, could count on many famous colleagues, and the phrase is puzzling when we remember what contemporaries thought of Einhard's character. 'So sweet and worthy a man' could never have given rein to malice or envy. The statement may be explained by Einhard's passion for economy in words. This, however, is the author's private conjecture. E.M.A.

14. Einhard, op. cit., chap. 29.

15. Cf. M.G.H., *Scriptores I*, p. 268.

16. Taylor, H. O., *The Mediaeval Mind*, Vol. I, p. 213.

17. 'It seems to me that the whereabouts of Charles's collection during his journeyings belongs to the realm of speculation. As for Einhard's use of the word *regum*, some nineteenth century scholars, connecting it with a statement by a late ninth century source, thought that this referred only to Charles's immediate

ancestors, but in view of Einhard's *antiquissima*, people now favour a less literal interpretation.

(a) The *Hildebrandslied* could have formed part of Charles's collection only if Einhard did not mean literally *regum*.

(b) Einhard does not state where the recording took place, and his only date is 800. From 794 onwards Aachen was Charles's principal residence, but he continued his travels through the realm, and according to Einhard, chap. 22, spent only his last years continuously at Aachen.

'The most definite thing that can be said is that the extant version of the *Hildebrandslied* seems to have been written approximately within a decade of Charlemagne making his collection of ancient lays, and at a centre which had strong links with England, where monks cultivated secular poetry, and with Bavaria. All the rest is speculation.'

I am indebted for the above information to Dr Kurt Ostberg, Bedford College, University of London. E.M.A.

18. Cf. Migne, *Patrologia Latina*, Vol. 88, p. 914 et seq.

19. The edition of Alcuin's letter here consulted is by Wattenbach and Duemmler, 1873. *Bibliotheca Rerum Germanicarum*, Vol. VI.

20. Ibid., p. 345. '*Haec est o dulcissime David gloria, laus et merces tua*'.

21. Ibid., p. 359. '*sed necessarie sciendum*.'

22. Ibid., p. 361.

23. Ibid., p. 162.

24. Cf. Matt., 26, v. 30, and Mark, 14, v. 26.

25. Ibid., p. 115.

26. Ibid., p. 481.

27. Ibid., p. 423 et seq.

28. Ibid., p. 412.

29. Ibid., p. 43.

30. Colchu was well known in Northumbria. Cf. Symeon of Durham, (*Historia regum sub anno 794, Rerum Britannicarum Medii Aevi Scriptores*, Rolls Series, ed. 1965), who mentions his death and adds a word of praise '*pro laboribus terrenis*'.

31. Alcuin, op. cit., p. 166.

32. Chambers, *Mediaeval Stage*, Vol. I. p. 26 et seq.

33. Alcuin, op. cit. epist. 124, sub anno 797.

34. Ibid, p. 643.

35. Chambers, op. cit., Vol. I, p. 36.

36. Alcuin, op. cit., p. 693.

37. Cf. Migne, *Patrologia Latina*, Vol. 95, p. 1583. The same volume contains all the extant works of Paul the Deacon.

38. Full text of the letter. Ibid., p. 1591.
39. Cf. Migne, M.P., Vol. 95, p. 1159 et seq. Migne used the text as it was printed in the Cologne Edition of 1539. *'Homiliarius'* had a great success in the Middle Ages.
40. Ibid., p. 1177. Migne refers to it as anonymous.
41. Notker, op. cit., Book I, 9.
42. English translation in Helen Waddell's *Mediaeval Latin Lyrics*, p. 97.
43. Taylor, H. O., op. cit., Vol. I, p. 214.
44. Cf. Migne, *Patrologia Latina*, Vol. 88, p. 1085. The quotation is, *'abba de baselica pecularis patronis nostri domni Dionisii marteris ubi ipse preciosus dominus in corpure requiiscit, climenciae rigni nostri sogessit eo . . .'* etc.
45. See below Part IX.
46. Notker, op. cit., Book I, 3, and 9.

VII

1. Einhard, op. cit. Preface. *'. . . de cuius nativitate atque infantia vel etiam pueritia, quia neque scriptis usquam aliquid declaratum est. . .'*
2. Ibid., II, 18.
3. Taylor, H. O., *The Mediaeval Mind*, Vol. II, p. 34.
4. Einhard, op. cit., II, 20. *'erat ei filius nomine Pippinus ex concubina editus.'*
5. Notker, op. cit. Book II, p. 13.
6. Ibid., Book II, p. 17.
7. Einhard, op. cit. 18.
8. Ibid., 19.
9. Ibid., 19 et seq.
10. After the break-up of her betrothal, Ruthrud joined her aunt Gisla at the Abbey of Chelles where she died about 810.
11. Cf. Einhard, op. cit. 26.
12. Cf. Ibid., 22.
13. Notker Balbulus, op. cit., Book I, 11.
14. Ibid., Book II, 8.
15. Ibid., Book I, 31.
16. Cf. Einhard, op. cit. 20.
17. Cf. Ibid., 19. *'Erat enim in amicitiis optime temperatus, ut eas et facile admitteret et constantissime retineret; colebatque sanctissime, quoscumque hac adfinitate sibi coniunxerat.'*
18. Cf. Ibid., 29.

VIII

1. Alcuin, *Epistolae*, Vol. IV, 288 et seq.
2. Alcuin had Canon Law on his side. Cf. Mansi *Concilia*, I, 1257.
3. Cf. Alcuin, *Epistolae*, IV, 387 f.
4. Cf. *Annales Regni Francorum*, sub anno 800.
5. Alcuin, *Epistolae*, IV, 118.
6. Cf. *Liber Pontificalis*, II, 7 and *Annales Laur.*, sub anno 800.
7. Einhard, op. cit. 28.
8. Notker, op. cit. Book I, 26.
9. Previté-Orton, C. W., *Outlines of Mediaeval History*, p. 315.
10. Einhard, op. cit., 28.
11. Jaffé, *Einharti Vita Caroli Magni*, pp. 49–50, f. 4. Cf. *Epistolae Carolinae* 29 et 40 in *Bibl. Rerum Germ.*, IV, 393 et 415.
12. Einhard, op. cit., 29.

IX

1. Einhard, op. cit., 29.
2. Ibid., '. . . sed de his nihil aliud ab eo factum est, nisi quod pauca capitula, et ea imperfecta. . .'
3. Previté-Orton, *Short Mediaeval History*, Vol. I, 323.
4. Alcuin, op. cit., p. 806.
5. Theodulf of Orléans, Migne, *Patrologia Latina*, Vol. 105.
6. Einhard, op. cit., 19.
7. '*Gloria, Laus et Honor*' (All glory, laud and honour:) A. & M. No. 98.
8. Einhard, op. cit., 17.
9. Thegan, *Vita Hludiwici Imperatoris*, Migne, *Patrologia Latina*, Vol. 106, 405 ff.
10. Ibid.
11. There are other variants saying that Charlemagne himself crowned his son, but all records affirm that not a single ecclesiastic took part in the ceremony.
12. Cf. E. Duckett, *Carolingian Portraits*, p. 17.
13. Einhard, op. cit. 18.
14. Ibid., 33.
15. Jaffé gives it a second spelling (*Vita Caroli Magni* 52 f.) of 'Walacho'.
16. Einhard, op. cit., 33.
17. Jaffé, op. cit., p. 56.
18. Ibid., p. 57.
19. Einhard, op. cit., 32.

20. Cf. W. P. Ker, *The Dark Ages*, p. 213.
    'A solis ortu usque ad occidua
    Littora maris planctus pulsat pectora
    Ultramarina agmina tristitia
    Tetegit ingens cum moerure nimio,
    Heu mihi misero.'
21. *'Francia diras perpera iniurias*
    Nullum tam talem dolorem sustinuit
    Heu mihi misero,
    Quando augustum facundumque Karolum
    In Aquisqrani glebis terrae tradidit.'
    The Latin text is quoted by Miss E. Duckett, *Carolingian Portraits*,
    p. 19. The present translation is the author's.
22. W. P. Ker, op. cit., p. 154.
23. Previté-Orton, *Short Mediaeval History*, Vol. I, p. 318.
24. In *Revue Belge de Philologie et d'Histoire*, 1923, p. 230.
25. W. E. H. Lecky, *History of European Morals from Augustus to
    Charlemagne.* Ed. 1911. pp. 271–72.

EPILOGUE

1. MacCullough, *Mediaeval Faith and Fable*, p. 47.
2. M.G.H., SS., II, p. 608.

SELECT BIBLIOGRAPHY

Abbreviations:
R.S. – Rolls Series.
M.P.L. – Migne, *Patrologia Latina.*
B.R.G. – *Bibliotheca Rerum Germanicarum.*
M.G.H., SS. – *Monumenta Germaniae Hist., Scriptores.*
M.G.H., S.L. – *Monumenta Germaniae Hist., Sectoi Legum.*
M.G.H., C. – *Monumenta Germaniae Hist., Concilia.*
P.L.A.C. – *Poetae Latini Aevi Carolini.*

Sources

Alcuin, *Epistolae,* Ed. Wattenbach and Dümmler. B.R.G., VI, 1873.
Amalar of Metz, *Opera,* M.P.L., vol. 105.
Angilbert, *Carminae,* Ed. E. Dümmler, P.L.A.C., vol. I.
Annales Regum Francorum, Ed. F. Kurze, 1895.
Capitularia Regum Francorum, Ed. A Boretius, M.G.H., S.L., (II), 1883.
Codex Carolinus, Ed. Jaffé, (vol. IV), 1867.
Concilia Aevi Karolini, Ed. A. Wermingoff, 1906.
Diplomatum Karolinorum, vol. I, Ed. Mühlbacher, 1956.
Einhart, *Vita Caroli Magni,* Ed. Jaffé, 1867.
Epistolae Merovingici et Karolini, Ed. Dümmler, 1957.
Flodoard, *Opera,* M.P.L., vol. 135.
Fredegarius, *Opera,* M.P.L., vol. 71.
Gregory of Tours, *Historia Francorum,* M.P.L., vol. 71.
Hincmar, *Annales Bertiniani,* Ed. Waitz, M.G.H., SS., 1883.
Liber Pontificalis, Ed. L. Duchesne, vols. I and II, 1886–1892.
Libri Carolini, Ed. H. Bastgen, M.G.H., C., vol. II, 1924.
Mansi, G. D., *Concilia,* vols. VIII and IX, 1769.
Monachus Sangallensis (Notker Balbulus), *De Caroli Magni,* Ed. G. M. von Knonau, 1920.
Paul the Deacon, *Opera,* M.P.L., vol. 95.
Perpetuus, Bp, M.P.L., vol. 71.

Rabanus Maurus, *Opera*, M.P.L., vols. 110 and 111.
Radbertus Paschasius, *Vita Adalhardi*, M.G.H., SS., vol. II.
Salonius, *Opera*, M.P.L., vol. 53.
Salvianus, *Opera*, M.P.L., vol. 53.
Saxo Grammaticus, *Danish History*, transl. by O. Elton, 1894.
Symeonis Monachi, *Opera*, R.S., Ed. 1965.
Thegan, *Vita Hludowici Imperatoris*, M.P.L., vol. 106.
Venantius Fortunatus, *Opera*, M.P.L., vol. 88.
Walafrid Strabo, *Opera*, M.P.L., vol. 113.
William of Malmesbury, *De Gestis Pontificum Anglorum*, R.S., vol. 52, 1870.

Other Books

Barker, G. P., *Charlemagne*, 1932.
Bettenson, H., Ed., *Documents of the Early Christian Church*, 1943.
Bloch, Marc., *Mélanges Historiques*, 2 vols., Paris, 1962.
Bryce, *The Holy Roman Empire*.
Bulfinch, T., *The Legend of Charlemagne*, 1863.
Cabrol, Ferdinand, *Les Origines Liturgiques*, Paris, 1906.
Calmotte, J., *Charlemagne, Sa Vie et Son Oeuvre*, Paris, 1945.
Chambers, *Mediaeval Stage*, vol. I., 1903.
Cipolla, C. M., *Money, Prices and Civilization in the Mediterranean World*. Princeton University Press, 1956.
Clercq, C. de, *La Législation Religieuse Franque de Clovis à Charlemagne*. Paris, 1936.
Daniel-Rops, E., *The Church in the Middle Ages*, trans. A. Butler, 1959.
Davis, R. H. C., *A History of Mediaeval Europe*, 1958.
Duchesne, L., *L'Eglise au VIème Siècle*, 1902.
Duckett, Eleanor, *Alcuin*, 1965.
Duckett, Eleanor, *Carolingian Portraits*, 1966.
Evans, Dr Joan, *Magical Jewels*, 1922.
Fichtenau, H., *Das Karolingische Imperium*, 1949.
Freeman, E. A., *Western Europe*, 1904.
Ganshof, F. L., *The Imperial Coronation of Charlemagne*, Glasgow University Publications, 79, 1949.
Ghellinck, J. de, *L'Essor de la Littérature Latine*, 1946.
Ghellinck, J. de, *Littérature Latine au Moyen Age*, 1949.
Gilson, E. *La Philosophie au Moyen Age*, Ed., 1944.

Guerber, H. A., *Myths and Legends of the Middle Ages*, 1909.

Halphen, L. *Etudes Critiques sur l'Histoire de Charlemagne*, 1921.

Halphen, L., *Charlemagne et l'Empire Carolingien*, 1947.

Hauck, A., *Kirchengeschichte Deutschlands im Mittelalter*, vol. II, 1958.

Hefele, C. J., and Leclerq, H. *L'Histoire des Conciles*, vol. III, 1910.

Henderson, E. F., *Select historical Documents of the Middle Ages*, 1907.

Hodgkin, T., *Charles the Great*, 1897.

Ker, W. P., *The Dark Ages*, 1904.

König, A., *Geistesleben and Unterrichtswesen zur Zeit Karls des Grossen*, 1902.

Latouche, F., *Les Origines de l'Economie Occidentale*, 1956.

Lecky, W. E. H., *History of European Morals from Augustus to Charlemagne*, Ed. 1911.

Lot, F., *Naissance de la France*, 1948.

Lowe, E. A., *The Legacy of the Middle Ages*, 1926.

McCullough, F., *Mediaeval Faith and Fable*, 1932.

Moss, H. St L. B., *The Birth of the Middle Ages*, 1935.

Pirenne, H., *Mahomet et Charlemagne*, 1937.

Previté-Orton, C. W., *Outlines of Mediaeval History*, 1916.

Previté-Orton, C. W., *Short Mediaeval History*, Ed. Philip Grierson, 1952.

Raby, F. J. E., *History of Christian Latin Poetry*, 1927.

Raby, F. J. E., *History of secular Latin Poetry in the Middle Ages*, 1934.

Revised Mediaeval Word List, O.U.P., 1965.

Stubbs, W., *Germany in the Early Middle Ages*, 1908.

Taylor, H. O., *The Mediaeval Mind*, 2 vols, 1925.

Waddell, Helen, *The Wandering Scholars*, 1932.

Waddell, Helen, *Mediaeval Latin Lyrics*, 1933.

Waddell, Helen, *Poetry in the Dark Ages*, 1948.

Waitz, G., *Deutsche Verfassungs – geschichte*, 1878.

Wallace-Hadrill, J. M., *The Long-haired Kings*, 1962.

Winston, R., *Charlemagne*, 1954.

INDEX